Research Methods fo Tourism Students

This introductory guide offers innovative ideas and strategies to students undertaking their first social science research work. Academically rigorous yet accessible, it uses a systematic step-by-step approach to illustrate the research process and its applications to the tourism industry. Students are presented with numerous examples and case studies, linking theory with practice.

The textbook provides a balanced coverage of both qualitative and quantitative methods, accompanying students throughout the process of selecting a research topic and specifying research questions, aims and objectives. A range of pedagogical features such as discussion questions, practical tips and examples enable students to review the literature, understand models and methodologies, analyse and interpret data (quantitative and qualitative) and ultimately write up their findings.

Featuring contributions by a group of academics with expertise in their respective fields, the book provides a comprehensive and engaging introduction to research methods. This is an essential resource to tourism students and will also be of interest to researchers in any social science subject.

Ramesh Durbarry is currently the Director General of the Civil Service College, Mauritius. He was appointed Professor in Tourism and Deputy Director at the Amity Institute of Higher Education, Mauritius. He has worked at the University of Bedfordshire as Head of Department, Marketing, Tourism & Hospitality. He was the CEO of the UOM Trust Business School in Mauritius and has also worked at the University of Nottingham as a Research Fellow, Lecturer in Research Methods of Tourism and Travel and then as Associate Professor in Tourism Management/Marketing. After successfully developing the School of Public Sector Policy and Management at the University of Technology, Mauritius, he was instrumental in the creation of the School of Sustainable Development and Tourism. His research focuses on tourism and travel, tourism taxation, price sensitivity of tourism and the impact of the tourism sector on the various economies, with a keen interest on climate change and sustainable tourism. He has published various articles in leading international journals and has contributed chapters in international books. He has worked on various projects for organisations such as WTO, UNWTO, EU, UNCTAD, VisitScotland and EMDA, among others, and on tourism destinations such as Malta and Cyprus.

Research Methods for Tourism Students

Edited by Ramesh Durbarry

LONDON AND NEW YORK

First published 2018
by Routledge
2 Park Square, Milton Park, Abingdon, Oxon OX14 4RN

and by Routledge
711 Third Avenue, New York, NY 10017

Routledge is an imprint of the Taylor & Francis Group, an informa business

British Library Cataloguing-in-Publication Data
A catalogue record for this book is available from the British Library

Library of Congress Cataloging-in-Publication Data
Names: Durbarry, Ramesh, editor.
Title: Research methods for tourism students / edited by Ramesh Durbarry.
Description: New York : Routledge, 2018. | Includes bibliographical
    references and index.
Identifiers: LCCN 2017031896 (print) | LCCN 2017051501 (ebook) |
    ISBN 9780203703588 (Master ebook) | ISBN 9781351336192 (Web pdf) |
    ISBN 9781351336185 (epub3) | ISBN 9781351336178 (Mobipocket) |
    ISBN 9780415673181 (Hardback : alk. paper) | ISBN 9780415673198
    (Paperback : alk. paper) | ISBN 9780203703588 (Ebook)
Subjects: LCSH: Tourism—Research—Methodology.
Classification: LCC G155.7 (ebook) | LCC G155.7 .R47 2018 (print) | DDC
    910.72/1—dc23
LC record available at https://lccn.loc.gov/2017031896

ISBN: 978-0-415-67318-1 (hbk)
ISBN: 978-0-415-67319-8 (pbk)
ISBN: 978-0-203-70358-8 (ebk)

Typeset in Frutiger
by Swales & Willis Ltd, Exeter, Devon, UK

Visit the eResource: www.routledge.com/9780415673198

Printed and bound by CPI Group (UK) Ltd, Croydon, CR0 4YY

Contents

Contents

Illustrations

Figures

Tables

Graphs

Contributors

Areej Shabib Aloudat is an Assistant Professor at the Department of Tourism and Travel, Yarmouk University, Jordan. She was Deputy Dean and Dean assistant for quality assurance in the Faculty of Tourism and Hotel Management, Yarmouk University (2012–15). Dr Aloudat's responsibilities include study plan development for both undergraduate and postgraduate levels, working with the faculty team to meet the requirements of the Tourism Education Quality (TEDQUAL). Her research interests include tour guiding, women's empowerment in tourism, and *Halal* tourism. Dr Aloudat has published work on tour guiding, grounded theory in tourism, natural heritage management and political stability.

Paul Beedie is Principal Lecturer in the School of Physical Education and Sport Science at the University of Bedfordshire, UK. He is fascinated with the sociology of adventure, and his publications, scholarly activity and teaching all reflect this theme. His research has been driven by an interest in adventure and includes explorations of risk, identity and community.

Anjusha Durbarry is a Research Officer at the Tertiary Education Commission, Mauritius in the Research and Planning Division. She has more than 15 years of experience in the field of higher education. She worked as a Research Fellow at the University of Nottingham, UK, and has taught Statistics and Research Methods modules at undergraduate and postgraduate levels at the University of Technology, Mauritius and University of Bedfordshire, UK.

Ramesh Durbarry is currently the Director General of the Civil Service College, Mauritius. He was appointed Professor in Tourism and Deputy Director at the Amity Institute of Higher Education, Mauritius. He has worked at the University of Bedfordshire, UK, as Head of Department Marketing, Tourism & Hospitality. He was the CEO of the UOM Trust Business School in Mauritius and has also worked at the University of Nottingham as a Research Fellow, Lecturer in Research Methods of Tourism and Travel and then as Associate Professor in Tourism Management/ Marketing. After successfully developing the School of Public Sector Policy and Management at the University of Technology, Mauritius, he was instrumental in the creation of the School of Sustainable Development and Tourism. His research focuses on tourism and travel, tourism taxation, price sensitivity of tourism and the impact of the tourism sector on the various economies, with a keen interest in climate change and sustainable tourism. He has published various articles in leading international journals and has contributed chapters to international books.

He has worked on various projects for organisations such as the World Tourism Organisation (WTO), United Nations World Tourism Organisation (UNWTO), European Union (EU), United Nations Conference on Trade and Development (UNCTAD), VisitScotland, East Midlands Development Agency (EMDA), and on tourism destinations such as Malta and Cyprus.

Sally Everett is Deputy Dean at the Lord Ashcroft International Business School, Anglia Ruskin University (Cambridge and Chelmsford), UK, and a Principal Fellow of the Higher Education Academy. She is the chair of the university's Disability Working Group, co-founder of its BME staff network and is co-lead of the Women's Network, which promotes gender equality in Higher Education leadership. Dr Everett was Head of Marketing, Tourism and Hospitality at the University of Bedfordshire (2009–13) before becoming a Deputy Dean at Anglia Ruskin University with responsibility for learning, teaching, quality and curriculum development. Her research interests include innovation in business education, inclusive and accessible learning and pedagogies, and food and drink tourism. Dr Everett has published work on folklore tourism, food festivals, sustainability, and research journeys, and has recently published the single-authored textbook *Food and Drink Tourism: Principles and Practices* (2016) with Sage Publications.

Hania Janta is a Visiting Fellow at the School of Hospitality and Tourism Management, University of Surrey, UK, where she is a co-investigator on a large collaborative project funded by the European Union's Framework Programme for Research and Innovation Horizon 2020, *Youth Mobility: Maximising opportunities for individuals, labour markets and regions in Europe* (www.ymobility.eu/). Prior to that, she was a Senior Lecturer and Head of Doctoral Programme at the University of Surrey and Lecturer and Senior Lecturer at Bournemouth University, UK. Primarily researching migration in the context of tourism, tourism employment and innovative research methods, Hania has published peer-reviewed articles and book chapters including in journals such as the *Annals of Tourism Research, Tourism Management, Technology, Work & Employment* and the *Journal of Further and Higher Education*. Recently she co-edited a special issue on 'Reconceptualising Visiting Friends and Relatives Mobilities' (with Scott A. Cohen and Allan M. Williams), which has been published in *Population, Space and Place*.

Prabha Ramseook-Munhurrun is a Senior Lecturer in the School of Sustainable Development and Tourism at the University of Technology, Mauritius. She holds a PhD in Services Marketing and Management from the same university. Her research interests include customer service experience, destination marketing and management, service quality, consumer behaviour and sustainable development with particular emphasis on sustainable tourism development and sustainable consumption. She has published in numerous journals and presented several conference papers in these subject areas.

Richard Sharpley is Professor of Tourism and Development at the University of Central Lancashire, Preston, UK. He has previously held positions at a number of other institutions, including the University of Northumbria (Reader in Tourism) and the University of Lincoln, where he was Professor of Tourism and Head of Department, Tourism and Recreation Management. He is co-editor of the journal *Tourism Planning & Development*, and a member of the editorial boards of a number of other tourism journals. His principal research interests fall under the broad areas of tourism, development and sustainability and the sociology of tourism; his books include *Tourism and Development: Concepts and Issues* (2002, 2015, with David Telfer); *Tourism and Development in the Developing World* (2008, 2016, with David Telfer); *Tourism, Tourists and Society*, 4th edition (2008); *The Darker Side of Travel*; *The Theory and Practice of Dark Tourism* (2009, with Philip Stone); and *Tourism, Development and Environment: Beyond Sustainability* (2009). His most recent book is *Mass Tourism in a Small World* (2017, with David Harrison).

Preface

After teaching for many years at various universities, I have noticed that many students tend to struggle when it comes to conducting independent research, especially when they have to do their dissertation or doctoral thesis. Although there is an amalgam of good textbooks written on research methods, some gaps were noted, for example, some were skewed towards quantitative or qualitative methods, some lacked a discussion on research paradigms and some were too theoretical. It is, indeed, often challenging for a student to get a companion textbook which covers essential elements to guide him/her when conducting an independent research. Taking these shortcomings and talking to students, I decided to embark on this project to write a book which would be suited to the needs of the students. We also reinforce the strengths of other books by making specific references to some of their chapters.

Listening to students' challenges, I structured this book so that it would guide you on your journey into how to conduct academic research. This textbook 'talks' to you, asks key questions and adopts a researcher's point of view. The book has been written assuming that you have not yet identified a topic for your research. The chapters take you through common issues that many students have (you are not the only with queries) and help you to make decisions at each stage so that you can progress further. The chapters are written in very clear language to communicate core concepts in an accessible and engaging way.

Research is not just distributing a few questionnaires or interviewing a few participants; it should be planned carefully. Knowledge generation adds value to your work. How do you know you are adding value? Have you approached the topic from the right perspective? Have you used the correct approach? Have you analysed your data carefully? In this respect, all the chapters have been designed to address these needs. I cannot pretend to be an expert in all methodological aspects and, for this reason, I have approached colleagues who are well versed in their respective subject to contribute chapters to this textbook. We all have used examples, case studies and illustrations to assist you to better understand the research process. We also explain how to write up your research and prepare you to present your findings to an audience.

I firmly believe that the skills and knowledge you will acquire when undertaking your research work will contribute to your self-development. The skills and knowledge will certainly prepare you for your future career. You will be better prepared to assess reports and make sound business decisions with objectivity. Employers seek employees with research skills that can contribute innovative ideas to, for example, delivering a service, creating a product, increasing productivity and improving production methods to stay ahead in this ever changing world environment.

I hope that you will enjoy reading this textbook and find it helpful to conducting your research study.

Ramesh Durbarry

Acknowledgements

It would have been quite difficult to write all the chapters on my own, and I, therefore, seize this opportunity to thank my colleagues for their valuable contributions enabling us to produce a complete textbook on this subject. I would like to acknowledge Gemma Lumsden, a third year student at the University of Bedfordshire, for giving her consent to use her research proposal for illustration purposes.

I wish to thank my wife Anjusha, who has been patient and supportive. She has also collaborated on three chapters with me. I would also like to thank my two daughters, Rheeya and Rushvi, for allowing me to skip some bedtime story sessions. I would like to extend my thanks to Emma Travis, who revived this project, and to Carlotta Fanton at Taylor & Francis, who have both been supportive and whose valuable assistance has made the publication of this textbook possible.

PART I

Nature of research and process

Chapter 1

Introduction

Ramesh Durbarry

Research is an exciting process as it adds to knowledge, curiosity and understanding of phenomena. How we look at a phenomenon depends on many factors, such as the way we think, our research philosophies, personal experience and the way we have learned to look at matters. The ability to conduct research and to interpret information is a key skill in both the academic and commercial worlds. There is no escaping from research, as nearly all jobs rely on research skills at some point.

So what is research? Why do we research? How we conduct research? These are some questions which we look at in this textbook. There is not a single formula to adopt to conduct research and we do not aim or attempt to provide one. This book is meant to be a guide on making appropriate decisions at each step of the research process.

1.0 Chapter objectives

Whether you are writing an essay, a project, carrying out a dissertation or a doctoral thesis, research into the subject matter is required. If you are undertaking an undergraduate or a postgraduate degree, you will most probably have to write a dissertation. This textbook will surely be a very useful companion to assist you in carrying out such a task.

Let's begin by explaining what a *dissertation* is. A dissertation is regarded as a structured piece of writing on a certain subject matter, which you have chosen, to seek out answers to some research questions which you are investigating. It is a scholarly piece of work where you are demonstrating your capability to conduct research independently. Compared to an essay, a dissertation is organised into chapters and there is a more thorough examination of the subject matter. It will include debating ideas from previous scholarly writings, application of research methods, collecting data, analysing and discussing findings, and providing concluding remarks.

In this chapter, we explain what carrying out research is all about. After studying this chapter, you will be able to:

- understand what research is;
- appreciate briefly the different types of research;
- recognise the importance of research in tourism; and
- have an overview of the structure of this textbook.

1.1 What is research?

When students are asked to conduct research in the form of a dissertation, many students hastily jump to start designing a questionnaire and collecting data. Collection of data is certainly not what research is all about, but is undoubtedly part of it. According to the *Concise Oxford English Dictionary* (2011) the term research is defined as 'the systematic investigation into and study of materials and sources in order to establish facts and reach new conclusions'. The word *research* has a French origin and is rooted in the term 'search'. At a closer look, research (*re*-search) implies search again. Almost in all studies, a researcher conducts a search (on existing knowledge) and then performs another search (re-) to generate new knowledge.

> ## What is research?
>
> It is the systematic investigation of data and inquiry to provide explanations, establish relationships, carry our experimentation or test hypotheses to generate (new) knowledge.

To you, what is more important is the phrase 'systematic investigation'. This means that the research is well thought out and carefully designed. We will look at these when we discuss the research process and research design. Research is carried out when we have a central question or problem we want to resolve. We first try to clearly formulate our question and then decide how we are going to answer it by looking at how others have addressed the problem. Creswell (1994, p. 51) defines research as a study that advances a research question and reports the data to answer the question.

1.2 Types of research

There are different types of research, which are explored later, but are briefly described below:

- Descriptive research: describes a particular phenomenon, focusing on the issue of what is happening, rather than why it is happening. This type of research increases your knowledge and you start getting an idea of the subject matter.
- Explanatory research: this type of research involves explaining why something happens, and assessing causal relationships between variables.
- Exploratory research: this takes place where there is little or no prior knowledge. Thus there is a need for an initial exploration before more specific research can be undertaken. Exploratory research is generally followed up by further research that tests any ideas or hypothesis generated.
- Predictive research: this forecasts future phenomena, based on the interpretations suggested by explanatory research.

The two main approaches to conducting research are: quantitative and qualitative. Quantitative research is said to be an inquiry into a social or human problem, based on testing a theory composed of variables, measured with numbers and analysed with statistical procedures, in order to determine whether the predictive generalisations of the theory hold true (Creswell, 1994, p. 2). Creswell (1994, p. 1) defines qualitative research as an inquiry process of understanding a social or human problem, based on building a complex, holistic picture, formed with words, reporting detailed views of informants and conducted in a natural setting.

The choice of using a particular approach depends on the researcher's ability to master it. Almost any research problem can be studied using either a quantitative or qualitative approach. Your philosophical position will influence the approach that you choose. For example, positivists tend to rely more on a quantitative approach, while interpretivists use qualitative approach. Many researchers, for pragmatic reasons, use both approaches to study a problem (a mixed method approach) to provide more support to their study results. In fact, the idea of using different methods to arrive to the same result is called triangulation.

In your research, you may be using an existing theory or aiming to test a proposition. However, how clear you are about the theory or your proposition at the beginning of your research raises an important question concerning the design of your research project (Saunders et al., 2003). This involves whether you are using a deductive or an inductive approach. In a deductive approach, you will be using an existing model or even developing a theory, stating a hypothesis and collecting data to test it, whereas in an inductive approach, you will be developing the theory or proposition based on data collection and analysis. Your philosophical thoughts also influence to a certain extent how to approach the research; for example, positivists tend to use a deductive approach, while interpretivists tend to use an inductive approach (but this is not always the case).

1.3 Why research in tourism?

With the growing importance of tourism, travel and leisure activities, the industry is becoming a global phenomenon and has particularly experienced rapid growth in the post-1945 period. The tourism industry is one of the largest and fastest growing industry sectors of the global economy, with the World Tourism Organisation (WTO) finding that:

> Tourism has become one of the world's major trade categories. The overall export income generated by inbound tourism, including passenger transport, exceeded US$ 1.2 trillion in 2011, or US$ 3.4 billion a day on average. Tourism exports account for as much as 30 per cent of the world's exports of commercial services and 6 per cent of overall exports of goods and services. Globally, as an export category, tourism ranks fourth after fuels, chemicals and food.
>
> (WTO, 2012)

The tourism industry has become not only the world's largest industry but has significant economic, social, cultural and environmental impacts. Predominantly, tourism was viewed as an economic activity and as an engine of growth for many developed and, especially, developing countries (Crompton and Richardson, 1986; Sinclair and Stabler, 1997). Tourism is an interesting field as it is interdisciplinary. Tourism has been braced by economists, geographers, sociologists, anthropologists, ecologists, environmental scientists and psychologists, among others. It is, hence, no surprise that a particular phenomenon could be investigated from various disciplines. Tourist behaviour, for instance, could be analysed by sociologists, economists and psychologists.

There are many topics which have warranted research at international, regional and national level and from the demand side (tourists) to the supply side (the tourism industry). Since the Brundtland Report in 1987 (World Commission on Environment and Development, 1987), attention has been drawn to tourist experience, behaviour on sustainable tourism and the impact of climate change has on tourism and vice versa. To appreciate the vast literature researched in tourism, the best places to start reading are the tourism related journals such as:

- *Annals of Tourism Research*
- *International Journal of Contemporary Hospitality Management*
- *Journal of Hospitality Management*
- *Journal of Hospitality Management and Tourism*
- *Journal of Hospitality Marketing & Management*
- *Journal of Hotel & Business Management*
- *Journal of Tourism Studies*
- *Journal of Travel Research*
- *Journal of Travel and Tourism Marketing*
- *Journal of Vacation Marketing*
- *Tourism Analysis*
- *Tourism Management International*
- *Tourism and Recreation Research*
- *Travel and Tourism Analyst*

American Hotel & Motel Association: www.ahma.com

ATA – Air Transport Association: www.air-transport.org

CHA – Corporate Hospitality and Event Association: www.eventmanager.co.uk/cha.htm

CLIA – Cruise Lines International Association: http://ten-io.com/index2.htm

HEDNA – Hotel Electronic Distribution Network Association: www.hedna.org

HITIS – Hospitality Industry Technology Integration Standards: www.hitis.org

IATA – International Air Transport Association: www.iata.org

IFITT – International Federation of Information Technology & Tourism: www.ifitt.org

IH&RA – International Hotel & Restaurant Association: www.ih-ra.com

Keynote Reports: www.keynote.co.uk

MINTEL: www.mintel.com

OTA – Open Travel Alliance: http://opentravel.com

TInet – Tourism Industries Network: http://info.trade.gov

TTI – Travel Technology Initiative: www.tti.org

TTRA – Travel and Tourism Research Association: www.ttra.com

WATA – World Association of Travel Agencies: www.wata.net

WTO – World Tourism Organization: www2.unwto.org

WTTC – World Travel & Tourism Council: www.wttc.org

For more tourism organisations visit: www.rmsig.de/tourism_organizations.htm

Figure 1.1 List of tourism organisations

Tourism organisations also can provide useful information and ideas for research. Some of them are listed in Figure 1.1.

1.4 About this book

This book is primarily written for students conducting independent research, such as a dissertation or even a doctoral thesis. We particularly use examples from tourism to illustrate to students how to conduct research and how to write their own research projects. The aim of the book is to assist students to develop essential skills while conducting their research. It also aims to provide tutors with a unique textbook to adopt for their Research Methods module, which covers topics that are taught at the undergraduate and postgraduate levels. This textbook aims to:

- provide a systematic approach to understand techniques used in (tourism) research;
- provide an understanding of different types of research and the procedures to engage students with the subject by making it more readable and accessible;
- make clear applications of theory in practice in the field of tourism;
- communicate core concepts in an accessible and engaging way;
- assist students to undertake a critical appraisal of previous research work;
- support students in conducting their research;
- support lecturers in delivering Research Methods modules;

- include a balanced coverage of qualitative and quantitative methods, as well as e-methods;
- enable students to collect and interpret data using qualitative and quantitative methods;
- familiarise students with the research process via theory and from practical experience;
- enable students to appraise and critically evaluate the appropriateness of data collection methods;
- develop students' ability to present research coherently;
- enable students apply research skills in the writing and designing of a project proposal; and
- prepare students for their dissertation.

The textbook is written from a researcher's point of view and will provide you with a step-by-step guide to accomplishing your research project or dissertation with examples from the field of tourism. It starts from how a topic is selected and continues to the writing up stage. The book aims to lay a solid understanding of research from base level up and to become essential reading for students. Students often complain that they are struggling to write research proposals prior to embarking on their dissertation and that they need more guidance. Those students who are enthusiastic about research tend to constantly seek advice from peers to supervisors and lecturers, while others, although passionate about research, do not often engage with others. This book has been designed to guide both sets of students.

1.5 The structure of the book

This book offers chapters written by experienced and well reputed academicians and practitioners who have conducted research, supervised and examined dissertations and PhDs, taught Research Methods modules and written articles in renowned journals. The chapters are organised in a systematic way so that readers can move from one chapter to another and at the same time engage with their research project. The book is divided into three parts. In the first part, we look at the nature of research; this is followed by a series of chapters in the second part on the conceptual framework and research methods; and in the third part we look at data analysis, research writing and presentation of the research.

Chapter 2 discusses the philosophy of social science to conduct research. Paradigms are the theoretical mindsets or beliefs that underlie the research approach. In the chapter, various research paradigms are introduced such as positivism, post-positivism, interpretivism, feminism, constructivism and critical theory. Two research paradigms are explored in this book: positivism and interpretivism. Paradigms are better explained by ontological, epistemological and methodical questions. An understanding of ontology and ontological concerns in relation to social research are further developed. The difference between objectivism and constructivism are explored. Similarly, an understanding of what is meant by epistemology and epistemological concerns in relation to social research and the differences between positivism and interpretivism are explained. The main features of the debate about whether quantitative and qualitative research approaches are epistemological or technical matters are discussed.

Chapter 3 introduces the elements of the research process. The chapter outlines the different stages of the process and describes the interrelationship between the stages as part of an overall process. This structure can be adapted particularly to those who are new in conducting research. The chapter illustrates how to start a research.

Chapter 4 provides an in-depth discussion on the various stages of the research and how to develop a research proposal. In the chapter an examination of how to narrow down your research topic to identifying a research title is detailed. It also explains how to conduct a preliminary literature review and write the research aim(s) and objectives. To decide on your research method, a debate is presented so that you can then select the one appropriate for your study.

Chapter 5 presents a framework to conduct the review literature and what is meant by a critical review. First, a discussion around why a literature is vital to conducting research is presented and what role it plays. Then the types of questions you should be asking when you are conducting the literature review are examined. The various sources where information can be obtained on the research topic are provided. An example of a literature review is provided as well.

Ethical issues are discussed in Chapter 6. In particular, the roles and responsibilities of the researcher are examined as well as ethical issues at different stages of the research process.

In Chapter 7, one of the fundamental elements of the research process, the development of a conceptual framework, is discussed. The reasons to develop a conceptual framework are elaborated and how it is different from a theoretical framework. How the conceptual framework works and where it fits into a research are elucidated. The terms *concept*, *construct* and *variable* are defined and explained.

Chapter 8 develops in more detail the inductive–deductive distinction introduced in Chapter 3 by concentrating on the former approach to research design. In particular, the chapter aims to show the importance of the interpretive paradigm in social science research, for example, in tourism research tourism professionals need to acquire insights into tourist behaviour from the perspective(s) of the tourists themselves if they are to more fully understand their behaviour and needs for the development of tourist products. The key components of a range of qualitative research methodologies are discussed and when to use a certain methodology. Also discussed is how to collect and analyse data by using a specific methodology.

Chapter 9 explains how to use quantitative research methods to study a phenomenon. Measurement issues in quantitative research and how surveys can be used to collect data – for example mail, telephone, street and on-site surveys – are described. Since collection of primary data relies significantly (but not always) on questionnaire surveys, there is a comprehensive discussion of how to design a questionnaire and its advantages and disadvantages.

Chapter 10 explores further the merits of using both the qualitative and quantitative approaches to a study. We discuss how the mixed method has become popular to support findings. We also look at what triangulation means and the types of triangulation.

Chapter 11 introduces the use of the internet as a tool to engage in research. The chapter provides an overview of netnography and the usefulness of this method in conducting qualitative research online. This innovative method has great potential as it uses rich data available online such as blogs, discussion fora or comments posted on social networking sites. The chapter provides an outline on how to perform a netnographic analysis.

Chapter 12 builds on Chapter 11 discussing how, with the growth of the internet, it has become possible to collect data. In the chapter, the author focuses on overviewing online surveys by discussing basic survey tools that can be used in research. She looks at different distribution channels: discussion fora, mailing lists, social networking sites and emails and assess their usefulness. She also looks at the challenges that we may face related to accessing various types of online communities. As with other types of research, the challenges and limitations that need to be considered when using online surveys are discussed.

Chapter 13 looks at how participants are selected in a study for data collection purposes. The significance of sampling is explained, how to use probability and non-probability sampling techniques, and how to choose an appropriate sampling technique.

Chapter 14 focuses on analysing qualitative data and looks at the key principles of qualitative data storage, coding and analysis. It discusses the ways in which qualitative data can be securely retained, analysed and interpreted – both manually and with the help of computer software. It helps you to understand your role as a data analyst. Given that qualitative data can be generated in many different ways and takes different forms, which range from detailed focus group transcriptions to recorded interviews to the content in marketing materials, the chapter provides an outline of how to make sense of the data you have collected. The authors also discuss how to analyse and interpret visual images and films.

Chapter 15 focuses on grounded theory, which is an interesting methodology commonly used to generate theories or to provide an explanation of phenomena. An introduction to grounded theory and its guiding principles are presented. The research process using this methodology is explained and how you can conceptualise data. A practical example is used to illustrate how grounded theory is applied.

Chapter 16 provides examples of how to use computer software to analyse qualitative data. The authors show how computer programmes such as QSR's NVivo can help you to analyse qualitative data. They demonstrate how to set up a coding system and guide you step-by-step to conducting your analysis.

In Chapter 17, some statistical tools which can be used to analyse the raw data collected are discussed. Further discussions are on how your data can be analysed using descriptive and inferential statistics. How data can be presented visually (using appropriate graphs) and how various statistics can be used to summarise data are also discussed.

Chapter 18 introduces the use of the SPSS software with worked examples, shows how to summarise data, explains how to conduct simple t-tests and perform analysis of variance, among many others. A brief explanation of a simple regression model and factor analysis is provided so that some initial analyses can be conducted. We use some case studies to illustrate how these methods can be applied.

Chapter 19 is concerned with writing up the research, which is arguably the most significant element of the entire research process. Indeed, the value of any research in general is measured by its outcomes while one of the fundamental criteria by which research in particular is judged is the extent to which it makes an original contribution to knowledge. However, the quality of that written work may have a significant influence on the grade awarded. The chapter discusses how to write in an appropriate academic style, use references effectively and correctly, and be more confident about writing up your research.

Chapter 20 discusses how to present your research to a wider audience. We explain as well how to structure the content of your presentation and how to prepare to deliver your presentation.

At the end of each chapter, there are discussion questions to help you to reflect on the journey that you are undertaking to complete your research study.

Chapter summary

- Research is mainly conducted to better understand a range of issues such as explaining a phenomenon, elucidating relationships, satisfying curiosity and generating new knowledge.
- For a scholar, research involves a systematic investigation into the matter.
- There are different types of research: descriptive, explanatory and exploratory, among others.
- Research in tourism is growing due to its importance and the contribution it makes to income and job creation.
- Tourism is interdisciplinary and has attracted the attention of many researchers.
- The purpose of this book is to provide a step-by-step guide for students who wish to conduct research at any level.

Discussion questions

1.1 State in your own words what you understand by *research*.
1.2 What topical issues fascinate you and prompt you to conduct research? Why?
1.3 List five tentative titles of your research.
1.4 How would you start your research on one of the topics you have selected? List the steps you would take to complete the research. (Keep this list for comparison later, after you have read the book.)

Further reading

Bryman, A. (2008). *Social Research Methods*. London: Oxford University Press.

Bryman, A. and Bell, E. (2007). *Business Research Methods*, revised edition. London: Oxford University Press.

Gayle, J. (2001). *Tourism Research*. Milton: John Wiley & Sons Australia Ltd.

Kalof, L., Dan, A. and Dietz, T. (2008). *Essentials of Social Research*. Maidenhead: Open University Press.

Neuman, W.L. (2006). *Social Research Methods: Qualitative and Quantitative Approaches*. Boston: Pearson, Allyn and Bacon.

Page, S.J. and Connell, J. (2009). *Tourism: A Modern Synthesis*, 3rd edition. Hampshire: Cengage Learning. [See the table of contents for topics.]

Saunders, M.N.K., Lewis, P. and Thornhill, A. (2009). *Research Methods for Business Students*, 5th edition. Harlow: Pearson Education Ltd.

Veal, A.J. (2011). *Research Methods for Leisure and Tourism*, 4th edition. Harlow: Prentice Hall.

Chapter 2

Philosophical disputes in research

Prabha Ramseook-Munhurrun and Ramesh Durbarry

'How do I know whether I have found the true relationship I am investigating?' asked an undergraduate research student. He further inquired what if he reported a finding which is contrary to popular belief.

I jokingly replied that *'the truth lies out there!'* (referring to the *X Files* TV series).

I explained to him that research is like an iceberg. At the tip of it, we apply research methods to test propositions and hypotheses of how the reality might look and we may use quantitative or qualitative methods, for instance. Beneath that tip of the iceberg, what we really need to know is what has been researched so far and what knowledge do we have on this 'reality'? The perspective from which we are conducting the research will also define the way we will be viewing this reality. The session on 'Research Philosophies and Paradigms' in the Research Methods module started to make sense to him.

2.0 Chapter objectives

Each researcher has different ways and beliefs of viewing the research domain. Consequently, the ways in which research studies are conducted vary. However, there are certain standards and principles that guide a researcher's actions and beliefs to provide a better understanding of why and how research is conducted. The aim of social science research is to explain and understand the phenomenon under investigation and this is possible by choosing an appropriate research paradigm.

The aim of this chapter is to explore the research paradigms adopted by researchers to justify the theoretical assumptions and fundamental beliefs underpinning a social science research such as in tourism.

After studying this chapter, you will be able to:

- identify various research paradigms;
- understand what is meant by ontology and ontological concerns in relation to social research, and the difference between objectivism and constructivism;
- understand what is meant by epistemology and epistemological concerns in relation to social research, and the differences between positivism and interpretivism;
- identify the main differences and the relationship between ontological and epistemological concerns and how these relate to methodological issues; and
- set out the main features of the debate about whether quantitative and qualitative research approaches are epistemological or technical matters.

2.1 Research paradigms

Researchers have defined paradigm as a basic set of beliefs and their associated research methods that illustrate a view of the nature of reality (Lincoln and Guba, 1985; Denzin and Lincoln, 1994). According to Saunders et al. (2003, 2009), a research paradigm depends on the way a researcher thinks about knowledge development.

Collis and Hussey (2003) explain that a paradigm provides a framework which consists of a set of theories, methods and ways in which the researchers can define their data when conducting research. Paradigm explains how researchers view the world, how they relate to the object under study and what they see as the nature of reality.

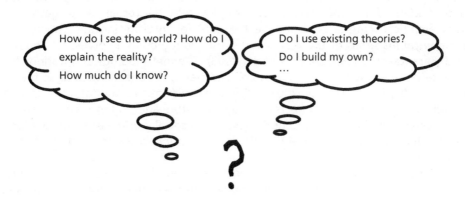

Paradigms are explained by three fundamental and interconnected philosophical assumptions: the ontological, epistemological and methodological questions. They relate to the nature of knowledge and the development of that knowledge, respectively. The understanding of the different paradigms is vital to the research process in all areas of study as they help understand the phenomenon under study within the social sciences and the possibility of embracing different research methodologies (Creswell, 2003).

2.1.1 What is ontology?

Ontology is concerned with the phenomena under investigation, whether the 'reality' to be examined is external or internal to the subject and whether reality is of an objective or subjective nature (Guba and Lincoln, 1994; Lincoln and Guba, 2000; Creswell, 2003). It is the view of how one perceives the reality. In social research, on one hand, this philosophical assumption explains the view of social reality undertaken in the study by the researchers, their interpretations of it, termed the objectivist. On the other hand, the subjectivist believes that reality is dependent on social researchers and assumes that individuals contribute to social phenomena.

2.1.2 What is epistemology?

Epistemology refers to how the individual perceives the world and communicates this as knowledge to others (Guba, 1990; Creswell, 2003). Understanding these philosophical assumptions and beliefs in social sciences is important as they describe the nature of the research design, how data will be collected and analysed, and knowledge gained (Easterby-Smith et al., 2008). The ontology and epistemology propositions and assumptions influence the research *methodology* to explore the nature of knowledge and the kind of entity that exists (Lincoln and Guba, 2000).

2.1.3 What is methodology?

Sarantakos (1998) defines methodology as a 'model, which entails theoretical principles as well as a framework that provides guidelines about how research is done in the context of a particular paradigm' (p. 32). It encompasses the study of methods, addressing the theoretical arguments and justifications for methods. Methodology is founded in the epistemological and ontological arguments about what social reality is. Methods are the specific tools employed by the researcher to gather data and/or empirical material and analyse the data for interpreting and (re)constructing empirical materials of the world and subsequently build 'knowledge' about the world (Sarantakos, 1998; Saunders et al., 2003). The methodological questions focus on the techniques used, such as surveys or interviews, to collect and analyse the data (Creswell, 2003; Saunders et al., 2003, 2009). The choice of a methodological approach for a subject of study deeply reflects not only the nature and exigencies of the study to be conducted but also the researcher's view of the social world. Each methodological approach has its own interests and realm of application in the research, setting and everyday life.

Ontology involves the philosophy of reality, epistemology addresses how the reality is known while methodology is located within these theoretical arguments and justifications and, consequently, identifies the particular practices used to attain knowledge of it. These assumptions are consequential to each other, such that the researcher's view of ontology effects his/her epistemological persuasion which, in turn, affects his/her choice of methodology. Thus logically following these assumptions, the researcher should be aware of his/her philosophical assumptions that might have a significant impact on 'what to research?'

Practical tips

The ontological questions

- What is the form and nature of reality and, therefore, what is there that can be known about it?
- Is there a real world out there which exists independent of our knowledge of it?

The epistemological question

- What is the nature of the relationship between the knower or would-be knower and what can be known?

The methodological question

- How can you go about finding out whatever you believe can be known?

2.2 Philosophical approaches

The objective and subjective approaches to research are the two major philosophical approaches explained by the assumptions made about ontology (reality), epistemology (knowledge) and methodology. In social science research, on the one hand, the objectivist approach has been developed from the natural sciences and the researcher employs the most successful methods of the natural sciences to investigate the social science phenomena. On the other hand, subjectivism belongs to reality as perceived by the subject and has an influence in the research outcome. As shown in Table 2.1, objectivism and subjectivism have been categorised differently in the literature. For example,

Table 2.1 Alternative philosophical paradigm names

Objectivist	Subjectivist
Quantitative	Qualitative
Positivist	Phenomenological
Scientific	Humanistic
Experimentalist	Interpretivist

Source: Adapted from Hussey and Hussey (1997)

Easterby-Smith et al. (2008) described them as positivism and phenomenology, and Hughes and Sharrock (1997) illustrated them as positivism and interpretive alternative.

2.3 Types of paradigm

There are many theoretical paradigms that can inform research, for example, positivism, post-positivism, interpretivism, feminism, constructivism and critical theory (Guba and Lincoln, 1994, 1998; Tashakkori and Teddlie, 1998; Creswell, 2003; Easterby-Smith et al., 2008). We do not discuss each of these paradigms here, as it is beyond the scope of this book. Readers are encouraged to refer to the list of 'Further reading' section at the end of this chapter.

The choice of paradigms in research is important as they act as a guide to the research design to generate answers for the research questions. A summary of the philosophical assumptions related to each paradigm can be found in Guba and Lincoln (1994, p. 109) and Jennings (2001, p. 56). The choice of the research paradigm is based on the aim and objectives of the research study, the data to be collected and the research area (Saunders et al., 2003, 2009). It is how the researcher views the nature of reality and how the knowledge is to be explained. However, the positivist and interpretive research approaches dominate the social science paradigms (Lincoln and Guba, 2000). We consider a few paradigms below.

2.3.1 Positivism

Positivists view the world as being guided by 'scientific rules that explain the behaviour of phenomena through causal relationships' (Jennings, 2001). According to Saunders et al. (2003), positivists employ the deductive approach to describe their worldviews and set of beliefs. Positivism is an ontological position of the world where the reality is external to the researchers, whereas the epistemological position is based on the belief that the researchers are objective and independent and applies the methods of natural science. A positivist researcher is independent of what is being investigated since the methodological decisions to conduct the research are established by the set of the study objectives (Easterby-Smith et al., 2008). Positivists think that there is a unique reality which is apprehendable (Guba and Lincoln, 1994). To investigate their research interest, positivist researchers use quantitative methods that employ large sample, surveys and statistical analysis as they view the world as an observable social reality, where hypotheses can be associated and tested quantitatively in the natural sciences (Creswell, 2003). Under the positivism approach, hypotheses are developed to test an established theory prior to data collection and using empirical analyses the hypotheses will be either supported or not supported (a *deductive* approach). Thus the key idea of positivism is that social world exists externally and has to be measured through objective methods rather than attitudes, intuitions or reflections (Easterby-Smith et al., 2008). Thus, positivist research is about objective research rather than subjective. The positivistic approach attempts to establish casual links and relationships between different elements of the study and relate them to a particular theory or concept. The methodologies adopted by positivists are surveys, experimental studies, longitudinal studies and cross-sectional studies.

Exercise 1

(a) Identify your own worldview to situate your research paradigm in your research.
(b) Identify a research study that illustrates the positivist paradigm. Explain why this study represents this paradigm by distinguishing the characteristics that led you to conclude that this study belongs to this paradigm.

2.3.2 Post-positivism

Under the post-positivism paradigm, the world is viewed to be independent of the researchers and open to different views (Easterby-Smith et al., 2008). The post-positivism paradigm is based on a scientific approach which aims to discover the cause and effect relationships and predict the future through hypotheses and research questions (Creswell, 2003). It takes an ontological position that external reality is real and exists (Guba, 1990). Methodologically, post-positivism uses qualitative techniques, experimental designs and surveys to better picture the real world. Post-positivism supports the development of models from existing theory to get closer to the reality, even though precise knowledge of reality is uncertain and imperfect (Saunders et al., 2003). A post-positivist approach is thus concerned with the concept that reality is subjective and recognises the complex relationships between individual actions, viewpoints and socio-cultural issues and the environment (Easter-Smith et al., 2008). Knowledge is developed based on observation and the measurement of reality by means of developing quantitative measures, that is, there is the theory, then data collection, and then the conclusion that the theory is right or wrong (Creswell, 2003).

Exercise 2

Identify a research study that illustrates the post-positivist paradigm. Explain why this study represents this paradigm by distinguishing the characteristics that led you to conclude that this study belongs to this paradigm.

2.3.3 Constructivist

The constructivist paradigm focuses on understanding the phenomenon under study. According to Lincoln and Guba (2000), constructivism attempts to explore the root of social phenomena, exploration being unique and its findings cannot be used to generalise to another similar phenomenon. Lincoln and Guba (2000) argue that constructivists believe that there is no subjective reality; instead, the reality is built on individual and collective experiences. A constructivist research is not to predict or control the world as positivists and even post-positivists might wish (Guba, 1990; Guba and Lincoln, 1994; Lincoln and Guba, 2000). Therefore, constructivism is developed and constructed in the individual's mind according to what he/she perceived or believed it to be. The methodological approach for constructivism must be hermeneutic (interpretation of texts) and dialectic (discourse between two or more people having different views on a subject matter) (Guba, 1990). Constructivism is associated with the qualitative method using the inductive approach. A constructivist researcher will consider the feelings and discourse of the subjects to understand and explain the world from the subjects' own perspective, thus following a subjectivist epistemological disposition. The findings of the constructivist approach are associated to the individual views of the world and such views cannot be compared with the views of other individuals (Bazeley, 2004).

Exercise 3

Identify a research study that illustrates the constructivist paradigm. Explain why this study represents this paradigm by distinguishing the characteristics that led you to conclude that this study belongs to this paradigm.

2.3.4 Critical theory

The critical theory is associated with the society and social theory (Guba and Lincoln, 1994). It is viewed as a synthesis of alternative paradigms, such as feminism, materialism and neo-Marxism as they share a particular set of basic beliefs. Under this paradigm, reality is formulated over time by social, political, cultural, economic, ethnic and gender forces and the researcher has a more authoritative role (Guba and Lincoln, 1994). According to the critical realist, knowledge of reality is a result of social conditioning and, thus, cannot be understood independently of the social actors involved in the knowledge creation process (Lincoln and Guba, 2000). The critical theory is different from post-positivism because it is grounded in real-world settings (Jennings, 2001). It further views the social actors as thinking and acting individuals rather than as individuals following defined rules and procedures (Jennings, 2001; Bazeley, 2004). Methodologically, critical theory aims to eliminate the false consciousness of participants and facilitate transformation, and could use any data collection techniques with a critical stance.

Exercise 4

Identify a research study that illustrates the critical theory paradigm. Explain why this study represents this paradigm by distinguishing the characteristics that led you to conclude that this study belongs to this paradigm.

A summary of the philosophical assumptions related to each paradigm is illustrated in Table 2.2.

Table 2.2 Basic beliefs of research paradigms

Paradigm	Positivism	Post-positivism	Constructivism	Critical theory
Ontology nature of reality	Naïve realism – 'real' reality but apprehendable	Critical realism – 'real' reality but only imperfectly and probabilistically apprehendable	Historical realism – virtual reality shaped by social, political, cultural, economic, ethnic and gender values; crystallised over time	Relativism – local and specific constructed realities
Epistemology nature of knowledge	Dualist/ objectivist; findings true	Modified dualist/ objectivist; critical tradition/ community; findings probably true	Transactional/ subjectivist; value-mediated findings	Transactional/ subjectivist; created findings
Methodology systematic inquiry	Experimental/ manipulative; verification of hypotheses; mainly quantitative methods	Modified experimental/ manipulative; critical multiplism; falsification of hypotheses; may include qualitative methods	Dialogic/ dialectical	Hermeneutic/ dialectical

Practical tips

The choice of paradigms in research is important as they guide the research design to generate answers for the research questions. Ontology and epistemology assumptions consequently influence the methodological questions, which focus on the techniques used, such as surveys or interviews, to collect and analyse the data (Creswell, 2003; Saunders et al., 2003). These questions should be addressed in order to determine whether research should follow a qualitative or quantitative approach or both. You would seek to understand the following:

● What is considered to be the subject of study and how is it viewed from the ontology perspective?
● What are the relationships between the subjects of study, objects and you (the researcher) from the epistemology perspective?
● How such data about the subject of study can be collected by you from the methodological perspective?

2.4 The methodological approach in social sciences

Appropriate methodologies have to be selected in order to satisfy the needs of any particular study (Saunders et al., 2003, 2009). When designing research, in particular when choosing the different methodological approaches, the ontological and epistemological position should be followed. In social science research, the qualitative and quantitative methodological approaches are primarily used to gather information. However, over the years there has been much debate about the paradigm positions and the qualitative and quantitative research paradigms. It is argued that the distinction between qualitative and quantitative methods is a technical matter and the choice of which methods to use should be determined by the research questions and how appropriate the method is for investigating them. For example, qualitative research is usually associated with induction and theory generation, but quantitative research is frequently undertaken in order to test theories rather than to generate them (also discussed in Chapter 3).

2.4.1 Qualitative approach

Qualitative research is interpretive in nature (Lincoln and Guba, 1985; Patton, 1990) and data are collected in natural settings either by interviews in the form of words, phrases or case studies using pictures or videos to understand and explain the social phenomena (Easterby-Smith et al., 2008). Some qualitative researchers have proposed that such data do not need to be analysed but simply presented, as the data often speak for themselves and the belief is associated with a constructivist paradigm position; the methodology is inductive in nature (Saunders et al., 2003, 2009). The qualitative approach involves subjects in order to provide the realism needed for theory building and developing the research propositions. Case study, ethnographic, phenomenological and grounded theory methods are commonly used in qualitative research data collection methods (Easter-Smith et al., 2008). Ethnographic is used when the subject is involved in an entire cultural group where participation observation is used to study and interpret values, behaviours and beliefs on the culture-sharing group (Saunders et al., 2003; Collis and Hussey, 2003), while grounded theory is used to develop and present a new theory based on core themes that emerged from the data under investigation (Glaser and Strauss, 1967; Saunders et al., 2003). The phenomenological research method is used to describe individual experiences of a phenomenon experienced by one or more individuals in their real-world life (Collis and Hussey, 2003), while case study involves an in-depth longitudinal investigation of a single case and aims at answering the 'why' as well as the 'what' and 'how' questions (Saunders et al., 2003, p. 93).

However, such an approach may lead to potential bias by the researcher because of the proximity of the researcher with the research subjects and may compromise the objectiveness of the research while describing, interpreting and explaining the phenomena of interest (Creswell, 2003). Moreover, in the process of gathering in-depth information, qualitative research involves a small number of subjects and does not represent the wider population. In addition, the issues of validity and reliability have also been criticised in the qualitative research approach. Because of its subjective nature, employing the conventional standards of reliability and validity in qualitative data is difficult (Creswell, 2003).

2.4.2 Quantitative approach

By contrast, the quantitative approach employs conceptual models, theories and hypotheses pertaining to the observed phenomenon from the real world to better understand, predict and manage processes, and uses experiment and survey to collect data (Creswell, 2003). Creswell (2003) further argues that the quantitative research approach tends to be associated with a positivist paradigm belief which reflects the scientific method of natural sciences. The methodological research approach for this paradigm is the deductive approach (Saunders et al., 2003). Quantitative researchers adopt the deductive approach by using established theory to address the research design and interpret the results of the study (Saunders et al., 2003). Instead of developing a theory, the aim of the quantitative approach is to empirically test or verify a theory through the conceptual model. Furthermore, the quantitative approach uses statistical techniques to analyse the data, thus making statistical and analytical generalisations of the findings under investigation (Onwuegbuzie and Leech, 2005). Consequently, quantitative researchers state that the research methods lead them to establish valid and reliable cause and effect relationships (Johnson et al., 2007).

However, one of the criticisms of the quantitative research approach is that it fails to consider the subjects' unique ability to interpret their experiences and behaviours, construct their own interpretations and act on these (Creswell, 2003). The quantitative research approach hardly captures complex phenomena that exist in the reality under investigation. Thus the challenge for quantitative methods is to incorporate qualitative methods to extend the richness of the investigation.

Many researchers now argue that the epistemological distinction between quantitative and qualitative research should be relaxed. There is growing interest in the combination of the two approaches, which is the mixed methods approach (discussed in Chapter 10).

Chapter summary

This chapter has explained the often confusing concepts of research paradigms and research methodologies. Conducting a research study should be started off by considering how the researcher views the observed social phenomena, which leads to the dominant research paradigm to be applied. The choice of a research paradigm leads to a relevant research methodology.

- A paradigm is a basic set of beliefs and their associated research methods that illustrate a view of the nature of reality.
- Paradigms are explained by three fundamental and interconnected philosophical assumptions: the ontological, epistemological and methodological questions.
- Ontology is about the form and nature of reality and, therefore, what is there that can be known about it.
- Epistemology is the philosophy of knowledge or of how we come to know.
- Methodology encompasses the study of methods, addressing the theoretical arguments and justifications for methods.
- Positivists are guided by scientific rules that explain the behaviour of phenomena through causal relationships and employ a deductive approach to describing their worldviews.

- Post-positivists view the world to be independent of the researchers and are open to different views.
- Constructivists focus on understanding the phenomenon under study.
- Critical theory is associated with the society and social theory.

Discussion questions

2.1 What are the advantages and disadvantages of positivistic, post-positivistic, constructivist and critical theory approaches in social science research?

2.2 Select a research topic, identify the research questions and discuss what approach would be best to study the question.

2.3 Describe three qualitative and quantitative research methods.

Further reading

Bryman, A. and Bell, E. (2007). *Business Research Methods*, revised edition. London: Oxford University Press.

Gayle, J. (2001). *Tourism Research*. Milton: John Wiley & Sons Australia Ltd.

Kalof, L. Dan, A. and Dietz, T. (2008). *Essentials of Social Research*. Maidenhead: Open University Press.

Neuman, W.L. (2006). *Social Research Methods: Qualitative and Quantitative Approaches*. Boston: Pearson, Allyn and Bacon.

Saunders, M.N.K., Lewis, P. and Thornhill, A. (2009). *Research Methods for Business Students*, 5th edition. Harlow: Pearson Education Ltd.

Veal, A.J. (2011). *Research Methods for Leisure and Tourism*, 4th edition. Harlow: Prentice Hall.

Chapter 3

The research process

Ramesh Durbarry

One of my undergraduate student studying the BSc (Hons) Tourism and Hospitality Management came to my office for a first meeting to discuss her dissertation. She sat down looking quite worried biting her fingernails. In fact, she was confused in that she had no idea where to begin, not to mention that she had not yet identified a research topic. I asked her which topic she would like to conduct her research. She replied: 'Give me a topic and I will do it.' I told her to conduct her research on estimating the tourism demand using the Time Varying Parameter model for the UK. She looked at me, her eyes wide open and she almost shrunk in her chair. Obviously, it was a paper that I was working on! She got my point that the topic should come from her and I then guided her towards a topic suited to her ability: we discussed the modules she liked most and why, which topic was interesting and why so. She finally came up with a vague topic on assessing the behaviour of tourists towards local residents. The next question she inquisitively asked was: 'What do I do now?'

3.0 Chapter objectives

The objective of this chapter is to introduce you to the elements of the research process. This chapter outlines the different stages of the process and describes the interrelationship between the stages as part of an overall process.

This chapter provides a structure which you can adopt, particularly if you are conducting research for the first time. This chapter will provide the basis of the different chapters in the book from selecting a title to conducting the literature review and writing up the research.

After studying this chapter, you will be able to:

● understand what a research process is all about;
● understand what the necessary steps are to conduct your research;
● outline the different stages of the research process; and
● provide an initial structure to your research.

3.1 What is the research process?

The research process is like a research map or a planner that will guide you through the journey. Once you know more or less the area you will be researching, the first part involves identifying key steps, locating resources (data and information) and analysing the stock of materials. The second part includes developing and expressing your ideas; this is where you are making your own contribution to research and knowledge. As we discussed in Chapter 2, there is a reality out there and as a researcher you are using ways and strategies not only to understand the world, but also to make known what you will eventually find out. How you understand the phenomenon, provide an explanation and make it known basically constitute the research process.

The best way to start is to, at least, chose a vague area of interest. Consider using a blank sheet and add ideas as you go along. Stick this sheet on the wall in front of your desk so that you get every opportunity to reflect on the ideas that you have jotted down.

Practical tips: what do I jot down on the blank sheet?

Ask yourself—what knowledge do I have on the topic? Do I know some authors who have written on this topic? What do I research on? What research questions do I ask? How will I answer these questions? Where can I get the data? How do I get the data? Is this a feasible research project given the time that I have?

Remember that there is strictly no such thing as a sequential process in research, although when the final piece is presented is looks very fluid from one step to the next. For this reason, you do not have to complete one step before moving on to the next. Initially, you may skip steps, undertake some steps concurrently or avoid some. This is why it is wise to scribble down ideas that relate to the research from which you can then design the research process in an organised manner with some fluidity. The next section shows you how to do this.

3.2 Understanding the research process

> Show me an example of the research process, I will understand it better.

If you are conducting your research, let's say on a tourism-related topic, probably the best way to understand the structure of research output is to read a journal article, from *Annals of Tourism Research*, *Tourism Management*, *Journal of Travel and Research*, among others. You will observe that several research articles have the following structure:

(i) Introduction
(ii) Literature review
(iii) Theory or model selection
(iv) Methodology
(v) Results and findings
(vi) Conclusion and discussions

The above structure is very superficial but is a good starting point. Remember that the published articles have been written by experienced researchers and scholars. There are many phases that have been considered before reaching this stage, such as revisions, reflections and articulation of the ideas, which we do not see.

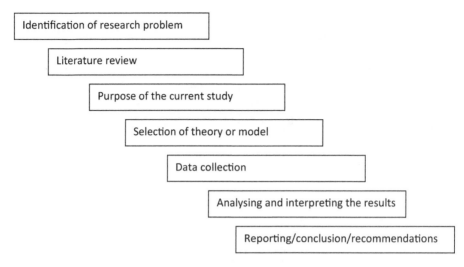

Figure 3.1 Steps in research

On your blank sheet you can consider expanding ideas on then themes specified in Figure 3.1 to form the initial stage of your research without any strict order.

The above process is not meant to be a linear process and is not a fixed set of steps. Neuman (2006) explains that the research process follows a sequence of steps. In fact, he identified a seven-step process which varies depending on whether the study involves a quantitative or a qualitative approach. A quantitative approach tends to follow a linear path, whereas qualitative research tends to be more recursive in nature. More importantly is that each step needs to be developed further. This is illustrated in Figure 3.2 showing the possible interconnections among the steps.

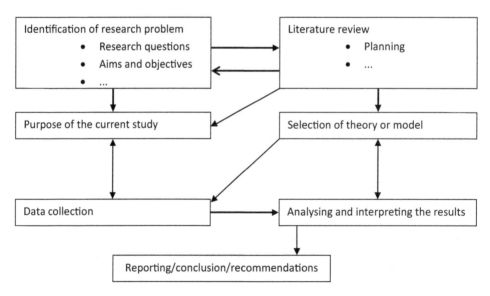

Figure 3.2 Connections between the steps

3.3 How to proceed?

To further understand the research process, we have identified five phases which are important to define the overall process. Moving from one phase to the next does not necessarily imply completion of that phase. Rather, the researcher has to constantly review the preceding phase given new information from the current phase. This will bring improvements to the overall process. The five main phases are:

1 Identify the research topic
2 Review the literature
3 Design the research strategy
4 Implement the research design
5 Evaluate and reflect

Phase 1: identify the research topic

Your initial starting point will be in identifying an area where you feel you can, at least, conduct research. The topic can be very broad in the beginning, for example, the behaviour of tourists, the motivation of tourists, perception of international tourists on a particular service, impact of tourism on the local community, residents' attitude towards tourists. Looking at the research problem from your perspective will define the way forward. Let's say you have chosen to research the behaviour of tourists; you can look at it from an economic point of view or from a social perspective or from a cultural dimension. Your academic background, knowledge on the topic or personal experience will tend to drive the dimension of your research. An article by Carr (2002) in *Tourism Management* provides you with an example of the researcher's interest in tourist behaviour. The title of the article 'A comparative analysis of the behaviour of domestic and international young tourists' is focused on providing a comparative analysis of the behaviour of young, single, international and domestic tourists during their holidays. We not only identify the research problem in Carr's topic from the title, but can also detect the narrowing down of the topic to tourists who are young.

The first thing that you already know is that you are going to conduct research in tourism in a broad area of interest to you. The next stage will be to narrow down the topic and to be more focused. How to narrow it down to a researchable topic is discussed in the next chapter.

Phase 2: review the literature

Where do we get ideas from? The most obvious thing to do is to take stock of the research other scholars have already carried out and this can only be done through a thorough literature review. How to conduct the literature review is discussed in Chapter 5.

What can we obtain from this exercise? These are a few important elements you can extract from a literature review, such as:

● ideas to formulate research questions;
● examples of aims and objectives;
● ideas of how the literature is to be reviewed;
● authors who have contributed on the topic;
● critical analysis of the topic by scholars;

- models or theories which have been put forward, adopted or adapted;
- hypotheses to be tested;
- research methodologies used;
- data analysis techniques; and
- identify gaps on research already conducted.

Hence, while conducting the literature review you can go backwards and reformulate your research topic based on what other researchers have already done. At this stage you need to start to identify key research questions that will sharpen your research and make it more focused. Try to seek one or two main research questions at this stage. In the next chapter, this is discussed in more details.

Phase 3: design a research strategy

In this step you are seeking ways to best answer your research questions. This will depend on the approach you use to collect your information needs such as data collection. Depending on your 'ism', that is your research philosophy, as discussed in Chapter 2, you will be choosing either a deductive or an inductive research approach. In the simplest definition, deductive research is theory or model testing (Figure 3.3) whereas inductive research is theory or model generating (Figure 3.4). The deductive approach is where you make use of a theory or develop a theory and hypothesise a relationship to be tested by collecting data. The inductive approach is where you collect data and then develop a theory to explain the phenomenon or relationship. While the former approach tends to rely more on positivism and employs more quantitative methods, the latter tends more to interpretivism and relies much more on qualitative methods.

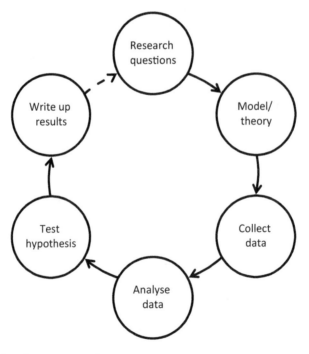

Figure 3.3 Deductive approach

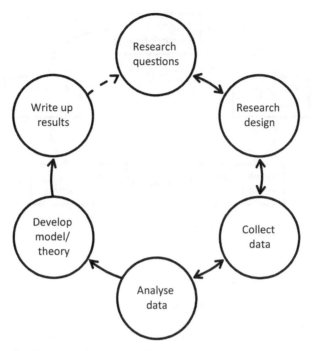

Figure 3.4 Inductive approach

Practical tips

After selecting your topic, work out your research plan in terms of whether you will use a deductive approach, which uses more a scientific and quantitative approach, or an inductive approach, which relies more on qualitative approaches. At this stage, you are in fact planning the research.

Phase 4: implement the research design

The implementation stage of the research design involves strategies to be used to collect and, subsequently, to analyse the data. The research strategy involves making use of, for example, a survey, case studies and grounded theory. These are discussed in Chapters 8 to 13. Data collection is very much linked with ethical issues relating to permission to conduct the study, gaining access to organisations and people and reporting the 'truth' about the data. These will be discussed in more detail in Chapter 6.

Practical tips

Assess the merits of some of the techniques you think might be applicable for your research to collect data. For instance, you may decide to use either online or mail surveys. List the merits as well as the limitations of using each method.

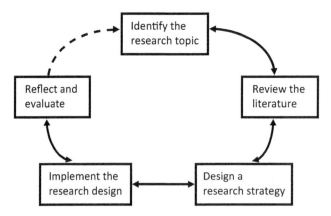

Figure 3.5 The research process phases

Phase 5: reflect and evaluate

At this stage you will have a first-hand picture of the research you will be conducting. It will be a good idea to evaluate your approach and try to foresee the merits, constraints and challenges you may face given your selected approach. If needs be, you can still review your research questions, approach and data collection strategy as it not too late to make changes now. It is always helpful to discuss your line of thinking with your supervisor or friends.

Practical tips

Re-examining your research process from different perspectives may bring, for example, innovative ideas, new research questions, new study methods and another data collection method. This will provide a comprehensive approach to your research.

The research process is an important stage that you must pass through, although it is a complex one. You have to adopt an iterative approach, that is, returning to the previous phase and re-examining it. This is illustrated in Figure 3.5. Revisions will lead to new ideas and improvements and you are more likely to bring creativity to your work. To be successful you must be open to change and observe fluidity in the process.

Chapter summary

- The research process is a research map and identifies key stages to locate resources and develop ideas.
- The research process is not linear and may require constant revisions to achieve the research objectives.

- There are five key stages: identifying the research topic, reviewing the literature, designing the research strategy, implementing the research design, and reflecting and evaluating.
- Adopt an iterative approach to make the process fluid.

Discussion questions

3.1 How do you identify a research topic?

3.2 Identify at least five journal articles related to your topic. List the similarities and differences among the articles using the structure suggested in Section 3.2, from (i) to (vi).

3.3 Why is the literature review important to your research?

3.4 Based on the literature you identified in Question 3.2, can you identify any research gap or identify weaknesses?

3.5 Using a journal article which is closely related to your chosen topic to conduct your research, apply the research process phases discussed in this chapter to demonstrate your course of actions.

3.6 Using a blank sheet, jot down your course of actions in each phase of the research process.

Further reading

Bryman, A. (2008). *Social Research Methods*. London: Oxford University Press.

Bryman, A. and Bell, E. (2007). *Business Research Methods*, revised edition. London: Oxford University Press.

Gayle, J. (2001). *Tourism Research*. Milton: John Wiley & Sons Australia Ltd.

Neuman, W.L. (2006). *Social Research Methods: Qualitative and Quantitative Approaches*. Boston: Pearson, Allyn and Bacon.

Saunders, M.N.K., Lewis, P. and Thornhill, A. (2009). *Research Methods for Business Students*, 5th edition. Harlow: Pearson Education Ltd.

Veal, A.J. (2011). *Research Methods for Leisure and Tourism*, 4th edition. Harlow: Prentice Hall.

Chapter 4

Developing a research proposal

Ramesh Durbarry and Anjusha Durbarry

Some students' points of view:

'Why do I have to write a research proposal?'

'Why should I tell you what I will be doing in my dissertation? I know exactly what to do.'

4.0 Chapter objectives

From the preceding chapter, you now have an overall picture of the research stages that you have to focus on to conduct your research. This chapter and the following ones will now elaborate further on those stages and provide tangible clues for you to embark on your study. Although the research process has become clearer, now it becomes important to provide a structure so that you stay focus on your research study and ensure completion within a set time period. The latter also implies some time management. This 'structure' is best presented in a research proposal so that a clear picture of the study is depicted and also it helps course leaders to identify a relevant supervisor to guide you through the research stages. Remember though that your research will not necessarily strictly follow the research proposal, this will most probably evolve especially if you are undertaking a doctoral research.

After studying this chapter, you will be able to:

- narrow down your research topic for your study;
- identify an appropriate title;
- understand what aims and objectives are;
- write down your research questions;
- provide a preliminary literature review relevant to your research;
- identify your research method;
- plan your time to complete your project using a Gantt chart; and
- work out a research proposal.

4.1 What is a research proposal?

A research proposal is simply a coherent summary of your proposed research. A research proposal not only clarifies what you have already decided to do but articulates your research ideas in a such a way that your supervisor or the Dissertation Committee is convinced you have a worthwhile research project. It is a piece of work which is used to evaluate the feasibility of the proposed study. It includes key elements in the research process (refer to Figure 3.3) and is presented in a structured form as to how your research will be conducted.

In writing the research proposal you will have to convince the person reading it why you are pursuing the chosen topic, what knowledge you have on the topic, what are the central issues and questions you will be looking at, how you will accomplish the aims and objectives and how much time you will take to conduct the proposed study.

If I write on these areas, are they enough?

Providing only sketchy details is not enough. First you will need to provide sufficient information and direction to indicate that your study is 'doable' and researchable in the set time frame (until the submission date). The research proposal should be well written, clearly expressing your arguments; it should be clear and compelling. The reader can determine whether your research will be completed within the defined time period by going through your research proposal (let alone decide whether it is a good one).

Practical tips: what does a research proposal address?

A research proposal addresses the following questions:

- Why you want to research a particular topic or phenomenon?
- What do you know on the subject?
- What you plan to accomplish?
- How you are going to conduct it?

4.2 What would normally be included in a research proposal?

The structure of a research proposal may differ from several disciplines – for example, a scientific research proposal tends to be shorter in length. However, one would expect the following elements to be present in a research proposal, regardless of discipline:

- Title
- Abstract (optional)
- Introduction/background/rationale
- Aims
- Objectives
- Research questions
- Literature review
- Methodology
- Time frame
- References

Although the structure provides a flow, it is not necessary to start in the order listed above. For example, to search for a meaningful title requires looking at past studies in the literature.

4.3 Getting started

Choosing a meaningful topic for your research study or your dissertation is always a great challenge. In fact, selecting a topic may feel like one of the biggest pressures, which add a higher degree of stress levels for students. In general, students are going to spend either one semester or two full semesters (depending on their respective university) on their research project. Therefore, you need to choose a research topic that is challenging and interesting. This could be solving a management problem, a social concern, addressing an environment problem, a policy issue and so on. The topic you choose to research should be in area where you have a certain 'liking' and interest; otherwise you might give up or it might be an additional stress at times. In other words, you will have to be very passionate about your topic, so choose a topic which fascinates you. Indeed, you should never be pressured by others while choosing your research topic. You may seek advice from your lecturers or from potential supervisors by having informal chats or discussions or from friends who have already (recently) completed their research studies/dissertations.

So where do I start?

As a tourism student, you are most likely to research a topic which is in the field of tourism. Having covered so many topics in your first or second year, you would probably have a certain preference for a topic or topics, such as buyer behaviour, attraction management, tourists' behaviour, service quality, employee motivation, tourists' perception, tourism marketing, tourism crime, crisis management, social impact, environmental impact, economic impact, to name just some of them. Try to narrow them down until you have two or three topics from which to choose from.

Since you will be working on your research for quite a while, try to find a research topic which is interesting but also one that you have some knowledge on. At this stage, it may still be vague. To be able to narrow it down further will require some more work, for example, try to have a brainstorming session with your friends or lecturers.

What should I be aiming for?

The most important thing is that you will have to produce research which contributes to knowledge and reaches new conclusions and findings. This means that your research will make a real or significant contribution, for example by filling a gap, solving a problem, clarifying a management problem, or testing or developing a model. The research will be valuable when it makes a contribution to the scholarly literature.

4.4 Where do I start searching?

There are many places where you can start searching.

4.4.1 Past dissertations (for your eyes only!)

With internet access, you can instantly access past dissertations through your university's digital library. Browse or download a few of them which are related to your chosen area of research, look at the titles, what does the title tell you, try to understand what the author was trying to investigate, look at the structure, and so on. This will give you some confidence in your endeavour by looking at how your previous peers have carried out their research. However, do not attempt to read too deeply, otherwise there is a tendency to replicate the work (in terms of style, literature, method, and so on) and the danger is that you do not know how good the work has been.

4.4.2 The internet

Use the internet search engines to explore the keywords on your topic. 'Googling' key concepts, for example, will generate book titles, research reports, unresolved issues, and so on. Browsing and reading these will perhaps provide you a direction. For example, Box 4.1 presents the results when the keywords 'tourism crime' was 'googled'.

Box 4.1: search results for 'tourism crime' on Google (accessed on 9 June 2017; extract from page 1 only and some details have been removed)

1   Tourism and Crime – Why Tourists become Victims – Safe …

   www.safecommunitiesportugal.com/.../Tourism-Crime-Paper-by-Maria-Bras-Pr...

2   Crime puts tourists off South Africa – Telegraph – The Telegraph

   www.telegraph.co.uk/travel/destinations/africaandindianocean/southafrica/737860/Crime-puts-tourists-off-South-Africa.html

3   Tourism and Crime – Center for Problem-Oriented Policing

   www.popcenter.org/problems/crimes_against_tourists/PDFs/Pelfrey_1998.pdf

4   Tourism, Leisure, and Crime – Oxford Handbooks

   www.oxfordhandbooks.com/view/10.1093/...001.../oxfordhb-9780199935383-e-009

5   Tourism and Crime in America – Universidad de Palermo

   www.palermo.edu/economicas/cbrs/pdf/.../paper1-Tourism-and-Crime-in-America.pd etc …

```
Searches related to tourism crime

    impact of crime on tourism          how does crime affect the tourism industry

    tourism increased crime             rate crime rate increase due to tourism

    crime rates affecting tourism       effects of crime on the tourism industry

    crime due to tourism                crime against tourists statistics
```

From the Google search, the researcher can decide to look at, for example, the impact of crime on tourist arrivals in a chosen destination, whether crime does have an impact on tourist arrivals or how much tourism has been affected, quantifying the impact, or whether tourism perpetuates crime. All these are relevant researchable topics. At the bottom of the search in Box 4.1, Google lists some related searches to 'tourism crime' and these can present you some ideas to explore some issues or relationships.

4.4.3 Social science databases

Ultimately you will have to search the literature, more importantly, scholarly literature. This means searching journal articles, peer reviewed publications (books, conference proceedings, and so on). You should, for instance, use journal databases. Social science databases such as EBSCO, Science Direct, Ingenta and Emerald are recommended to find relevant journal articles. Some tourism related journals are:

Annals of Tourism Research

International Journal of Hospitality Management

International Journal of Contemporary Hospitality Management

Journal of Hospitality Management and Tourism

Journal of Hospitality Marketing & Management

Journal of Hotel & Business Management

Journal of Tourism Studies

Journal of Travel Research

Journal of Travel and Tourism Marketing

Journal of Vacation Marketing

Leisure Studies

Tourism Analysis

Tourism Economics

Ramesh Durbarry and Anjusha Durbarry

Tourism Management

Tourism and Recreation Research

Travel and Tourism Analyst

Visit www.ciret-tourism.com/index/listes_revues.html (accessed 10 June 2017) for further journal titles.

4.5 The sections

4.5.1 Title

By reviewing the literature, you will be in a better position to choose a title that is interesting and is communicating what your research is all about. When refining your title, you may wish to use verbs/adverbs that could make an impact on the reader. Remember that your title should neither be too long nor too short. When someone reads your title, he/she will immediately have an idea of what you are undertaking in your study (see Box 4.2 for examples of vague and acceptable titles).

> ## Box 4.2: examples of titles submitted by Year 2 students for their dissertation
>
> **Vague or over ambitious titles:**
>
> > Sustainable tourism in Brighton
> >
> > Environmental impact of tourism
> >
> > Destination tourism marketing
> >
> > Customer satisfaction in travel and tourism
>
> **More refined titles:**
>
> > Motivations to attend music events
> >
> > Local impacts of 2014 winter Olympics
> >
> > Residents' perception on tourism impacts: Birmingham
> >
> > Impact of tobacco regulations on event sponsorship
> >
> > Residents' attitudes towards local events
> >
> > Travel motivations to Bucharest by residents in Luton
> >
> > Attendance behaviour modelling: sport events

4.5.2 Introduction

The introduction will not necessarily be the first section that you will write. In fact, most of the time, this is written after the literature has been searched, the title has been identified and the research aims and objectives have been specified.

After you have a clear picture of the research study, you can write the introduction. In particular, you will provide some background information on the topic, current trends in the literature and what has been researched and found. You can highlight the implications of current research. You can then provide a rationale for what you will try to achieve in your research study, given the time frame. This is where you can state what your contribution to knowledge will be and which gap you are filling.

4.5.3 Aims and scope of your study

For any study, it is important to define the main aim or purpose in broad terms. For instance, the main aim of a study could be to assess the level of customer satisfaction at a visitor attraction. Having the main aim or purpose ensures that the researcher or student knows exactly what he/she wants to do.

In addition to the main aim or purpose of study, it is equally important to define the scope of the study. The main reason in the case of a student is that he/she has a limited time to complete his/her research. As a result, the scope of the study should be well-defined. This is done by formulating appropriate research objectives and research questions.

4.5.4 Aims, objectives and research questions

To help you write your research aim, and possibly further refine your title, you should be formulating some key research questions. There can be only one central question, and at most two or three, or your research will be too huge a task given the time that you have to complete and submit it. The main research question can then be complemented by subsidiary questions. By going through the literature review, you will be able to set your own research questions, for example based on the gaps you have identified or questioning whether similar conclusions will be reached in a different context (region, country, time, and so on). Using the example of customer satisfaction, if a paper has found that customer satisfaction in a restaurant is significantly determined by the price and quality of food, you may wish to investigate: 'Does customers' age have any influence on customer satisfaction in a branded restaurant?' or 'How does customer satisfaction differ by the behaviour of employees?'

Practical tips

Research questions inform us what you are trying to do and are very specific.

From the research questions we can only get an indication of the various questions which will be answered. However, still we are not sure of the end product of the research.

We can encircle all the research questions into a statement to inform the reader what you are going to achieve. This 'statement' is referred to the *aim* of the research.

What are aims?

An aim is a broad statement stating the intention(s) of the research. It is basically stipulating what will be accomplished but not how it is going to be accomplished. For example, 'To assess the level of customer satisfaction in branded restaurants.' The reader can now understand what will be achieved in the research. You can observe that the statement *does not say how* this will be achieved. The aim addresses the long-term outcome of the research.

Practical tips

To state the aim, it should be in the form 'To . . .', for example, 'To assess . . .', To evaluate . . .', 'To analyse . . .', 'To determine . . .'.

Objectives

How will the aim(s) be achieved? These are achieved by setting objectives. Objectives are the steps you are going to take to answer your research questions to achieve your aim(s). They are specific tasks needed to accomplish the goals of the research. They emphasise *how* the aims are to be accomplished. As Brotherton (2008) explains, objectives should be 'action-oriented, specific, achievable and clearly be making a contribution to the achievement of the aim' (p. 53). Each objective states how a specific output is to be accomplished.

Specifying objectives lead to greater clarity to the reader than the research questions. They explain how the aim(s) will be accomplished. The objectives also establish the limits of the study.

Practical tips

Objectives are usually expressed in the following form using action verbs: 'To describe . . .', 'To compare . . .', 'To test . . .', 'To develop . . .', 'To conduct . . .'.

4.5.5 Literature review

In a research proposal for a dissertation you need to select at least around ten journal articles which are closely related to the area you are looking into (you may need around 40 to 50 for PhD research). Familiarise yourself with what has been researched in the area. Read the most recent articles, as they are most likely to identify gaps in the research area for future work (this might give you a head start). These most recent journal articles would also have reviewed the literature, hence presenting you with a detailed critical analysis of past work. At this stage you should be looking at the aim of the study, the research question(s) the author(s) is (are) posing, how the author(s) is (are) addressing those questions, the research approach, the methodology used, the (academic) writing style and examining how the results and findings are analysed and presented.

Take notes as you read the articles and use coloured pens to highlight interesting aspects. Reflect on the few articles you have read and write up a summary of what you have on each of the articles. For the literature review section in your research proposal, if you just write, let's say, the summaries of five articles one after the other, it does not add any value. At this stage you are becoming more aware of discussions on the topic and starting to obtain some ideas for your research. What is more important is that you look at the five articles in parallel and critically look at similarities or contrasting arguments, ideas, questions and methodologies that the authors have used. For example, you can say: 'While author X has used a mail survey to investigate customer satisfaction, author Y has used an internet survey.' You can even group articles which have supported the same hypothesis and reported the same findings against those that have different findings. This type of writing is called *synthesising* compared to just summarising.

Most importantly, the purpose is to determine what has been done up to now, what the gaps are, what methodologies were used, and so on; all these will guide you on what you will be doing and why you believe that your chosen research study is an interesting piece of research work. In Chapter 5, we look in more detail at the literature review: the different types of literature review, how to conduct a review and how to review the literature critically.

4.5.6 Methodology

How you accomplish your objective will depend on which methodology is most appropriate. This will also depend on the research paradigm. If you are a positivist, you are more likely to use a quantitative approach. If you are adopting an interpretivist approach, you are more likely to use qualitative methods such as focus groups, interviews and ethnography. You may also use mixed methods, particularly if you wish to check the robustness of your results (we will discuss this further in Chapter 10).

4.5.7 Time frame: the Gantt chart

Research must have a timescale for submission. Your research needs planning if you want to deliver it on time. Research activities are very demanding and proper planning will ensure timely submission, although in many cases they can take longer than anticipated. Proper time management will avoid the need for requesting an extension, which is stressful in itself to obtain.

Activities	Month 1	Month 2	Month 3	Month 4	Month 5	Month 6	Month 7	Month 8	Month 9
Literature search	■	■							
Outline research questions			■						
Aims and objectives			■						
Literature review				■					
Methodology				■					
Draft questionnaire				■					
Pilot questionnaire				■					
Conduct survey					■				
Collect and input data						■			
Analyse data						■			
Conduct statistical test						■			
Write results and findings							■		
Submit preliminary chapters							■		
Update chapters								■	
Write conclusion								■	
Format as per guidelines									■
Submit dissertation									■

Figure 4.1 Gantt chart for a research project

Although the plan may not be accurate, the reader can assess the viability of the research given the timescale. Many researchers use a Gantt chart, which was developed by Henry Gantt in 1917. It illustrates the research schedule: the start and finish dates and the summary elements of the research. The Gantt chart is a visual interpretation of the tasks or activities that make up your research project, each plotted against a time line. Figure 4.1 gives an example.

Practical tips: guide for a good research proposal

What the research proposal must address the following questions:

- What do you plan to accomplish?
- Why do you want to accomplish this research?
- How are you going to accomplish the research?

Ensure the following:

- The title is clear and enthuses the reader.
- Aims and objectives are clearly written.
- The research questions are consistent with the aim and objectives.
- Influential and landmark studies are cited.
- A critical literature review is conducted.
- The boundaries of your research are defined.
- The main theories, models, hypotheses and ideas developed by other researchers are presented.
- The focus stays on the research questions.
- Major issues in your research are identified.
- How you are going to accomplish the research in terms of the research methodology is explained.
- You provide a time plan.

In Box 4.3 an example of a 'Table of Contents' from a research proposal prepared by a tourism student at the University of Bedfordshire is provided. In Box 4.4, an extract from the research proposal, illustrates the 'Introduction' and the 'Aims and objectives' sections.

Box 4.3: table of contents

Project proposal:

'How effective is the marketing communication strategy of Woburn Safari Park in encouraging repeat visitors to the attraction?'
By Gemma Lumsden

(continued)

(continued)

Table of Contents

Permission was obtained from Gemma Lumsden to make use of her research proposal.

Box 4.4: extract from the research proposal of Gemma Lumsden

'How effective is the marketing communication strategy of Woburn Safari Park in encouraging repeat visitors to the attraction?'
By Gemma Lumsden

1 Introduction

Marketing has become an integral part of maintaining growth and development in the leisure sector; visitor attractions are continuously improving and developing their marketing strategies as more and more competition is entering the market (Briggs, 2001). The American Marketing Association (2007) define marketing as, 'Marketing is the activity, set of institutions, and processes for creating, communicating, delivering, and exchanging offerings that have value for customers, clients, partners, and society at large'. Marketing has become an important aspect for managing visitor attractions as it allows the organisation to communicate with the public and encourage people to visit; therefore, generating revenue for the attraction (Page and Connell, 2006). It is vital that marketing is continuously monitored and evaluated within organisations with the aim of improving the quality and success of the strategies utilised. The purpose of the study is to research the ways in which Woburn Safari Park employs marketing tools and techniques and how these are perceived by visitors to the attraction.

1.1 Area of study

Woburn Safari Park is part of the Woburn Estate comprising of: Woburn Abbey, The Inn at Woburn, and Woburn Golf Club. The estate is owned by the Duke of Bedford and the safari park was opened by the Duke in 1970 as the first visitor attraction of its type. The attraction allows visitors to view animals in their natural environments; able to roam freely as opposed to the traditional version of zoos hosting animals in pens and cages (Woburn Safari Park, 2012). The safari park boasts 360 acres of parkland making up the 'road safari' in which visitors can drive through and see the animals out in the open. There is also a 'foot safari' presenting smaller animals in walk-through enclosures and offering visitors the experience of feeding times as well as shows and demonstrations. When the park opened in 1970, no form of marketing was undertaken; the attraction thrived within its first year of opening, with visitor numbers exceeding 1 million solely from its unique appeal being the first attraction of its kind (Woburn Safari Park, 2012). However, in the years following the opening, visitor numbers began to drop; the Duke came to the conclusion that money needed to be invested in marketing strategies to promote the safari park and once again attract visitors.

1.2 Aims and objectives

The proposed research question is as follows:
'How effective is the marketing communication strategy of Woburn Safari Park in encouraging repeat visitors to the attraction?'
The aim of the study is to evaluate how effective the marketing communication strategy used by the safari park is in the view of those who have visited the attraction; either for the first time or as repeat visitors.
The objectives of the study are:

- Identify the different marketing communication channels used by Woburn to attract visitors.
- Collect data on how visitors to Woburn Safari Park perceive the marketing techniques used by the attraction.
- Determine whether visitors perceive the marketing techniques to be effective in attracting new visitors as well as encouraging repeat business.
- Identify the importance and impact of discounted rates and offers used in marketing strategies.
- Analyse trends in visitor numbers alongside different marketing techniques used by Woburn Safari Park.

Chapter summary

- Writing a research proposal does take some time. However, it is time well spent if it has been properly carried out.
- A research proposal will enable your potential supervisor to know what you want to do as part of your final year dissertation or research project. In some universities, it is assessed either by your potential supervisor or by a panel of academic staff.
- You will be given feedback in terms of whether it is appropriate for the level and programme of study, including whether it is feasible. In addition, based on your research proposal, you may be allocated an appropriate supervisor who will be guiding you throughout your study.
- Select a topic on which you have some knowledge.
- Read journal articles to familiarise yourself with the writing style, to identify future research work and to draw up a title for your research.
- The structure of your research proposal should include: Title, Introduction, Aims and objectives, Literature review, Methodology and Time scale.

Discussion questions

4.1 Explain how your research proposal will be similar to or different from a structure proposed for scientists. (You may use the following web link: www.anc.ed.ac.uk/dtc/index.php?option=com_content&task=view&id=136&Itemid=0.)

4.2 What is grey literature and scholarly literature?

4.3 Why is it important to conduct a literature review?

4.4 What is the difference between aims and objectives?

4.5 What will determine the choice of your research methods?

Further reading

Cooper, D.R. and Schindler, P.S. (2003). *Business Research Methods*, 8th edition. New York: McGraw-Hill.

Davis, D. (2005). *Business Research for Decision Making*, 6th edition. Mason, OH: South-Western College Publishing.

Hussey, J. and Hussey, R. (1997). *Business Research: A Practical Guide for Undergraduate and Postgraduate Students*. Basingstoke: Macmillan Business.

Chapter 5

Reviewing the literature

Anjusha Durbarry and Ramesh Durbarry

'Why should I conduct a literature review? What will I gain from doing such an exercise? How the review will inform my research? Can I be critical of others' work?' These are among the many questions students ask.

Before you start your own research spend some time knowing how and why other researchers have carried out their research. Read journal articles (a must for scholars), books, newspapers, magazines, blogs, among many others.

5.0 Chapter objectives

This chapter explains why the literature review forms an integral part of any research study and provides an insight into how the literature review is conducted. We present a systematic way to conduct a literature review. The proposed framework consists of the following: sources of information (collecting data), the review process and composing the literature review.

After studying this chapter, you will be able to:

- understand the importance of conducting a literature review;
- select the relevant literature to assist you in carrying out your research;
- critically review the literature; and
- identify a structure to write your literature review chapter.

5.1 Importance of conducting a literature review

A literature review provides a historical overview of the theory and the research literature. It aims to support the argument put forward by you using existing evidence. A literature review plays a significant role to:

- validate your choice of research question;
- produce a theoretical or conceptual framework;
- demonstrate that you are familiar with up-to-date research regarding the topic;
- determine the importance of the topic;
- identify gaps in the literature;
- provide background information required to understand the study; and
- fulfil the requirement of your study.

You should be aware of the body of knowledge that exists on a particular subject, topic or research question. Awareness on what has been written allows you to track intellectual progressions on your research topic. A methodological review of existing literature is also a crucial endeavour for you to apprise the various methods which have been employed. The need to uncover the existing body of knowledge before embarking on any research study should not be underestimated. It is imperative that you analyse existing literature related to your research topic and review it systematically, especially if you are working towards generating new knowledge. An effective literature review ensures that you do not have to start 'from scratch', running the risk of producing irrelevant work by investigating approaches that are already known.

5.2 The literature review

A literature review is taking stock of the current or existing knowledge that has been generated on a particular subject, topic or research question. Generally it takes into consideration what has already been published by attributed researchers and how the findings are reported. The literature on a particular topic can be found in textbooks, journals, magazines, newspapers, and so on. Nowadays almost all of the literature is published electronically and is accessible, for example, from the digital library of your university, depending on subscriptions.

By carrying out a literature review you will be aware of the current state of the knowledge relating to the topic which is being investigated and also gives you the opportunity to examine how various researchers have conducted their research. This process of engagement increases the knowledge of the reader in many aspects as it answers the following questions:

- What has been researched?
- Why was the research conducted? (Purpose)
- How was the research conducted? (Conceptual framework, research methodologies, research design, and so on)
- If any, how data were collected?
- What came out of the research? (Such as conclusions, model, theory, and so on)
- How do I design my own research?

A literature review enables the researcher to learn from others and stimulate new ideas (Neuman, 2006).

5.3 Conducting the literature review

You can see from the above that a lot of information can be obtained from the literature review and it is an important exercise, otherwise, you may be conducting research which has already been investigated and will, hence, be of no value. So now that you know what a literature review is, the question is how to conduct it. Your literature review should be guided by a central research question. This central question may be fine-tuned as you acquire more knowledge on your topic. In fact, as you progress with the literature review you will be able to tighten your research questions.

To enable you to conduct the literature review, a simple framework can be used, as illustrated in Figure 5.1. The framework for conducting literature review is divided into three phases:

- Phase 1: Sources of information – the key issues related to gathering relevant information.

Figure 5.1 A framework for conducting and writing an effective literature review

- Phase 2: Critical literature review – the data processing, evaluation, assessing for relevance.
- Phase 3: Synthesising – writing the literature review including the bibliographic details.

Phase 1: Sources of information

Researchers search for information on existing published research from a number of sources. The matrix in Figure 5.2 indicates some common sources of information.

The first part of the framework is related to locating information for the literature review. Always start by reading from the current year and proceed to previous years. In this way you will be able to learn the latest developments in the field. Novice researchers often face the problem of identifying the correct sources of information. The academic librarian is usually the best person to talk to, as he/she can guide you to the best resources that your institution has. We discuss some important sources here.

Peer-reviewed papers

It may be noted that academic research work gains significance when it is published. Peer-reviewed papers usually undergo rigorous quality control and the academic research community has implemented a process that eliminates setbacks prior to the publication of the research paper. Hence, using peer-reviewed paper to gather information can be an initial step. However, it is important to note that not all published materials are of high quality. For example, research journals have impact factors determining the quality, impact and influence of the research being published (see Box 5.1).

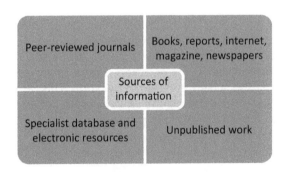

Figure 5.2 Common sources of information for conducting a literature review

---

Box 5.1: journal ranking database

There are many journal ranking databases such as:

- The SCImago Journal & Country Rank: www.scimagojr.com/index.php
- Australian Business Deans Council – Journal Ratings List: www.abdc.edu.au
- The Social Sciences Citation Index: http://ip-science.thomsonreuters.com
- See also an article by McKercher et al. (2006). 'Rating Tourism and Hospitality Journals', *Tourism Management*, 27 (6), 1235–1252.

In fact, we recommend that you read strategically by looking at the validity and reliability of the publications. To do so inquire about:

- author(s)
- date of publication
- title of the journal
- impact factor of the journal
- number of citations

Databases and electronic resources

The speed at which researchers identify relevant literature increased dramatically with the advent of electronic resources and databases. You must be thoroughly aware of online databases relevant to the field of your study and identify suitable literature and narrow down the search. The following process may be adopted to conduct searches electronically:

- Start initially with broad descriptors or well defined descriptors.
- Use synonyms of key concepts to broaden your search.
- Redefine the required topic and try to narrow down the search to a specific area of interest.
- Be sure to identify classic (landmark or influential) studies, as these provide the researcher with a framework for the study.

Books

Books would perhaps be the most obvious source in the library and do provide useful information on a topic. Nowadays, many textbooks guide the readers to various sources and include links to web pages, have blogs and are connected to a network of resources.

Assessing relevant research articles

After locating and identifying research articles, you must read and assess them. A journal article title provides a good indication of the nature of the research without describing the results; it informs you the context of the study. Next, the abstract summarises the important information about the study. It includes the study's purpose, the methodology used and highlights major findings. You should be able to decide on the relevance of the research article based on the title and abstract. If the research article appears relevant then you must probe further into it. The introduction and the conclusion are two important sections that indicate whether it is worth investing time in a detailed analysis of the paper. The introduction section, for example, has three main purposes:

- To present a broad topic and demonstrates a transition to a specific research question;
- To show the expanding knowledge in relation the topic and establishes connections with past work; and
- To provide an overview of theoretical framework and defines major concepts utilised.

A good literature review should be comprehensive, that is, it should include past to current studies that are relevant to the topic. It should be selective and should not just include everything that is written in a particular field. More importantly, the literature review should provide a critical evaluation.

Practical tips: how many should I read?

Many students cannot determine how many journal articles they have to read to be able to move to the next phase. You may have downloaded hundreds of articles which bear resemblance to your chosen topic, but not all might be relevant to your research. What to do? Use a 'skimming' technique:

1   Divide the pile of articles into two groups: relevant and not relevant. Read the title and abstract and immediately you will know whether it is relevant or not.
2   Discard the irrelevant ones and with the relevant pile divide them further into groupings as you think is more appropriate. It may be in chronological order, or it may be by themes, by theories, by models, by research paradigms, by research methodologies, and so on.

This process should enable you to read relevant ones. Note that it is the quality of the articles and their importance which matters not the quantity of articles that you use in your research.

There are several types of literature review. The type of review will depend on the purpose of your research and the research questions. Some types are highlighted below:

1   An *argumentative review* examines selected literature which, on one hand, offers support and, on the other hand, offers contradictory viewpoints on certain relationships, suppositions, theories, and so on.

2 A *historical review* is a review which is focused on research throughout a period of time and traces how the phenomenon has emerged, conceptualised, operationalised and shaped.

3 An *integrative review* includes all studies that address related research problems. Such a review synthesises representative literature on a topic in an integrated way.

4 A *methodological review* focuses on how the reality has been presented by looking at research approaches, data collection and analysis techniques.

5 A *systematic review* consists of reviewing all those studies related to a central research question. In such a review, you would collect multiple research papers and critically analyse them. Conclusions are evidence based.

6 In a *theoretical review*, the purpose is to examine the body of theories that has been proposed and investigated on a certain subject matter.

For more details, see Neuman, 2006, p. 112.

Phase 2: critical literature review

Once you have identified the articles for your review, you need to analyse them. You must bear in mind that a literature review is not a brief summary of each article reviewed with an annotated bibliography. A literature review goes beyond a summary of what you have read, it should incorporate a critical analysis of the relationship among different studies and is centred around your specific topic of interest.

The literature review can provide you with a theoretical framework and rationale for your research study. Besides enlarging your knowledge, a literature review allows you to gain and demonstrate skills in two areas:

- information searching skills, which is the ability to skim through the literature efficiently and to identify relevant publications, and
- the ability to evaluate critically.

The following may be useful when undertaking the literature review:

- Define the topic: you must identify a topic and some research question(s) at the initial stage.
- Get an overview of the articles: skim through the articles to identify the general purpose and content. The abstract, introduction, first few paragraphs and the conclusion of each article provide a general overview.
- Organise the articles into different themes and sub-themes.
- The relevant aspects of the topic must be presented in a logical order so that readers understand the context and significance of your study.
- A well-structured literature review presents the relevant aspects of the topic in a logical order that leads readers.
- Keep track of the supporting ideas, examples and sources that you will be using for each point as you organise the ideas for writing.
- Be centred around the topic or research questions.
- Critically analyse the information and identify controversial areas and loopholes in the literature.
- Identify areas that need further research.

Composing

You will have to take notes while you are reading the articles. First, decide on the format in which you will take notes as you read. These are some suggestions:

- Highlight key definitions and identify differences in the definition of the terms/concepts.
- Select useful quotations, copy the exact words from the article and ensure that you cite the page number.
- Note the important statistical data that have been used.
- Identify the strengths and weaknesses of different research studies and make an evaluation as you read.
- Identify main trends or patterns reported in a range of articles of your topic and analyse them.
- Identify relationships among studies such as which of them were the major ones which led to subsequent studies.
- Identify groups of authors supporting a particular view.
- Identify gaps in the literature, why the gaps exist and what can be done to address them.
- Ensure that your review is focused and relevant to your topic.

Reviewing the literature critically

It is important that the relevant articles are read critically, which usually involves questioning rather that accepting what is read. The strengths and the weaknesses of previous work must be assessed. Key academic theories pertaining to your research area must be identified as far as possible and included in the review. It is important that you provide necessary background information and arguments supported by referencing previous work.

Critically reviewing the literature enables you to generate new knowledge and justify a particular approach to research your topic: it assists the research design and helps build a conceptual framework, provides evidence or support when you select a particular research method and demonstrates how the study will contribute towards new knowledge.

Phase 3: synthesising

As we mentioned above, writing a summary of an article you have just read provides you with important information about the source, but synthesising the gist of the article is a re-organisation, or a reshuffling, of that information. Some strategies to write the review are:

- Provide a structure to the literature review. A literature review should contain an introduction, a body and a conclusion, and should be focused on a main topic or research question.
- Generate section headers or sub-sections, especially for longer literature review, for example, to highlight the different points of view, time period and debates.
- Indicate what other authors have written on the topic. You should avoid listing a series of research reports with a summary of the main findings from each one; rather, you must explain what the information or quoted material means

in relation to the literature review. The connection between a specific quote or information and the corresponding argument must be explained.

● Organise common findings together. A well-accepted approach is to deal with most important ideas at the beginning and to logically connect important findings or statements.

At the end of this chapter we provide the literature review section of Gemma Lumsden's research proposal following the 'Introduction' and 'Aims and objectives' sections presented in Chapter 3.

Practical tips: good practice when writing a literature review

● Organise your ideas and provide a structure.
● Focus your writing on the research topic.
● Avoid repetition.
● Ensure that the literature includes landmark and influential papers.
● Evaluate the research – question the articles that you are reading rather than just accepting them.
● Provide a synthesis of the papers that you have reviewed.
● Provide a conclusion of what you found in the literature.

Chapter summary

This chapter has discussed why it is important to conduct a literature review and, more importantly, how to conduct a critical literature review.

● A literature review provides the current or existing knowledge on a topic and probes into what is already known.
● It provides many sources of ideas about approaches to the topic, theories, models, research methodologies applied, and so on.
● Three phases for an effective literature review are: sources of information; critical literature review; and synthesising.
● Use a 'skimming' technique to detect materials relevant to your research.
● Read and assess the papers and materials identified.
● Question rather than accept what you read.
● Writing will occur smoothly once the main ideas of the literature review have been framed.
● Provide a logical structure to present the literature review.

Discussion questions

5.1 Why is a literature review is important?
5.2 Explain the process to undertake a literature review.

5.3 What is meant by 'critical literature review'?

5.4 Refer to the literature review at the end of the chapter; rewrite it in your own words.

Further reading

Brotherton, B. (2008). *Researching Hospitality and Tourism: A Student Guide*. London: Sage.

Neuman, W.L. (2006). *Social Research Methods: Qualitative and Quantitative Approaches*. Boston: Pearson, Allyn and Bacon.

Saunders, M.N.K., Lewis, P. and Thornhill, A. (2009). *Research Methods for Business Students*, 5th edition. Harlow: Pearson Education Ltd.

Veal A.J. (2011). *Research Methods for Leisure and Tourism*, 4th edition. Harlow: Prentice Hall.

Appendix: example of a critical literature review

Extracted from Gemma Lumsden's research proposal

2 Literature review

2.1 Marketing communications

The focus of the evaluative research will be on the marketing communication strategy of Woburn Safari Park. Communication is one of the main elements of the marketing process, allowing companies to promote their brand alongside creating impressions of their products and services in order to target potential consumers (Kotler, 2011). Devashish supports this by stating, 'The purpose of marketing communications is to add persuasive value to a product or service for customers'. These strategies have therefore become an important factor allowing organisations to reach their marketing objectives, consequently determining their overall success (Bennett & Strydom, 2001). Due to increasing competition within the visitor attractions sector, marketing communications also allow organisations to make their product or service recognised for its best qualities, Keller (2001, p. 823) states, 'In a cluttered, complex marketplace, marketing communications can allow brands to stand out and help consumers appreciate their comparative advantages'. Another key development in marketing communications is the continuous advances in technology; marketers must keep their marketing programs up to date with the introduction of mass communication methods (Varey, 2002). Kotler & Armstrong (2009, p. 433) elaborate on the process of creating effective marketing communication, identifying the following steps: 'identify the target audience, determine the communication objectives, design a message, choose the media through which to send the message, select the message source, and collect feedback'.

In terms of visitor attractions, marketing is more complex than that of manufactured goods as the visitor attraction industry is offering a service product. Swarbrooke (2002) outlines 5 primary characteristics of visitor attractions as service products causing implications on the marketing process. These characteristics include: staff – contribute to the production and delivery of the product, intangibility – customers cannot try the product before purchasing, perishability – the product cannot be stored and has no value if it is not sold, customers – different attitudes and behaviours affect the experience had by visitors, the product it is not standardised – moods and behaviour of staff differs creating a lack of quality control. These variables have to be considered carefully in the management and planning process to ensure the service is marketed effectively. Thompson (2001) also notes the importance of marketing through staff at visitor attractions stating, 'Word-of-mouth recommendation is considered as the best form of advertising – a satisfied visitor is telling someone on your behalf that they should visit your attraction', this supports Swarbrooke's focus on staffing and customer attitudes.

2.2 The marketing mix

One of the key terms in all forms of marketing is, 'marketing mix'; Cooper (1998) describe the combination of elements as, 'tools that may be manipulated to meet specific objectives and attract pre-defined target markets'. The marketing mix originated in its simplest form by McCarthy (1960) who identified 'the Four P's' these being; product, place, promotion and price. These 4 elements provide marketing personnel with a basic framework when creating marketing strategies (Goeldner & Ritchie, 2009). However, in terms of services marketing such as visitor attractions, customers base their perceptions of an organisation on elements such as their previous experiences and association with the company, the views of others, as well as any information they have gathered independently (Brown et al, 1991). Thus, Booms and Bittner (1981) suggested an extra 3 P's, these being; people, process and physical evidence. Services are intangible, perishable and heterogeneous; the additional 3 variables distinguish the marketing of services from that of manufactured goods (Kumar, 2010). 'People' refers to the interactions of staff and visitors, 'process' is the elements of the overall delivery of the service and physical evidence refers to the physical environment in which the organisation operates (Fyall & Garrod, 2005). The marketing mix is a flexible set of variables and is constantly being developed and added to in order to satisfy the needs of different organisation's marketing strategies (Hooley et al, 2008). The different components of the marketing mix need to be evaluated effectively in order to ensure that the right message is reaching the right audience, and that the right media channels have been used to target that audience (Dahlen et al, 2010).

2.3 Evaluating effectiveness

With regard to evaluating the effectiveness of marketing and advertising strategies, Wells (1997) notes that there are many difficulties facing researchers as other elements within the marketing mix contribute to the performance of an organisation. Wells (1997) also goes on to stress the importance of recognising whether presumably effective campaigns show any forms of pattern in order to determine their true effectiveness. In terms of visitor attractions, this would relate to a rise in visitor numbers at the time of perhaps seasonal campaigns throughout the year. However, Schwartz (1969) describes the difficulties in identifying a relationship between advertising and sales stating, 'a considerable time lag may exist between exposure to an effective advertisement or series of advertisements and the actual purchase'. Schwartz (1969) goes on to suggest a program for evaluating marketing effectiveness, comprising of measuring the following elements; exposure to different media forms, consumer message retention, consumer level of preference over other brands, consumer attitudes towards the product and recent consumer marketing behaviour. The work of Schwartz (1969) is relevant to the research topic as the program outlines a structure which the basis of the questionnaire can be formed around.

2.4 Repeat visitors

Visitor attractions are challenged with creating effective marketing strategies in order to both attract new visitors as well as encouraging repeat business. Litvin (2007) researched repeat visitors to destinations with focus on paid visitor attractions; his study revealed that marketing strategies used by attractions in Charleston were concentrating on the repeat visitor, despite this, his findings indicated that first-time visitors contributed more to the revenue of the attraction sector. Although Litvin's study is limited to the area of Charleston, his findings give an indication to the difficulties faced by attractions in retaining loyal customers, trying to improve their service to visitors and incorporate new products to encourage customers to return. However, this is a complex process for marketing departments entailing in depth market research of customer needs, analysis of resources available as well as careful consideration of how the product or service will be marketed to the consumer (Dibbs, 1995). One method of retaining visitors is to provide season tickets, loyalty schemes, local resident discounts or membership programs to offer more incentives to return to attractions and maintain attendance levels (Fyall et al, 2008). However, as Kinser & Fall (2005) recognise, when implementing such systems, communication with members is key to success and customer retention. Kinser & Fall (2005) undertook research in order to provide insight into the topic of repeat visitation as the industry was previously lacking relevant knowledge. Therefore, this study is intended to expand on the literature regarding the communication methods between the repeat visitor and host tourist attractions.

Chapter 6

Research ethics

Ramesh Durbarry

Paul is a third year student and has been working on his dissertation. The deadline for submission is in two weeks. He has been so busy with other assignments that he eventually found himself with limited time to conduct a survey to collect data. To cut corners, he has designed a survey questionnaire and piloted it on ten respondents. He also conducted a face-to-face interview with his cousin to gather information on his piece of work.

He has completed his writing up. In his data analysis section, he reports that surveys were conducted on 100 respondents (when in fact he did only ten). He also mentions that 15 face-to-face interviews were conducted. His result and discussions are based on these premises.

What would be your reaction to such a scenario?

6.0 Chapter objectives

After studying this chapter, you will be able to:

- understand why research ethics are important when conducting a research;
- understand the process for research ethics at your institution;
- know the information that are requested in an ethical form; and
- negotiate your research ethically at various stages.

6.1 Introduction

Research ethics are a set of principles that guide moral choices about how you should behave and your relationship with others. In social sciences research, ethics are associated with projects involving study participants, including use of questionnaires and focus groups, and you must ensure that research is conducted in line with ethical standards so that no harm is caused to the participant or to yourself. Such research must conform to a *code of ethics* which confirms that the research meets a set of ethical guidelines. Neuman (2006) enlists some of the basic principles of ethical social research as follows:

- The researcher is responsible for the ethical issues.
- Do not exploit subjects for personal gain.
- Some form of informed consent is highly recommended or required.
- Respect privacy, confidentiality and anonymity.
- Avoid coercion.
- Use an appropriate research method that suits the topic.
- Undesirable consequences to the participants must be removed.
- The sponsor of the research must be identified.
- Interpret results which are consistent with the data.
- Strive for accuracy.
- Do not conduct secret research.

6.2 Policies and code for research ethics

Ethics are very important for the conduct of research and in this regard many professional bodies, government agencies, universities and research institutions have come up with specific codes, rules and policies related to research ethics. The ethics codes can be divided into four main areas as illustrated in Figure 6.1: honesty and integrity; objectivity; intellectual property and the law; and confidentiality.

6.3 Research ethics at research institutions

Many universities and research institutions ensure that integrity and ethics are at the core of their research activities. As a result, these institutions have developed their own

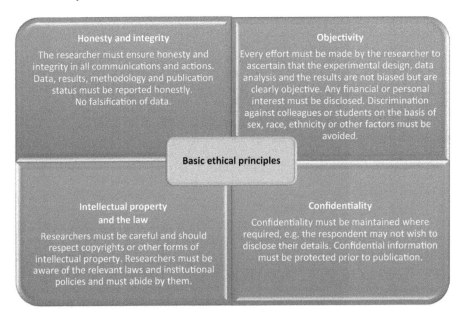

Figure 6.1 Basic ethical principles

Research Ethics Policy and Procedures which govern the ethics of research. At universities, the ethics policy is generally applicable to all researchers including all staff and students carrying out research under the auspices of the university. Universities and research institutions therefore have Research Ethics Committees to ensure that research projects meet the requirements. The main aim of the Research Ethics Committee is to ensure that all stakeholders involved in the research, such as participants, institutions, funders and researchers, are protected during the lifetime of the research. You should therefore be aware of the Research Ethics Policy in place before embarking on a research project.

Normally a research proposal should spell out all the ethical concerns and implications of the research study. The research proposals of undergraduate and postgraduate students are usually individually submitted for approval to the University Research Ethics Committee. The research projects require approval before any research can commence. The University Research Ethics Committee must convince itself that the research project poses no ethical issues, or that ethical issues have been properly addressed, before approval can be given for the research to proceed. An ethical form may request information as listed in Box 6.1.

Box 6.1: information which may be requested in an ethical form

Institution:_____

Department:_____

Type of project (*whether undergraduate/postgraduate*):_____

Researchers name(s):_____

Principal investigator(s)/Supervisor(s):_____

Research title: _____

_____

Date:_____

Rationale (*brief description of the project*):_____

_____

1　**Duration of the study:** _____

2　**Tentative start date of the project:** _____

3　**Potential implications of the research:**

　　● 　is there any conflict of interest? _____

　　● 　what is the data collection method ?_____

　　● 　has permission been sought to use unpublished data?_____

4　**About the respondents:**

　　● 　details about the intended participants

　　● 　sampling method used

　　● 　duration of the respondents' involvement

　　● 　location of field work/research

　　● 　permission to use the location for the research activity

5　**About the research funding**

6　**Other ethical checklist**

　　● 　details regarding permission to use the site of research

　　● 　any research collaboration

　　● 　informed consent

　　● 　participant information sheet

　　● 　the right to withdraw

　　● 　written consent

　　● 　recording

　　● 　confidentiality

　　● 　data security

Exercise 1

Find out the following at your institution:

● 　Who to contact to get the ethics form.
● 　To whom the form is submitted.
● 　How long it takes to get approval.

6.4 Ethical issues and the research process

Ethics must form part of each and every stage of the research process. The research project must therefore be designed in line with the ethical principles. In particular, ethical issues must be considered when seeking initial access. Potential participants should not be pressurised to grant access and consent to participate in a research project is not a simple issue.

6.4.1 Informed consent

Usually, the individuals must understand the purpose of the research project and must be provided with relevant knowledge pertaining to risks and benefits. The individual must then consent to participate without compulsion. An extensive checklist with regard to informed consent has been put forward by De Vaus (1995, p. 334) and he promotes that informed consent needs to provide the individuals with the following knowledge:

- the research process and purpose
- any related risks
- how the participants were chosen
- the benefits of the research
- the ability to ask questions concerning the research
- the voluntary nature of their participation
- the identity of the researcher and any funding sources
- how the findings will be utilised

Therefore, an informed consent letter must be either given or read to the potential participant by you. If you are using a mail survey, the consent from the respondent can be included in the covering letter itself. Apart from protecting the participant's right, you must also ensure anonymity and confidentiality wherever relevant. Try to simplify the consent form as much a possible so that the form itself does not look like a survey questionnaire!

6.4.2 Ethics during data collection stage

It is important that you do not infringe on the participant's privacy and you should not go beyond the scope of the agreed access. Data collection must be conducted objectively otherwise the results will be biased.

Confidentiality and anonymity are two important issues to be considered during the data collection and data handling process. Anonymity means the participants remain anonymous; the subject's identity is protected. Usually you can code the questionnaire and refrain from using the participant's name in case you need to chase up a response. Confidentiality means that the information may bear the names of the participants but the information is kept secret. It may happen that you provide anonymity without confidentiality or vice-versa.

6.4.3 Authorships

It is important that all those who have contributed towards a particular research project should receive appropriate credit.

Anyone involved in the research design, data collection, data analysis, drafting the manuscript and the final approval is considered as an author. If a research project was conducted as a team effort, the name of the principal investigator is placed first, followed by the other researchers in alphabetical order. Sometimes leadership is shared and the names are placed alphabetically. The main author usually takes the responsibility for ensuring that the data are accurate, responds to all the inquiries after publication and all also ensures that other deserving authors are recognised. Funding bodies and mentorship may usually not be considered as authors, but you must acknowledge their contribution towards the research. Also, contributions that are primarily technical do not warrant authorship. Researchers who have contributed to a lesser extent to the research should be appropriately acknowledged, such as in footnotes or in an introductory statement.

6.4.4 Plagiarism

Failing to give recognition to other people's work in your own work is known as plagiarism and is considered an academic offence. Nowadays, computer software is available to check plagiarism. Plagiarism can be avoided by ensuring that the work has been properly referenced and gives due recognition to the author(s) whose work has (have) been used in your research. To avoid the risk of plagiarism, you can use quotes from an article and cite the author(s). The trouble sometimes is how much you can quote. As a rule of thumb, for every line quoted you develop it into your own words on two lines. Another way to avoid plagiarising is to paraphrase. This means rephrasing the idea or information in your own words.

Chapter summary

- Ethics are important when carrying out a research.
- Ethical codes can be classified into four main areas: honesty and integrity; objectivity; intellectual property and the law; and confidentiality.
- Research ethics must be considered at different stages of the research process.
- You must give an informed consent letter or read it to the potential participant at the start.
- You should not breach the participant's privacy and should not go beyond the scope of the agreed access.
- Grant authorships if researchers have contributed to the research design, data collection, data analysis, drafting the manuscript or the final approval.
- All research work must be properly referenced and due recognition must be given when using other people's work.

Discussion questions

6.1 Why do we have to consider ethics in our research?
6.2 Who is responsible for research ethics at your institution?
6.3 What are the procedures in place?
6.4 You are planning to conduct a survey. Design a consent form to be presented to the participants.

Ramesh Durbarry

6.5 How would define the terms 'confidentiality' and 'anonymity'?
6.6 What can you do to avoid plagiarism?

Further reading

De Vaus, D.A. (1995). *Surveys in Social Research*. New South Wales: Allen and Unwin. www.plagiarism.org.
Neuman, W.L. (2006). *Social Research Methods: Qualitative and Quantitative Approaches*. Boston: Pearson, Allyn and Bacon.
Saunders, M.N.K., Lewis, P. and Thornhill, A. (2009). *Research Methods for Business Students*, 5th edition. Harlow: Pearson Education Ltd.
Veal A.J. (2011). *Research Methods for Leisure and Tourism*, 4th edition. Harlow: Prentice Hall.

PART II

Conceptual framework and research methods

Chapter 7

Developing a conceptual framework

Ramesh Durbarry

When talking to one of my colleagues who has been supervising and marking dissertations at the undergraduate and postgraduate levels, including PhD supervisions, she tells me that 'poor grades in dissertation tend to be mostly because of a poor conceptual framework; the pieces simply do not tie up'. For the research to be tied together requires a good conceptual framework. This is perhaps the most difficult part of the research.

So what is a conceptual framework?

This chapter addresses the main crux of conducting research. Somewhere in the research there need to be a structure to explain how the 'pieces' fit together. The 'pieces' link the concepts, variables, constructs, theories or models to develop the conceptual framework.

7.0 Chapter objectives

You have now looked at what other authors have researched on topics similar to yours through the literature review. Whether you are using a positivist or an interpretivist approach, the literature review is important to know what has been researched. So now you are better equipped to plan your research and decide on the specific area your study will focus on. This is why you will need to design a conceptual framework.

After studying this chapter, you will be able to:

- understand what a conceptual framework is;
- know why the conceptual framework is necessary in your research;
- understand what the conceptual framework does;
- understand where the conceptual framework fits into quantitative and qualitative research;
- understand how to present the conceptual framework; and
- understand how to develop the conceptual framework.

7.1 Introduction

From the literature review, you can get an idea of what have been used as models, theories, methodologies, hypotheses, research methods and sampling methods, among others. The critical review provides a path towards your research, the research questions become sharper, your aims and objectives are becoming clearer (not necessarily finalised, though) and you know pretty much what you will be researching on. However, your ideas may still be sketchy because you are yet to connect the concepts or variables to form relationships and this needs tidying up to put the 'pieces' together. Depending on the way you 'frame' the relationships, this will guide the research design. This is the idea behind devising a conceptual framework.

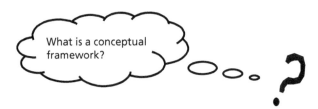

7.2 Defining the conceptual framework

A conceptual framework can be defined as a set of broad ideas and principles taken from relevant fields of inquiry and used to structure a subsequent presentation (Reichel and Ramey, 1987).

The most popular definition of concept framework cited in many research method textbooks (see the list in the 'Further reading' section) is that of Miles and Huberman

(1994) because of its clarity in understanding what is actually meant. They describe the conceptual framework as follows:

> A conceptual framework explains, either graphically or in narrative form, the main things to be studied – the key factors, constructs or variables – and the presumed relationships among them. Frameworks can be rudimentary or elaborate, theory-driven or commonsensical, descriptive or causal.
>
> (Miles and Huberman, 1994, p. 18)

From the literature you will have identified key concepts, constructs or variables which are important to your research; our next task is to put the 'pieces' together and to provide a structure that will identify and present the connections among them in a logical way. This connectivity, not only in terms of the concepts or variables, but between the research problem, purpose, literature review, methodology, data collection and subsequent analysis, is important. The framework you present can be simple or highly structured depending on how far you are prepared to explore. The complexity of the structure depends on the lens of the researcher, how much you are prepared to zoom in or zoom out.

Depending on the research design, the conceptual framework tends to be more dynamic in qualitative research using an inductive position than in quantitative research using a deductive approach. This is because in the former case you start collecting and analysing the data while developing the theory; they are intertwined. The 'to and fro' from one stage to the other will feed more information (improving the theory and the data collection and analysis process) until the researcher is satisfied that a clear representation of connections between the concepts is reached. Obviously when you start your research under this approach, you can use a simple framework, which may be drawn from the literature review, unless you are a very experienced researcher using, for example, grounded theory (even then a knowledge of what is already out there is important, otherwise how would you know that whatever you are researching has not been researched). You may start from a model or a theory you believe does not adequately explain the phenomenon and seek to continuously make improvements or replace it. Miles and Huberman (1994) further note that researchers generally have some idea of what will feature in their study – at least a tentative rudimentary conceptual framework, which can then be changed or replaced. The conceptual framework in inductive research becomes the output of the empirical investigation from which theoretical explanation emerges.

In deductive research, the conceptual framework is the guide for the research; it links the concepts using models and theories to test hypotheses using empirical data. The framework plays an important role in how the empirical study is designed and conducted.

7.3 The elements of a conceptual framework

The elements of the conceptual framework consist of concepts, constructs and variables.

7.3.1 What is a concept?

A concept can be defined as an idea expressed as a symbol or in words (Neuman, 2006). It helps to identify the key dimensions and elements relating to the phenomena that are being studied and facilitate their measurement (Brotherton, 2008). A concept can have one dimension or more. Concepts do not exist in the real world, they are abstractions created to help organise thoughts and understanding. For example, 'quality' and 'customer satisfaction' are abstract terms, but we do have some ideas as to what they communicate. What 'quality' means can vary from persons to person, depending on one's interpretation. Identifying dimensions can lead to a better understanding the concept, for example, price, attributes and brand names.

7.3.2 What is a construct?

Constructs are much broader than concepts. While concepts group related dimensions (factors) together, constructs tend to group related concepts. Both constructs and concepts are essential in developing the conceptual framework. They help to structure the path to understand the phenomena under study.

7.3.3 What is a variable?

Constructs or concepts are abstract in form and cannot be measured directly, the former being more abstract than the latter. Customer satisfaction, for example, may entail a series of concepts such as the product, design and service quality. Measuring these concepts will enable a better understanding of what is meant by customer satisfaction. These will bring clarity in the conceptual framework, but to test relationships, associations or effects between the dimensions there is a need to operationalise the constructs and concepts; this is what variables do in the conceptual framework. Variables are derived from constructs and concepts.

7.4 The importance of a conceptual framework

The conceptual framework is like a map to the researcher. The conceptual framework provides a logical and coherent structure for the study. It develops an awareness of the topic on the literature, the methodology, and so on. It is the starting point for reflection about the research and its context. It sets the boundaries of the work to answer the research questions. The framework then 'forces' the researcher in a process of negotiation with the literature, models, methodologies and data collection.

The conceptual framework provides the researcher with the ability to not only describe, but, more importantly, to move beyond descriptions to explanations of the 'why' and 'how' of the phenomena. It is a means of providing an explanation of the data that flow from the research questions.

The conceptual framework is used to outline the possible courses of actions to an idea. It encourages theory development. In fact, theories can be deduced from it. The conceptual framework assists you in giving meaning to subsequent findings. It also provides a framework for reporting and interpreting results.

7.5 Difference between conceptual framework and theoretical framework

There are many students who are confused between conceptual framework and theoretical framework. Often they are treated synonymously, but indeed there is a significant difference. A theoretical framework offers a theoretical perspective on something. The model can become a basic approach to understanding the phenomenon under investigation. It is a system of knowledge which can be made up of concepts, laws, principles and hypotheses. For example, in studying the demand for tourism in a destination, Durbarry (2008) uses a gravity model to explain tourism demand for the UK. The theoretical model is based on the law of gravity and has concepts such as price, income and distance to explain how tourism demand is determined. Various hypotheses are empirically tested as to whether there are significant relationships among the variables. The framework is a cause-and-effect model. The theoretical framework uses interrelated concepts to give a systematic view of how tourism demand is determined by specifying relationships among the variables.

A conceptual framework can make use of one or more theories depending on the researcher's ability to investigate the topic. The conceptual framework is your viewpoint on how the problem statement will be explored, while the theoretical framework provides the basic relationship between the different concepts and variables involved in the study.

7.6 Developing a conceptual framework

The complexity of a conceptual framework depends on the type of research. For instance, descriptive research will not require an elaborate conceptual framework as would explanatory or evaluative research (Veal, 2011). The main purpose of research is to systematically explore, describe and explain observed phenomenon, understand relationships, explain how the world works or establish relationships.

7.6.1 Where do I start?

At this stage, you are most probably trying to explain relationships, how the world works. It is complicated to explain where to start from, as it depends on many factors related to your capability of undertaking research, knowledge on the phenomena (gathered from the literature review), experience, research background and, possibly, data collected. The elements of the conceptual framework as explained above consist of constructs, concepts and variables, which may all be taken from the literature. Your role consists of developing a structure. You can present it as a flow chart, tree diagram or mind map.

Start with an idea, concept or term and brainstorm. You can brainstorm alone, with friends, in a group, with your tutor, and so on. I find using a mind map very useful. This can be then structure in a flow chart as well. The best way is to use a piece of paper or flip chart and throw in your ideas (the process is similar to the research process explained in Chapter 3 – see Figure 3.3). Let's say you are interested in doing research on customer satisfaction. Start by asking a few question: What is it that I am interested in? Is it about *measurement* of customer satisfaction, how it is *determined*, how it is *influenced*, and so on. Place the theme 'customer satisfaction' in the middle of the piece of paper and write related concepts as you read through the literature; an example is illustrated in Figure 7.1.

Refine your ideas and decide on the relationship you are going to explore. Don't hesitate to colour code your thoughts and ideas. Think of the linkages between these concepts (e.g. from theories and hypotheses). For example, you may wish to explain the relationship between employee satisfaction and customer satisfaction and use the framework of Heskett's et al. (1994) service–profit chain as a basis to conduct your investigation. This step is already *setting boundaries* to your research. The boundaries will depend, as we explained earlier, on your research lens. Another student may wish to explain the relationship between waiting time and customer satisfaction. From Figure 7.1 so many relationships can be explored. Use solid lines or dotted lines to express relationships between the concepts. A solid line may indicate an obvious direct relationship while a dotted line may indicate an indirect relationship through another concept, as illustrated in Figure 7.2.

Figure 7.1 Concepts related to customer satisfaction

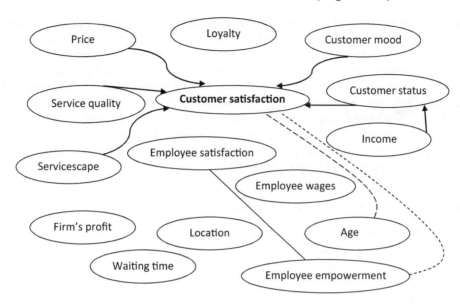

Figure 7.2 A tentative connection of the concepts to the concept of customer satisfaction

Practical tips

Use different colour pens to label the concepts, encircle them, think of synonyms for the concepts and gather more ideas. Sometimes working backwards from variables to concept might help to identify relationships.

The next step will be to list all associated or would-be associated concepts to the relationships you are exploring. As soon as you set the boundaries to your study, some concepts, variables or constructs may become redundant and will not fit the framework. For example, if you believe that you will not be exploring the relationship between customer satisfaction and loyalty, you can then remove 'Loyalty' from the diagram. These decisions would emanate from the literature review, your experience or from your own interpretation or hypotheses you are putting forward. For example you may be retaining those concepts such as reward, employee loyalty, empowerment and motivation. You can use flow charts, tree diagrams, concentric circles and overlapping circles to further structure the conceptual framework (see e.g. Jennings, 2001).

The next step will be to *define the concepts*. The literature review will be the obvious place to look for definitions, especially scholarly written definitions. The definitions should be related to the context you are investigating. For example, 'empowerment' should be clearly defined in the context of work–employee empowerment rather than, for example, political empowerment. You have to revisit the previous step of mapping the concepts again.

The next step is to 'put a face' to the concepts you have identified, that is, to operationalise the concepts. This will depend whether the concept is quantitative or qualitative in nature. If it is quantitative in nature, the next step is how the concept is to be measured, for example, 'reward' can be in terms of wages measured in pounds earned annually. Mind you, that 'reward' can also be qualitative such as being nominated as the employee of the month or getting a promotion. How you operationalise your concepts is an important issue with regard to whether it is a *valid* measure. For qualitative concepts, operationalisation will involve deciding how to describe or identify the concept when conducting the research, for example, how 'empowerment' will be described or identified if an employee is empowered. Operationalising your concepts will help you to decide on the methodology and collection of data. Variables are created to operationalise the concepts.

7.6.2 Revisiting the conceptual framework

It is important that you that you think of the process of developing the conceptual framework as being iterative. You may not get it right in the beginning. Explore inter-relationships and uncover unexplored areas – this is where you will make a contribution to knowledge and the literature.

Positivists, using quantitative research, often use cause-and-effect relationships to explain the world. They make use of theoretical frameworks within conceptual frameworks to further analyse relationships or inter-relationships. They use theoretical models to further quantify the relationship – for example, Durbarry and Sinclair (2003) used an Almost Ideal Demand System (AIDS) model to explain how tourism demand is determined. The model is built using the theory of demand, where tourism demand is a function of the price of tourism in the destination, price of tourism in other destinations and consumer's income. Relationships are tested – for example, it is hypothesised that there is an inverse relationship between tourism demand and price and a positive relationship between tourism demand and income. Time series data are collected and the parameters are estimated using econometric techniques. The significance of the relationships is statistically tested.

7.7 Where does the conceptual framework appear?

Not many dissertations will have a chapter on 'Conceptual Framework' as such. It is mostly used a guide to develop your research. However, in many PhD theses, researchers tend to present a dedicated chapter on it. This is because they want to illustrate their research design in an explicit way.

Depending on the type of research, the conceptual framework either provides a structure for the research or of the research. In quantitative research, the conceptual framework is developed while conducting the literature review where you are using existing theory to formulate your research questions and objectives. The conceptual framework provides the structure and content for the study based on the literature review. Models are then used and relationships are hypothesised and stated. Data are then collected and analysed. The results are interpreted to confirm or revisit the conceptual framework. Figure 7.3 illustrates the possible course of actions in quantitative research.

For qualitative research, particularly where an inductive approach is used, you start collecting the data, code and categorise them, and then explore the emerging themes and concepts. This can be a really hard exercise to conduct if you are an inexperienced

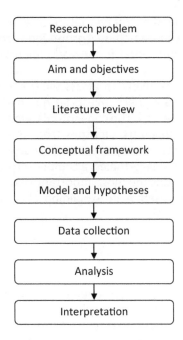

Figure 7.3 Possible course of actions in quantitative research

researcher as Yin (1994) explains. Any researcher has some idea of what will feature in the study and this forms, at the very least, a tentative conceptual framework. An inductive approach is commonly used where no literature or theories exist or

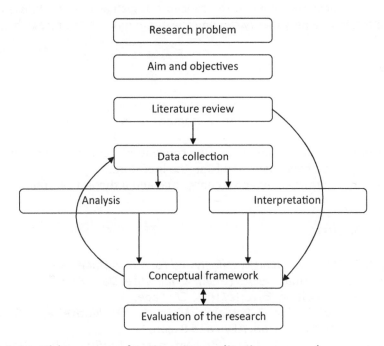

Figure 7.4 Possible course of actions in qualitative research

where the theories are misleading. In the latter case, you will start by wiping the slate and starting afresh. Such research uses grounded theory (see Chapter 15), where themes come out and the conceptual framework emerges from the process of data collection and analysis.

As a student, you are more likely to assess what other researchers have found and written about in the area you are investigating. In effect, you will be analysing the data as they are being collected. The conceptual framework will be developed and revisited. The conceptual framework emerges from this process of data collection and analysis. Figure 7.4 depicts the possible course of actions for qualitative research.

The conceptual framework is nevertheless a complex process, whether in quantitative or qualitative research. It remains the most important stage in terms of structuring and tying up the research study together in explaining phenomenon and understanding relationships.

Chapter summary

- The conceptual framework provides a guide for you to conduct your research.
- The conceptual framework is like a map.
- It provides a logical and coherent structure for the study.
- It helps to structure the presentation of the research, linking the literature review and the empirical research design.
- It tends to be more dynamic in qualitative research, using an inductive approach, than in quantitative research, using a deductive approach.
- It can make use of one or more theories depending on your ability to investigate into the topic.
- From the connections between the concepts as well as the variables, hypotheses can be tested or a new theory can emerge depending on the research approach.

Discussion questions

7.1 What is the difference between constructs and concepts?
7.2 Explain the role of the conceptual framework in quantitative and qualitative research.
7.3 Revisit Figure 7.2 and design your own conceptual framework. Start with one or two concepts you have identified from the literature.
7.4 Explain the difference between a conceptual and a theoretical framework.

Further reading

Brotherton, B. (2008). *Researching Hospitality and Tourism: A Student Guide*. London: Sage.
Miles, M.B. and Huberman, M.A. (1994). *Qualitative Data Analysis: An Expanded Sourcebook*, 2nd edition. Beverley Hills, CA: Sage.
Neuman, W.L. (2006). *Social Research Methods: Qualitative and Quantitative Approaches*. Boston: Pearson, Allyn and Bacon.
Veal A.J. (2011). *Research Methods for Leisure and Tourism*, 4th edition. Harlow: Prentice Hall.

Chapter 8

Qualitative research

An application to tourism

Paul Beedie

Anju wants to examine whether a relationship exists between tourist spending at attractions and tourism experience. She has weighed up the pros and cons of quantitative and qualitative approaches and she has concluded that her research should be carried out using the latter approach. Although tourism spending data can be collected numerically, collecting data on tourism experience is very challenging.

How will Anju collect her data? What are the methods she can use?

8.0 Chapter objectives

This chapter develops in more detail the inductive–deductive distinction introduced in Chapter 3 by concentrating on the former approach to research design. In particular, this chapter aims to show the importance of the interpretive paradigm for tourism research by arguing that tourism professionals need to acquire insights into tourist behaviour from the perspective(s) of the tourists themselves if they are to more fully understand their behaviour and needs for the development of tourist products.

After studying this chapter, you will be able to:

- more fully understand the differences between quantitative and qualitative research design;
- understand the interpretive perspective of tourism research;
- articulate the key components of a range of qualitative research methodologies;
- recognise when to use a certain methodology;
- understand how to collect and analyse data by using a specific methodology; and
- develop your knowledge and application of the key ideas outlined here by exploring further indicative sources.

8.1 Tourism experience: a case for qualitative research

Tourism is a broad area of social activity variously defined using distinctions from other areas of social life. Tourism activities involve, for example, time spent away from a person's home, time away from work routines and the consumption of sights, sounds and experiences that are extraordinary rather than quotidian. Tourism is a business endeavour and like all commercial activity it can operate markets that range from small scale and local to large scale and international. The market dimension has lent itself to alignment with business development models, and these, in turn, are supplied with market research which purports to offer empirical data relevant to tourist needs, and thus inform tourism development.

People and organisations, professionals, who invest in tourism development monitor markets and require facts and figures to inform the entrepreneurial strategies they might apply to their potential investments. In this way of thinking tourism products are market commodities in which the provider (e.g. travel and tourism service supplier) and the consumer (i.e. the tourist) enter into a business agreement in which money is exchanged for tourism experiences (e.g. an overseas package holiday, a white-water rafting descent, a guided tour of Westminster Abbey). Both groups (tourists and service providers) are concerned with value for money, costs off-set against benefits or gains, but tourists are particularly concerned with the transferability of this economic capital into the symbolic capital of touristic consumption.

Practical tips – before you start

- Read existing relevant published research.
- Check the research aim(s).
- Check the research validity – i.e. that the chosen methods are appropriate for achieving the aim(s).

Tourism can therefore be thought of as the accumulation of experience(s) and this has led to a market research culture that emphasises quantitative methodologies that can deliver facts and figures to a specific timescale so that strategic planning can thereafter consider the tourist 'needs' that the research identifies. Market researchers typically present findings from questionnaires in the form of reports, flow diagrams and graphs that can only illuminate the tourist 'experience' in so far as the methodology allows personalised articulation from the tourists being studied. Given that most tourists, because they are away from their familiar environments, want to feel nurtured and cared for – comfortable – it is not surprising that market researchers will want to find out how the tourist rated the food, the accommodation and the friendliness and helpfulness of the service provider's employees. To this end questionnaires and feedback forms abound and the quantifiable data accumulates. There is, however, a growing momentum towards exploring the tourist experience via the qualitative or interpretive paradigm, and there are a number of reasons for this important development.

One of the limitations of traditional questionnaire-based methodologies is that the construction of questions and analysis of data is undertaken by people who have an established worldview based on their own background, education and training. Given that organised tourism has emerged from industrial models first seen in developing countries such as Britain – it is a moot point whether Thomas Cook in nineteenth-century England might be seen as a founding father in this respect – inevitably it is the people who run tourism services whose views are reflected in the way research is conducted: such people are typically projecting a white, educated, heterosexual, middle-class, Christian able-bodied perspective.

Meanwhile, the rest of the world is catching up. For example, for western tourists a visit to China might have originally been seen as a classic tourist experience of the exotic and otherness. This might still be the case today, but China (certainly in the cities) has developed through its rapid and extensive adaptation of market principles, and through drawing on its own natural resources, an industrialised economy to rival any of the existing super-powers in Europe and North America. And with such social change has come an emergent, relatively affluent middle-class who are themselves interested in tourism so that now China 'exports' far more tourists into global tourism than it receives. This example is indicative of processes of globalisation that accelerate the pace of life whilst simultaneously shrinking the world, but one of the key consequences is that there are more tourists, engaging with a greater range of tourist products than at any time in history. Moreover, the social and cultural mix has never been so diverse. This amounts to a greater breadth and depth of tourist experience and a growing realisation that understanding tourist needs is inevitably an increasingly complex undertaking. Ryan (1998) observed that research that denies the opportunity for holidaymakers to speak of their own experience in their own words is itself limited. Qualitative research methodologies engage the interpretive paradigm and endeavour to articulate the tourist experience from the tourist's perspective.

8.2 A critique of quantitative research

It has been suggested above that quantitative tourism research methodologies have limitations with regard to the potential they offer to understand the subjectivity of the tourist experience. Tourists are often viewed as a homogenous group when in

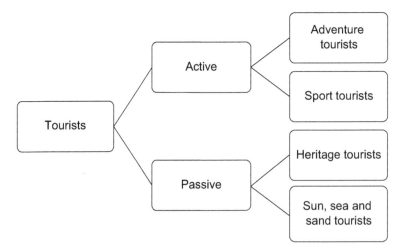

Figure 8.1 Indicative tourist typology

reality they are likely to be a collection of individuals who are sharing a common experience but may have many differences in background, aspirations and motivations.

As an indicator of diversity among tourists some studies demonstrate the range of capacities, interests and motivations within a group brought together for a tourist activity (see Beedie (2010) for an example from mountaineering adventure tourism). Additionally, a tourist experience is not usually an isolated event but is commonly part of a series of activities, journeys and visits. Quite how these experiences satisfy and stimulate our appetites for more of the same is highly individualised. However, tourism providers are interested in returning clientele (hence the regular circulation of brochures and email promotions) and tourists are likely to be constructing a tourist career (Ryan, 1998) from the building blocks of their individualised experiences. The mechanisms through which this symbiotic relationship is nurtured are well documented throughout tourism studies, for example the analysis of push and pull factors. However, when a tourist is credited with having a tourist career there is a commensurate need to understand this construction over time. Because as humans our own capacities, motivations and social circumstances do change over time, longitudinal studies of tourism behaviour offer the most appropriate means to gather data. Longitudinal studies are rarely dominated by quantitative methodologies given the desire to monitor these evolving characteristics over time. However, partly because they are time-consuming, difficult to administer and relatively expensive to mobilise, longitudinal studies are quite rare in tourism research.

A second critique of quantitative methodologies develops the notion of diversity introduced above. It has been noted that tourism is diversifying in terms of the products it offers. In particular, there is a growing trend, certainly among tourists originating from developed countries, towards forms of tourism that are active and experiential rather than a more passive consumption of sights. Part of this changing emphasis is evidenced by the rapid growth of adventure tourism which, as Varley (2007) has shown through his 'adventure commodification continuum', is heavily slanted towards 'soft' and carefully risk managed tourist provision such as safari trips, hot air balloon rides and white-water rafting. Today, walking tours are just as likely to feature on a tourist's ambition as visiting the Taj Mahal. Any assumptions that one research method fits all forms of tourism do therefore have limitations. Additionally, when significant differences in the tourist experience (such as those between passive and active consumption) are identified and combined with cultural differences among tourists the case for re-thinking research methodologies to reflect this diversity is strengthened.

A third point of critique considers the relationship between data collection determined by commercial interests and the form(s) this takes as well as its availability for general perusal. Commonly with sponsored research, it is not possible to disassociate the vested interests of the sponsor and the construction of the methodology, including the analysis and presentation of outcomes. This concern to be professional and scientific favours quantitative techniques which, as argued here, don't necessarily reflect nuanced tourist behaviour but do present impressive reports which provide sponsors with facts and figures to use as fits their purposes. Governments, for example, are concerned with the economic benefits of tourism and therefore need certain forms of data to argue the case for executive decisions that may (or may not) be in the public's interest. This is well illustrated by the British government's construction of the case to bring the Olympic Games to London in 2012. The data promoting the economic benefits of additional tourism featured prominently in the original arguments which are being subject to more detailed scrutiny and are being found wanting. Moreover, such research is not always available in the public domain, and when it is statistics may be presented in ways unintelligible to non-academics.

Summary of quantitative critique

- Tourists are not a homogenous group.
- Tourist careers are best monitored through longitudinal studies.
- There is a diversification of tourism into sub-genres.
- There is a growing trend to active rather than passive tourist consumption.
- Positivist methodologies produce statistics which can be manipulated and presented to support vested interests.
- Human behaviour is complex and changes over time and place.
- There is a fluidity in boundaries between tourism and other lifestyle choices.

Fourth, again developing the discussion above, quantitative methodologies do not readily uncover tourist motivations and track and illuminate our sometimes complex behaviours. Tourism is an extraordinary experience and necessarily engages the tourist at an emotional level. Monitoring excitement, boredom, fear, anticipation and satisfaction is difficult because our responses are determined by environmental and social factors that are constantly changing and we all carry a history of experiences (e.g. education, family, previous tourist activity) through which we make sense of our ongoing experiences but which operate to individualise emotional responses to each new situation we find ourselves in. Additionally, because of changes in environmental and social frames our responses change over time and place. So, not only is the timing of data collection crucial, each person's responses might be different and the same person's responses might be different in different places at different times. Standardisation in operating research methodologies that contain assumptions that tourists will behave in line with a pre-determined set of typologised expectations thus brings its own limitations.

Finally, elements of postmodernism explored by various academics (see e.g. Bauman, 2000) indicate that social boundaries are becoming less clear as we live in 'fluid' times. Tourism is an important element of today's consumer society but it is becoming increasingly difficult – particularly in the developed world – to differentiate tourism products from other lifestyle choices. The many ways of being a tourist have led some commentators (e.g. Urry, 1995) to suggest 'we are all tourists now'. An example, in the form of an imaginary story can illustrate this point.

Example of fluid boundaries in tourism and lifestyle choices

A group of friends buy a day return rail ticket to London to visit tourist attractions such as the Houses of Parliament and Trafalgar Square; whilst there they find roads closed because the climax of the Tour of Britain Cycle Race is happening, which they enjoy watching. Inspired by the race, and back home now they buy bicycles and start to explore their local environs; they meet others and join an informal cycling club that posts meeting details on its website; an advert on the site alerts them to a company that will provide a support service (e.g. luggage transportation, food and accommodation, mechanical breakdown support) for a trans-Britain multi-day cycle tour; they set the dates and book the holiday.

In this not untypical example it is difficult to draw boundaries between tourism, recreation, sport and identity formation. Such typological intentions would literally only be of academic interest as the group of friends just go on enjoying the experiences they have discovered, and would unconsciously be forging a tourist career as they did so. Qualitative researchers, especially those using ethnographic methodologies, would aspire to understand this group's new found tourism interests from the participant's point of view not from some externally determined perspective.

The following sections explore four forms of qualitative research methods. These are focus groups, interviews, ethnography and auto-ethnography. These four forms move from the group to the individual and offer different levels of subjectivity such that the researcher is located more and more centrally in the study from the focus groups through to auto-ethnography. Examples will be used in the discussion to illuminate how these methods operate, the role of the researcher(s) and the outcomes and analyses that can be anticipated.

8.2.1 Focus groups

It is too simplistic to think of focus groups as being a form of interview because data collected is from a group, not an individual. Setting up and managing focus groups entails careful planning and execution.

Practical tips for focus groups

- Researcher as organiser/facilitator.
- Six to ten participants.
- Researcher accepts all views offered.
- Researcher can collate additional data such as body language and engagement.
- Produce broad but often shallow data.
- Works well when different groups are likely to have a range of views about a tourist development.

Group sizes are typically six to ten participants and the researcher operates as a facilitator of the emergent discussion. The advantages are that the researcher can determine the 'setting up' and 'control' of the focus group – as in selecting the sample, organising the space and the time as well as framing the discussion – whilst simultaneously recording the range of views offered about the subject providing the focus. You, as a researcher/facilitator, as in all forms of qualitative research in the social sciences must be cognisant of engaging the participants and moderating to a level commensurate with the type of group and the stage the research is at (for example the facilitation would be low if the group were set up to explore the potential understanding of a subject but high if the group purpose was to explore patterns already identified within the subject). You must take care to accept all views offered and are responsible for the recording of the session and any additional field notes which, for example, might note body language, levels of engagement and participant activity over and above what was actually said. Focus groups benefit from multiple intra stimulation and can produce rich data in a relatively efficient manner; however, this data is generally shallower even if it is broader than other qualitative methods such as interviews.

Example of successful focus groups

When Harrison (1991) used focus groups to investigate attitudes to recreation and tourism in the British countryside she produced a set of conclusions that challenged the broadly accepted views, drawn from predominantly quantitative research designs using questionnaires and surveys, of who used the countryside and in what ways. In particular she demonstrated that, far from being a white middle-class preserve whose interests were cultural, educational and romantic, countryside recreation and localised tourism trips were enjoyed by a much greater range of people and for a much greater range of anticipated benefits than had hitherto been considered. For example, black and ethnic minorities were found to enjoy picnics and low-level walks although

(continued)

> *(continued)*
>
> they tended towards family based gregarious configurations rather than the 'solitudinous contemplation' of nature preferred by many middle-class white people. Harrison made these 'discoveries' because her research design took her out of her own white educated middle-class enclave into inner city neighbourhoods where she set up focus groups and was prepared to listen and record the attitudes and views presented.

The place and constitution of the group are therefore important, and although a group needs some element of commonality to avoid overly antagonistic views that would make analysis overly complex, it remains important to listen and record all inputs. The group samples and time and place of occurrence will be determined by the research question or subject, the range of participants available and the practicalities of getting them together in one place at a set time. Focus groups could, for example, be used at the beginning and end of a package tour holiday at the point where the group requires 'briefings' from the tour provider's staff; or they could be used to explore local views of a proposed Centre Parcs complex to be built as a tourist attraction in Bedfordshire. In both cases a range of views and attitudes might be discovered with, in the latter case especially, a clear necessity to run a series of focus groups that might comprise local residents (most immediately affected), people from the regional catchment area it would serve (including inner London) and the planners, economists and officials most obviously connected to the proposal.

Recording, collating and analysing the considerable amount of data that focus groups can generate is not easy. The analysis can take different forms, determined by the research subject and question, and might draw upon discourse, content or narrative analysis, but broadly speaking the researcher is aiming to identify themes in the data that draw out individual contributions from the participants which can then be positioned using a systematic coding. This emergent structuring of data can lead to discussion of these themes in ways that may produce conclusions from this research and/or generate hypotheses that can be further explored in the existing study or form the starting point for further studies.

8.2.2 Interviews

Interviews have been a core constituent of qualitative research for as long as the social sciences have conducted empirical investigation – indeed, if one does consider focus groups to be a form of collective interviewing, interviews in one form or another feature in all the research methods discussed in this chapter. It is the form of the interview that determines where and how it is used, but interviewing is also a methodology in its own right. Forms of interviewing vary depending upon how rigidly defined the interview situation is. At one extreme of a continuum there are structured interviews which are closer to quantitative methodologies in that the set of clear questions are planned and presented in the same way to all interviewees with no deviation from the pre-determined text. At the other extreme are unstructured interviews in which the interviewer's interventions are minimal whilst the interviewee

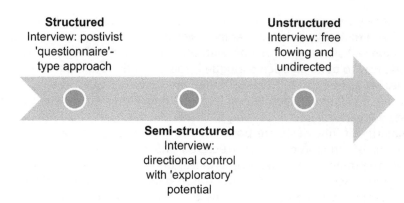

Structured
Interview: postivist
'questionnaire'-
type approach

Unstructured
Interview: free
flowing and
undirected

Semi-structured
Interview:
directional control
with 'exploratory'
potential

Figure 8.2 Interview forms

is allowed to meander through a subject in ways undetermined by the rigor of set questions. Somewhere in the middle ground are semi-structured interviews which draw on both methods with an aim of guiding responses but without closing down avenues of explanation that might arise in the dialogue. The form of interview that is used will be determined by the usual variables of research aim, resources, access to participants and practical constraints of time, place and allowance for transcription. In general terms structured forms are used when there is a proposition to test and unstructured forms are used to establish possible avenues to explore.

When a research project is being formulated pilot studies can be used: 'to become familiar with phrasing and concepts [to help formulate] hypotheses about motivations underlying behaviour and attitudes' (Fielding and Thomas, 2008, p. 248). The phrasing of interview questions is important because the interviewer must endeavour to gain spontaneous rather than rehearsed answers. Moreover, the questions should try to encourage communication of attitudes, beliefs and values.

Practical tips

You will get the most from interviews by:

- preparation of questions consistent with the aim(s) of your research
- starting with 'recall' questions before moving to 'response' and 'exploratory' inputs as required
- keeping time to manageable proportions
- transcribing the interview as the starting point for identifying themes and issues
- using the transcription document to check support for your accuracy and as a means of extending the dialogue in key areas you have identified.

Interviewing is a skill that will improve with practice, allowing the interviewer to get below the surface of the glib and the factual to illicit emotional responses, even when the interviewee may not be comfortable with this such as when they are led into describing their own behaviour as inconsistent, irrational or otherwise abnormal. Because there will always be problems with the articulation of feelings, attitudes and beliefs, one way to build an open dialogue is to start with 'recall' questions (e.g. how many times have you been to Norway?), then use 'response' questions (e.g. why were you attracted to Norway?) before 'exploratory' questions (e.g. can you explain the ways that your expectations of Norway matched the reality of your experiences?)

The majority of interviews are positioned somewhere on the scale between the two extremes of structured and unstructured and therefore the onus is upon the interviewer to prompt and to probe in order to uncover the deeper, more significant emotional responses that constitute the *raison d'être* of the interpretive paradigm. Whilst the probing will be determined by the individuality of each interview situation, follow-up questions of the exploratory type in the example set out above might include: What images in particular excited you about your trip to Norway? What impact did the tourist professionals have on your planning and enjoyment of the experience? What parts of the trip were especially meaningful and why? What tensions existed before and during the trip? If you were to go to Norway again what would you do differently and why? In this respect the requisite skill of the interviewer becomes apparent through the need to control the form, the pace, the direction and the emphasis of the dialogue, even when, as in the case of a semi-structured interview, some of the lines of questioning will not have been pre-determined.

When the interview data has been collated decisions have to be made about transcription. The basic question is does the researcher transcribe all interviews fully, or just some interviews or parts of interviews or use software to transcribe (Lewins and Silver, 2007). The answers lie in the time available, the amount of data and access to software, and the proposed analytical framework. Being selective does run the risk of slanting the data towards expected outcomes but if the data collected from a series of interviews is analysed in stages over time then themes and patterns may already be emerging that justify a more selective approach to the time-consuming aspects of full transcription. The time-consuming elements of transcription can be off-set by using dictation software that, apart from a 'combing through' process required because of the difficulties of achieving 100 per cent accuracy with voice recognition programmes, can significantly accelerate the data processing stage. However, the process of hand transcription does give the researcher time and space to reflect upon the data, and thereby begin the analysis. It also creates a manuscript that offers the potential to re-visit the interviewee and/or get that person to check that the transcription matches the dialogue that took place. Once transcribed, coding of themes and patterns can be used to compare and contrast data from different interviews and discussion, hypotheses and/or conclusions developed.

Problems with interviews

- There is a bias implicit in all human interaction.
- Language is a limited way of conveying thoughts and feelings.
- There are no guarantees of consistency and 'truthfulness'.

There are problems with interviewing as a data collection method. For example, as across a range of qualitative methodologies, it is difficult to ignore the human bias implicit in all human interaction, this is especially significant in cross-cultural research. It is also important to recognise that interviews record dialogue and language may be a limited way of communicating feelings and thoughts. Similarly, there are no guarantees that interviewees will be consistent and even truthful. In making the case for the validity and reliability of interviewing, assuming the circumstances of the research permit, there is a case for the cross-referencing of data through ethnography.

8.2.3 Ethnography

Ethnography is a research method combining documentation, interviewing and observation. Rather like a case study, the emphasis is upon depth, context and intensity. Interviewing can form a part of ethnography but the requirements for the researcher to be immersed in the social field of investigation make this method distinctive in its demands upon a researcher's time and capacities to negotiate gate-keepers and generally position themselves in the particular culture of investigation. Ethnography draws on the interactionist's premise that groups of people, such as tourists, develop ways of being and behaving that can be studied from an 'insider's' perspective. The patterns of behaviours being observed are 'natural' in so far as the researcher(s) goes to the setting rather than creating an 'artificial' setting to bring the participants to, such as with a focus group for example. The ambition of ethnography is to illuminate the worldview(s) of the participants (Hammersley and Atkinson, 2007). Ethnography is demanding of time and organisation as well as requiring considerable interpersonal skills.

Ethnographic data is gathered by participation in the culture of a group whereby mental and written notes are made of observations, informal discussions, the dynamics of groups and sub-groups, rituals and other forms of social intercourse. The approach when applied to mainstream tourism is illustrated by Tim Edensor's book about tourism at the Taj Mahal (Edensor, 1998) in which the site become his focus

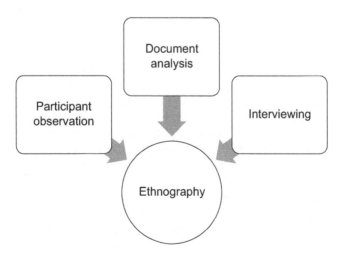

Figure 8.3 The multiple methodologies of ethnography

for observations of and dialogues with a range of tourists and tourism operators over several weeks: without a clear intent to plan each day, the people (data) literally came to him. A key idea is that ethnography is open ended and works on the principle of progressive focusing whereby themes, ideas and analysis emerge from the writing up of the data. The circumstances of ethnographic investigation will vary but the principles remain the same. A key component of progressive focusing is that field notes are written up on a regular basis: this is not always easy or straightforward, and this will be illustrated in the indicative case study below which will address some of the planning and activation required to make the methodology effective. The important elements of this are: negotiating access to a group culture, overt or covert positioning and related ethical issues, making field notes, dealing with 'reactivity', reliability and validity, transcription and analysis and the concept of relativism.

Key definitions

- *Gate-keepers*: people who control access to certain groups, e.g. the museum director at Lords Cricket ground permitting entry to and observation of the behaviours of visiting sport tourists.
- *Fieldwork*: immersion in the physical space(s) frequented by the research target group for purposes of data collection, e.g. travelling about with a coach tour of Scotland group.
- *Participant observation*: being among a group in an active or passive way and taking note of relevant aspects of behaviour, e.g. noting dress codes, camaraderie and bonding rituals among a group of football supporters.
- *Progressive focusing*: using the gaps between sessions of data collecting to start the analysis in ways that inform the details you particularly want to explore as the data collection advances.

Case study: inductive research in action

In my book about mountain adventure tourists (Beedie, 2010) I describe and explain how the ethnography that I developed for my research project evolved. The research focus I developed emerged from my background experiences as a mountaineer combined with an interest in how the way a person might assume the identity of 'mountaineer' now that adventure tourism providers appeared to be offering tourist products that changed the traditional 'apprenticeship' patterns of identity construction. I was interested in the way social boundaries appeared to be more fluid and the way that mountaineering holidays were being packaged to create commodified adventure.

I knew I needed to enter the communities of mountaineers/adventure tourists to find some answers and my experience and qualifications as a mountain guide enabled me to achieve this. Nevertheless, it was not as easy as I thought to gain access to sample groups and I was turned down by several gate-keepers (mountain adventure tourism company directors) before I was successful with two Sheffield-based companies (Foundry Mountain Activities and Jagged Globe). Over a period of a year I undertook five fieldwork trips as part of different groups of paying clientele with one of these two companies to locations in Britain and Europe. I had access to all promotional materials used by these companies, was able to talk informally to other guides and equipment and local transport suppliers, and in one case a 'rival' group from another adventure tourism company met by chance in a bar in northern Spain whilst with 'my' group. I also arranged to conduct follow-up interviews with as many of the clients as I could at a time and in a place convenient to them (typically an office, a quiet public place or the person's home). The interviews alone generated 60,000 words of data and this was supplemented by five booklets of field notes (roughly one book per trip) which emerged from my participant observation in the places we spent time together, most obviously the mountains but also in huts, hotels, bars, shops and the offices of the two companies I was a part of for the purposes of this research. My ethnography was, therefore, fragmented as periods of intense involvement in the mountaineering culture were separated by periods in which I could collate data, transcribe interviews, work through my field notes to identify patterns and generally advance the study by progressive focusing. However, although I did not know this was how the study would emerge when I started, it enabled the ethnographic process in many ways.

Ethnography, then, is defined by the principles set out above but is a methodology that must adapt to the circumstances created by the culture being studied and any practical constraints generated by the researcher(s) and the focus. The ethnographer has to learn the language and meanings used by the people in the culture and this takes time. When ethnography was first developed by anthropologists whose intention was to investigate native people in remote locations such as Amazonia, such was the depth of cultural immersion – meaning long periods of time (typically months, sometimes longer) and isolation from contacts and communication with normal life – that the researchers had to be wary of 'going native'. This is because a certain detachment is required if a researcher is to make sense of the data being collected. However, as tourism has become a global phenomenon and access and boundaries more fluid in all aspects of contemporary times, so authentic native peoples have diminished and ethnographers turned their attention to urban ethnographies that explore, for example, delinquent youth cultures or political extremist groups. There is also a trend towards internet-based ethnography now that technologies have facilitated social networking and the creation of online communities (Hine, 2005). For the researcher, the ethnographic principles remain the same and the concern about the extent to which researchers reveal their *role* remains.

The decision by you to adopt an *overt* or *covert* position in the culture remains regardless of the form of the ethnography. The decision has ethical implications. To be covert, that is not to declare one's position as a researcher, has the advantage of maximising the 'naturalness' of the behaviour of the participants in language and in action. It may be necessary in some circumstances – such as gang culture – where there may be dangers to setting oneself up as an outsider, and there are certainly ethical issues in acquiring data from participants without some form of consent and an articulation of how the data is likely to be used. However, in most tourism research situations – and certainly in the case of my own ethnography – being overt about one's role addresses these ethical issues, although it does introduce other problems. Most notable here is the problem of *reactivity*.

The problem of reactivity

Reactivity recognises that, by introducing oneself to a group as a researcher one is positioned as an 'outsider' on the inside and thus the way people speak and behave may not be 'natural' as degrees of self consciousness are introduced so that a person enters into a *performance* that may not be how they might speak and behave if you were not present.

Reactivity is a problem that cannot be completely overcome, but two points can be made. First the interpretive paradigm draws on interactionism and, following the pioneering work of Erving Goffman (1959), it can be argued that people act or perform a role in all aspects of social life. Second, as researchers spend more time inside a culture so their presence becomes more normal and accepted. This acceptance is enhanced as the language and behaviours are learned and internalised so that a closer proximity to 'naturalness' is achievable in most instances. In my own ethnography, for example, I quickly learned from early discussions not to refer to the participants as 'adventure tourists' because being a tourist had certain connotations that these people clearly wanted to distance themselves from. The ethnographer, then, despite being immersed in the culture, floats between a world of 'self' and a world of 'other' whilst never being completely attached to either. But it is the synthesis of insider and outsider views that is the strength of this methodology.

Recording field notes became a challenge for my ethnography. My participation as a mountain guide required me to undertake practical activity that was not conducive to making notes in the field – I was too busy navigating, monitoring client well-being, checking ropes and harnesses and operating as a decision-making leader. Note making was mental at times of action but I wrote things down as soon as the opportunity emerged after the climb. The process of writing up field notes initiates the analysis stage because by describing what happened – recording remembered dialogue and behaviours such as positioning and stance, group intercourse and forms of motility – it becomes possible, over time, to identify patterns. In a similar way to interview transcripts, field notes can be thematically organised, the data annotated, coded and re-sequenced around the emerging themes. The analysis is provided by articulating the differences between self and others within the overall aim of bringing to the fore the participants' views. In the case of my ethnography I could set my own traditional mountaineering apprenticeship, hard earned over many years of independent mountaineering endeavour, against the lived experiences of mountain adventure tourists who, because their experiences were essentially a tourist product, appeared to achieve a fast track career to the same social identity.

Collecting and analysing data

- Writing up field notes is often impractical during participant observation but should be completed at the first opportunity thereafter.
- Record verbatim quotes whenever possible and note behaviour changes during the period of participation.
- Start the analysis as you write up your notes by identifying themes and coding as part of progressive focusing.
- Follow Fielding's (2008) application of 'situational ethics' and acknowledge the subjectivities of yourself as central to the research process.

Validation of this research procedure remains a problem which has been subjected to much academic debate. Fielding (2008, p. 276) notes: 'the concept of relativism tells us that the ethnographer is never a fully detached observer: our view is inescapably relative to our own perspective'. Rather like the overt–covert debate, there are no straightforward responses to this issue, although by learning the cultural operating rules, and by passing this information on to other researchers, it should be possible for others to verify outcomes; Fielding (2008) calls this a 'test of congruence'. Lofland and Lofland (1995) go further by suggesting that we should assess the quality of ethnographic findings by scrutinising the details of the research design. Variables in this respect include: the amount of direct observation, the social and spatial position of the researcher, the consistency of data from group members, the coherence of observations when compared to other sources and studies, and the extent to which the data appears to have been manipulated to fit pre-determined themes.

Finally, ethical issues emerging from ethnography appear to continue to exercise academic debate. The arguments range from those who point out it is unethical to acquire and use data for any purpose without the participant's consent – a circumstance aggravated by the difficulties of articulating the direction and outcomes of a study before the research process has started. At the other extreme there are arguments which suggest that it is unethical *not* to investigate and scrutinise all social groups, for example to uncover the machinations of powerful elites. The best fit solution is proposed by Fielding (2008) as 'situational ethics'. By this he means a common-sense approach whereby general ethical principles are applied in ways that facilitate formation of guidelines sensitive to the social group and its culture being investigated. To help this process – and this is certainly possible in my own experiences of tourism research – honesty, transparency and feedback on transcripts and draft reports should be encouraged from participants commensurate with the context of the study. There is one last form of tourism research methodology to consider and, in auto-ethnography, that rationale takes a postmodern turn.

8.2.4 Auto-ethnography

Postmodernism is the complex set of social conditions alluded to in the introduction to this chapter created, it is suggested, by the acceleration of social activity in a global context leading to fluidity, ambivalence and the merging, for example, of tourism with other social forms such as sport, recreation and education. In these unprecedented social conditions tourism continues to thrive and by the emergence of ever more complex, client-focused tourism forms the case can be made for research methodologies that can illuminate the subjectivities of the tourist experience. Ellis et al. (2011) suggest:

> Auto-ethnography is an approach to research and writing that seeks to systematically analyse (graphy) personal experience (auto) in order to understand cultural experience (ethno). This approach challenges canonical ways of doing research and representing others and treats research as a political, socially-just and socially-conscious act. A researcher uses tenets of autobiography and ethnography to do and write auto-ethnography. Thus, as a method, auto-ethnography is both process and product.

This research method emerged from the 'crisis of confidence' inspired by the postmodern writers of the 1980s such as Lyotard and Barthes. The idea of 'writing stories rather than theories' became a reaction against the perceived strictures of existing social science research forms. The limitations in this respect included having to produce research that met the expectations of funding bodies, dense statistical reports produced by experts for selective consumption and 'pretending' that the personal bias and experiences of the researcher have no bearing on the outcomes of the study. Auto-ethnography inverts this position by prioritising the production of accessible, personalised reports; it is an approach that acknowledges and accommodates subjectivity, emotionality and recognises researcher bias.

The process of writing auto-ethnography involves retro-actively writing, which is by definition selective as our recall will be partial and influenced by the impact of the experiences we are writing about. Ellis et al. (2011) refer to these events as 'epiphanies', that is, significant occurrences that hold significance for the person experiencing them. Whereas ethnography entails participant observation, field note analysis from an examination of clothing, social activity, texts such as photographs with an aim to illuminate the collective voice of the culture being studied, auto-ethnography takes the logic a stage further. Auto-ethnography involves writing about what is happening to you by being immersed in a certain culture or assuming that cultural identity. Ethnography is about the collective, auto-ethnography is about you, the individual, and the differences between your story and that of others. Auto-ethnography engages by leading the reader into the story and then illustrating the story with detailed descriptions of personal and interpersonal experiences. The story is evidenced by field notes and interview data.

The critical debates concerning auto-ethnography extend from the issues identified more broadly with the qualitative methods set out in this chapter. These include: a lack of consensus about how much emphasis should be on self and how much on others across different studies; the extent to which our own stories inevitably implicate those of our colleagues and friends who are not involved in the research but who have shaped the researcher's history and worldview; and the assumption that people can articulate by speaking and writing a re-construction of what may be highly subjective and emotionally charged experiences. So, the different forms of auto-ethnography, relational ethics and issues of reliability, generalisability and validity all remain, although the context, meaning and utility of these terms is altered (Ellis et al., 2011).

Reliability becomes the narrator's credibility and the reader is required to ask whether the storyteller really has had those experiences and does the account relate these without poetic licence. Validity becomes the 'truth' that the story evokes for the reader's own experiences in the way it creates a story that is life-like and plausible. Generalisability becomes the move from the respondent's account to the reader's experiences and the extent to which the story can illuminate the unfamiliar. The reader of an auto-ethnographic account is encouraged to think about how similar or different their own lives are from that of the narrator, and the reasons for this. Despite criticisms which suggest a lack of rigor, theory and analysis, or in some extreme cases a self-absorbed narcissism, auto-ethnography does not claim to be exclusively scientific but rather exists to disrupt the science–art binary. Holman-Jones (2005, p. 764) puts it thus: 'Auto-ethnographers view research and writing as socially-just acts; rather than a pre-occupation with accuracy, the goal is to produce analytical, accessible texts that change us and the world we live in for the better.'

Practical tips

Choosing a research design and its commensurate data collection methods will be determined by:

- what you want to find out about tourism and how much time is available to do so (e.g. what is your research question and how easy or otherwise will answering it be);
- whether you are a lone researcher or part of a bigger team and the resources available to you (e.g. you may not be experienced in using qualitative data analysis software but a member of your team may be);
- your capacity to negotiate gate-keepers and thereafter operate appropriate 'situational ethics' (e.g. you cannot conventionally collect qualitative data without access to real people);
- the scale of your research (e.g. local issue or national consensus); and
- who your research will be seen by (e.g. a university supervisor or a tourism development professional).

8.3 Conclusions

This chapter is not a complete explanation of qualitative research methods in tourism but is, rather, a discussion of some of the possibilities that collectively offer an alternative to the top-down principles of research design which aim to capture tourist responses to pre-determined criteria (with the ethnocentricity of the designers foremost) by submitting to a much more subjective and inductively grounded approach to data collection and analysis. There will inevitably be decisions to be made by researchers using these and other qualitative methods concerning which method is best, and such decisions will be influenced by the research question and practical considerations such as time, resources, gate-keepers, potential degrees of immersion, the number of participants among many others, but there are a number of principles which these approaches collectively adhere to. First, the object under study is the determining factor for choosing a method and not the other way round. Second, objects are not reduced to single variables but represented in their entirety in their everyday context. Third, the fields of study are not artificial situations but the practices and interactions of everyday (tourist) life.

Chapter summary

- The interpretive paradigm is becoming more and more important in tourism research in particular when studying tourism behaviour.
- Qualitative research methodologies engage the interpretive paradigm and endeavour to articulate the tourist experience from the tourist's perspective.
- Qualitative researchers may use focus groups, interviews, ethnography and auto-ethnography to conduct their research.

Discussion questions

8.1 What are the merits of using qualitative research?

8.2 What are the limitations of using quantitative research in explaining tourism experience or tourism behaviour?

8.3 How can qualitative research overcome the issues you have raised?

8.4 Why is qualitative analysis not a linear process?

8.5 Which qualitative method would you recommend Anju undertake? Why?

Summary of key points about this selection of further reading

- The Kellehear book (1993), although a little dated, is well written and full of definitions and practical advice and examples from across the social sciences that can be applied to tourism studies.
- Lemelin's (2006) study is a good example of how tourism research is undertaken and written up for an academic journal.
- Weber (2001) sets out the argument for using the interpretive paradigm to investigate outdoor recreation – which by definition includes tourism (especially adventure tourism and wildlife tourism).
- Smith and Weed (2007) present the case for narrative research as an alternative methodology, hitherto unused in sport and tourism research.
- Anderson (2006) aims to clarify the terminology, the status and the strengths and weaknesses of auto-ethnography as a research methodology. He acknowledges the growing importance of this subjective position and its potential, but there are few examples (yet) in tourism research.

- McCarville (2007) Is an example from outdoor sport that uses an auto-ethnographic approach which leads to theoretical propositions. The fact that this account is published in an academic journal indicates that the range of possibilities in qualitative research is being recognised in the extant literature.
- The Travel and Tourism Research Association (TTRA) is a professional organisation for tourism research. This is for dedicated researchers and requires membership to access the full range of professional benefits (such as opportunities, networking and other support services).
- The World Travel & Tourism Council is a representative body for tourism business leaders around the world. Its utility for tourism researchers lies in its databases, organised by country.
- Tourism Research.com is the latest manifestation of Dynamic Frontiers and it facilitates access to a huge range of resources relevant to tourism research, including databases of statistics (quantitative) and blogs (qualitative). The links are global in their reach.

Further reading

Anderson, L. (2006). 'Analytic Autoethnography', *Journal of Contemporary Ethnography*, 35 (4), 373–395.

Kellehear, A. (1993). *The Unobtrusive Researcher: A Guide to Methods*. Sydney: Allen & Unwin.

Lemelin, R. (2006). 'The Gawk, The Glance and the Gaze: Occular Consumption and Polar Bear Tourism in Churchill, Manitoba, Canada', *Current Issues in Tourism*, 9 (6), 516–534.

McCarville, R. (2007). 'From a Fall in the Mall to a Run in the Sun: One Journey to Ironman Triathlon', *Leisure Sciences*, 29, 159–173.

Smith, B. and Weed, M. (2007). 'The Potential of Narrative Research in Sports Tourism', *Journal of Sport & Tourism*, 12 (3–4), 249–269.

Weber, K. (2001). 'Outdoor Adventure Tourism: A Review of Research Approaches', *Annals of Tourism Research*, 28(2), 360–377.

Websites

Travel and Tourism Research Association (TTRA): www.ttra.com/about-us
World Travel & Tourism Council: www.wttc.org/our-mission
Tourism Research.com: www.tourismresearch.com

Chapter 9

Quantitative research

Ramesh Durbarry

A researcher wants to analyse the sensitivity of tourism demand of theme parks in UK. One of the first tasks would be to work out how to measure tourism demand. Will it be measured in terms of the number of visitors or the amount visitors spend per head or per household?

If the researcher assumes that ticket prices have an influence on demand (using the theory of demand), he/she then has to collect data on the tourism demand variable (e.g. number of visitors over a certain time period) and the ticket prices charged.

Depending on the measurement of the variables, the results can differ. Whether we have 'correctly' measured the variables will depend on the reliability and validity of the variable measurement. How the data were collected can also influence the results.

Can you think of other methodological instances that can affect the results?

9.0 Chapter objectives

The objective of quantitative research is to explain phenomena by collecting numerical data and to employ statistical methods to test developed theories, mathematical models, hypotheses, and so on. Measurement is hence central to quantitative research. How you collect your data from empirical observation or surveys and apply statistical analyses can influence the explanation of the phenomenon under study.

In this chapter, we will look at the types of survey that can be used to collect data such as mail, telephone, street and on-site surveys. Online surveys are dealt in Chapter 13. We will also look at questionnaire surveys, and the design and the advantages and disadvantages of using questionnaires. Measurement issues in quantitative research will be explored as well. The reliability and validity of measures will also be discussed.

After studying this chapter, you will be able to:

- demonstrate an in-depth knowledge of the different types of surveys;
- design questionnaires for different types of surveys;
- conduct surveys;
- code responses; and
- consider reliability and validity aspects when conducting surveys

9.1 Survey vs. questionnaire

Students often get confused about the terminologies 'survey' and 'questionnaire'. They are sometimes used synonymously. Students regularly stipulate that they have conducted 100 surveys but what they mean to say is that 100 questionnaires were distributed or received. 'Questionnaire' is simply a 'structured' list of questions that you set to collect data and information. It is an instrument to collect data, which consists of open and/or closed questions. It can also take the form of e-questionnaires. A 'survey' is simply a method for collecting data. This can take the form of mail surveys, street surveys, telephone surveys, household surveys, on-site surveys, e-surveys, and so on. Veal (2011) defines a survey as 'the *process* of designing and conducting a study involving the gathering of information from a number of subjects' (p. 256).

Surveys can include questionnaires, interviews, observations, reports or documentaries. Quantitative research tends to use questionnaire-based surveys to gather information. How the data are collected depends on the type of survey. We first discuss a few types of survey which are commonly used (e.g. in the field of tourism) and then discuss *how* to design questionnaires.

There are many elements that you will have to look at before you select the type of survey that you will use for your study. This will depend on:

- the purpose of your study: what information you are looking for?
- the amount of time that you have to conduct your study
- the population you are targeting, hence, the sample size
- the cost

9.1.1 Mail surveys

Mail or postal surveys are very commonly used where residents or members of organisations are being surveyed. Questionnaires are mailed to respondents who fill in and return them to the researcher. The success of a mail survey will depend on many factors such as:

- the interest of the respondent
- the literacy of the respondent
- the language used
- the length of the questionnaire
- the complexity of the questionnaire
- the design of the questionnaire
- the cost to the respondent (in terms of sending the reply)
- the geographical coverage of the study
- any incentive such as token or prize

Another factor which is important to consider is to be able to explain to the respondent the purpose of the study and his/her invaluable input to the study. This can be conveyed in a covering letter. Confidentiality is another important issue for the respondent. Many studies require personal information such as income, age, gender and ethnic group, which are sensitive to the respondent. As long as the respondent is given assurance that the questionnaire will be treated anonymously, he/she is more likely to fill in the questionnaire. A post-paid reply envelope is usually provided so that there is no cost to the respondent. A stamped envelope is very likely to increase the response rate according to Jennings (2001), 'as the respondents can see that someone has gone to the trouble to place stamps on the envelopes' (p. 230).

Sending reminders to respondents who have not returned their questionnaires can increase the response rate, but there are some implications. First, only if you are able to identify those who have not returned their questionnaires will you be able to send a reminder; in such a case the respondent will know that his/her responses are not anonymous. Otherwise, you can send a reminder to all the participants thanking them if they have filled in and returned the questionnaire, and, in case they have not yet done so, encourage them to return the completed questionnaire and explain how valuable their response is. A response rate of 20–30 per cent is usually reported in many studies and deemed satisfactory.

Practical tips

Whether you are able to use a mail survey for your study will depend how far you can identify your population and select a sample from it. Let's say, you want to study the activities that the residents of a particular village have engaged in on their most recent vacation. In this case, you will have to identify the village population by, for example, visiting the local council or municipality, then use a sampling method to select your sample. You may then choose to use a mail survey and send the questionnaire by post (if you can, you may deliver them yourself).
What constraints can you envisage in this case?

9.1.2 On-site surveys

Most surveys undertaken in tourism take the form of on-site surveys. Examples include surveys at visitor attractions, leisure and recreation facilities, hospitality accommodation, restaurants, modes of travel (such as airlines) and tourist destinations. Many studies assessing service quality, customer satisfaction and customer motivation use this type of survey. Often this type of survey is combined with a street survey where visitors are interviewed in town centres, for example. You have to be aware of the advantages and disadvantages when selecting this form of survey (discussed below).

On-site surveys are mostly conducted by owners/managers in leisure, recreation, travel and hospitality. At hotels, for example, the manager would be interested to know whether guests are satisfied with their service offerings to improve guest satisfaction. A short questionnaire is then designed and left on the table in the guest room. The guest can fill it when they are relaxed and have free time. A pen and a short covering letter normally accompany the questionnaire. You have to find a time when the selected respondents (based on the sampling technique discussed in Chapter 14) are not too busy – for instance, if you are conducting a survey at a museum, the best time would probably be when the tour has been conducted but not when the tour is in progress (the respondents might feel they are being disturbed and are 'wasting' time talking to the interviewer and may miss out on information about the displays). The best place to approach visitors would be at the souvenir or coffee shop, at the exit or in the parking area when they are leaving. You can also distribute the questionnaires at the entrance and collect them at the exit. A reward, such as key rings and discount vouchers, is likely to increase the response rate. If you are conducting a study on visitor expectation, you can interview participants at the entrance while they are queuing up.

To achieve a high response rate:

- questions have to be carefully written;
- the questionnaire must be well designed;
- you should give the respondent an estimate of the time it will take to complete the questionnaire (whether it is for respondent completion or for interviewer completion); and
- you should explain the purpose of your study to the respondent, e.g. whether it is to improve the level of service or improve the welfare of the community.

To select your respondent, you may use the random method, for example, using the table of random numbers, you arbitrarily chose a number. If, let's say, the number is four, then every fourth individual who passes by or is in the queue will be approached to participate in the survey. Purposive sampling can be used as well as quota sampling, or the sampling methods can be combined.

9.1.3 Street surveys

Street surveys are conducted on the street, in town centres and busy areas where you expect to find respondents fulfilling the profiles you are looking for. For example, if you are conducting a study on the impact of increasing petrol prices on vacations, you could conduct the survey on a caravan site.

The process for conducting a street survey consists of stopping people in the street or selected areas for an interview. Now think of stopping an individual carrying a handful of shopping bags, pushing a pram and requesting him/her to fill in a questionnaire! Does this mean that we cannot stop individuals with this sort of profile and what if the study requires this type of profile?

For the success of this type of survey you have to consider a few things. First, you need to have some form of identification to make yourself known to the respondents, e.g. a student card. Second, and perhaps most importantly, the interview should not be too long. This also implies that much attention has to be spent in designing the questionnaire to make it short and relevant to your research. Generally, street surveys tend to take around or less than five minutes. There are, however, some street interviews which can be long if the respondent has time to spare. Having a respondent standing for 15 to 20 minutes in a busy area is going to be challenging unless you have an allocated spot with a table and chair. Think whether as a student you will have access to dedicated spots with some logistics. Very often interviewers can be seen in an area where benches are located so that they can invite the respondent to take a seat if required. Third, this type of survey calls for an interviewer-filled and pre-coded questionnaire. If you, as the researcher, are the only one conducting the survey you may have open questions; however, jotting down the answers quickly enough to move to another question is quite daunting. Recording is an option but ethical issues will crop up and this means tends to be unpopular in street surveys. If there is a group of interviewers conducting the survey, it is highly recommended that closed questions be designed in the questionnaire to ensure consistency. And, fourth, it is also recommended that you have a proper dress code to look professional when approaching individuals.

Street surveys can be biased, especially when the researcher is achieving a low response rate. The interviewer then starts selecting individuals around his/her own profile, e.g. in the same age group, as these individuals will be thought to be more responsive. If a group of interviewers are employed, then to avoid such bias, you can use quota sampling, where a pre-determined quota with a certain profile (e.g. age, gender, nationality) is clearly specified. This can give a better representation of the population.

Warning: A street survey can be tedious and time consuming for a student if he/she is the only interviewer.

9.1.4 Telephone surveys

Telephone surveys are interviews conducted over the telephone where the interviewer seeks information or an opinion from respondents. Respondents are normally selected randomly using a telephone directory. The length of the interview is typically not more than 15 to 20 minutes. To encourage response, the questions are closed, that is, where respondents respond to questions with answers such as: 'Yes', 'No', 'Strongly Agree' to 'Strongly Disagree', and 'Number 1', 'Number 2' etc. Because the responses are short and pre-coded, the answer can be recorded simultaneously. With technology, there are now many software packages available to record and analyse the responses immediately. This method is very popular with political pollsters, especially in the run up to an election. This is due to the speed with which the results can be analysed and the widespread coverage of the sample. This method also maintains the anonymity and confidentiality of the respondents, as well as being cheaper. A more comprehensive discussion on the merits and limitations of using a telephone survey can be found in Jennings (2001, Chapter 8).

There are some aspects that need to be considered before using a telephone survey:

- The length of the questions.
- The number of questions.
- The design of closed questions.
- Which day and at what time to make calls – for example, during weekdays, retired people or housewives can be reached but evening and weekend calls can capture more respondents.
- Who is the targeted population: head of households, for example?
- Non-telephone users are excluded from this survey. How much will this affect the validity of the study?
- Mobile users are also excluded, as their numbers are not listed in any directory.
- The representativeness of the sample then becomes an issue that will need to be addressed.
- It isn't possible to use images/cards/lists; other ways have to be devised.

9.2 Questionnaire design

The questionnaire design needs to be carefully thought about. Very often as soon as students decide to research on a certain topic, they jump to designing the question-naire or start listing a series of questions for the interview. This is the wrong approach and shows that you have not given enough thought to what others have done, what the limitations of your strand are, what improvements need to be done and how you have reached your decision to include the questions from a carefully designed conceptual framework.

From the conceptual framework, you will be able to identify the concepts and then build the causal links among the concepts. You will probably be specifying hypotheses among the concepts and will operationalise the concepts by creating measurable variables. In a causal relationship, the dependent and independent variables will be identified for data collection. It is only when the variables have been identified and the hypotheses to be tested are confirmed that you can begin to make a list of questions to be included in the questionnaire. The process starts after the research questions have been identified and the research objectives have been clearly set.

Practical tips – list of questions

The list of questions has to be related to the research questions and purpose of your study. If you are conducting a comparative study with other studies, you might as well add questions which figured in those studies to be able to make comparisons.

For each question or item that you are listing to be included in the questionnaire, ask yourself questions such as: 'Why is this question important?', 'What benefit is there in including this question?', 'How do I use the data collected from this response?' and 'Will I be using this question to create a variable for hypothesis testing?'

Figure 9.1 illustrates the steps that will produce a relevant and carefully worked out questionnaire for your study. This will provide you with more ideas on the questions to be included in the questionnaire. Going back to the literature and see what others asked respondents, for instance, will be helpful to make comparisons with their results. Once you are satisfied with the list of questions you can then work on the questionnaire design.

The types of survey and whether the questionnaire is be completed by either the interviewer or interviewee (discussed below) will both influence the design of the questionnaire. The design elements of the questionnaire, such as layout, wording, whether questions are closed or opened-ended, are further discussed below. After designing the questionnaire, it needs to be piloted. It always helps to get a second opinion. Sometimes it is difficult to spot minute mistakes such as spelling or omission of words despite reading the questions over and over again. This can be done by inviting some friends, the supervisor or a small number of individuals to pilot the questionnaire. A pilot study can include 10 to 20 participants. The idea is to see how the respondents answer the questions, whether they understand how to answer the questions, remove mistakes and to check whether the questionnaire produces the intended outcomes. When the feedback from the pilot study is taken into account, the finalised questionnaire is ready for conducting the survey.

9.2.1 Interviewer-completion or self-completion questionnaire

As pointed out above, who completes the questionnaire can make a difference in terms of design and conduct. An interviewer-completion questionnaire takes less time to design, when selecting the appropriate font type and size, devising filters, and so on. This is because the respondents do not complete it and therefore do not need to see the questionnaire, hence requiring less time refining the design; for example, the number of pages is not as important as it would be if the respondent was completing it. As Veal (2011) explains, it can be less 'user-friendly'. This is more so especially when the interviewer is also the researcher. However, in large-scale studies, such as household surveys, where interviewers are employed, attention must be paid to the design of the questionnaires to avoid bias and ensure consistency. In such cases, questions are rigidly structured and are generally closed questions. An interviewer-completion

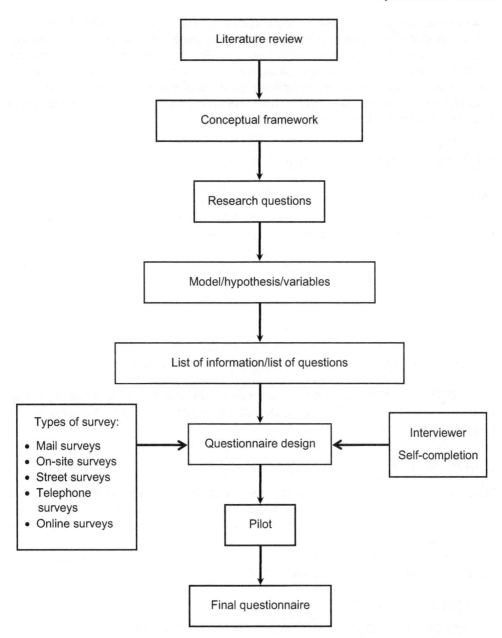

Figure 9.1 Questionnaire formulation and design for a deductive approach

questionnaire encourages the respondent to answer all the questions, hence there is no need to send reminders; the interviewer can clarify questions where needed and can use cards and images to conduct the survey.

Interviewer-completion does allow for clarity and more information when open questions are included. The disadvantages of this form of completion are that it is time consuming, costly and respondents are not anonymous and may give inaccurate information in answer to sensitive questions.

A self-completion questionnaire requires careful design as it should be formatted in such a way that the respondent is encouraged to complete the questionnaire. The lay-out should be clear and the number of pages should not be too long. Two columns on one page can maximise the number of questions to be included in the questionnaire. It is a cheaper than an interviewer-completed questionnaire as several questionnaires can be distributed to many respondents at the same time, hence it is less time consuming to conduct the survey. It is also relatively anonymous.

9.2.2 Designing the questionnaire

The content

Although you may have listed the questions which you will be including in the ques-tionnaire, you still need to present a structured questionnaire, that is, in terms of flow, presentation, format and open or closed questions.

Let us analyse the types of information that are commonly found in a question-naire. Let's say that you are conducting an on-site survey at an attraction or facility, the following might just be enough to design a questionnaire:

(a) the profile of users of the site/attraction/facility
(b) the activities/usage of the site/attraction/facility
(c) the evaluation/perception/satisfaction of the site/attraction/facility

Veal (2011) states that the questionnaire can be divided into three main headings: Who? What? and Why? We use some examples to illustrate how this may assist you in designing your questionnaire.

Who?

Most surveys request information about the characteristics of the respondent, such as age, gender, income, occupation, educational qualifications, marital status, ethnic group, family size, nationality and residential location. These are sought, first, to describe the profile of respondents representing the sample. Second, and most importantly, these characteristics can be used as control variables to explain differences or patterns in certain variables of interest. Let's say you ask the following questions:

1 **What is your age?**

   ☐ **15–24**   ☐ **25–34**   ☐ **35–44**   ☐ **45–54**   ☐ **55+**

2 **How much did you spend on your visit to London? £____**

From these two questions you can observe the spending pattern of the four age groups: *age* is the control variable and *spending* is the variable of interest (which we may call the dependent variable in this case). The data which are derived are describ-ing the spending pattern of the sample only. Descriptive statistics can be used to get a better picture of spending patterns, for example, you may find that, on average, the 35–44 age group spends twice that of the 55+ age group. To be able to generalise for the population, you have to use inferential statistics. Whether the observation made in the sample is the same for the whole population is mainly what you must be interested in. In Chapters 17 and 18 we show how to perform statistical tests to, for example, test whether there are any significant differences in spending pattern by age groups.

To facilitate data analysis, the responses need to be coded. For example the responses from Question 1 can be coded as follows:

☐ 15–24	☐ 25–34	☐ 35–44	☐ 45–54	☐ 55+
1	2	3	4	5

As for Question 2, the numerical value can be used without the need for coding.

What?

The activities that take place on a site, at an attraction or in a destination interest managers, policy-makers, the government, among others. Some examples are: the activities tourists engage when they visit a destination (shopping, swimming, visiting museums, enjoying local cultures, and so on), number of nights spent, number of times they have visited an attraction, total expenditure, mode of transport used to reach a destination and where they are staying. The format of the questions will depend on the purpose of the study. For example, you may wish to know the type of activities that visitors mostly do while visiting London.

3   **Which of the following places did you visit while in London?**

    London Zoo   ☐

    Buckingham Palace   ☐

    Trafalgar Square   ☐

    Covent Garden   ☐

    Piccadilly Circus   ☐

From this question you will know the places most visited by visitors in London. The preferred way to code the responses is to use dichotomous coding; this is because it is a multi-response question and the respondent can tick all the options. If the respondent has ticked a box, a value of 1 is given, otherwise 0.

If the purpose was to find out the most preferred place that visitors liked, then the question could be specified as follows:

3   **Please rank the following as your most preferred place visited. Rank them from 1 for the most preferred to 5 for the least preferred.**

    London Zoo   _____

    Buckingham Palace   _____

    Trafalgar Square   _____

    Covent Garden   _____

    Piccadilly Circus   _____

In this case each response will be coded the numerical value the respondent ranks the place. The intention is to discover the relative importance of the places to the respondents.

Alternatively, you could specify the question as follows:

3 **Which of the following is the place you have liked best? Tick only one.**

London Zoo	☐
Buckingham Palace	☐
Trafalgar Square	☐
Covent Garden	☐
Piccadilly Circus	☐

In this case the respondent is guided to tick only one box. The response can be coded as:

London Zoo	☐	1
Buckingham Palace	☐	2
Trafalgar Square	☐	3
Covent Garden	☐	4
Piccadilly Circus	☐	5

You may also make use of an open question if you believe the respondent may answer differently from the list provided, for example:

3 **Which place did you best like while visiting London?**

_____

As you can see, from the way the question is styled the responses can yield different answers and the coding will be different. Hence, it is important that you know what the research intention is to be able to set the 'right' question and code it appropriately for data analysis.

Why?

The 'why?' list of questions are probably the most important part in a questionnaire where you are seeking explanations about, for example, behaviour, opinions and attitudes. Most evaluative or explanatory studies tend to use a series of statements to explore concepts and constructs. For example, in a study exploring customer satisfaction at a restaurant only one question might not be sufficient to understand the concept of 'satisfaction'. For instance:

Were you satisfied at the restaurant?   ☐ Yes   ☐ No

This will group respondents into two groups and can be coded 1 for 'Yes' and 2 for 'No'.

Using scales can improve the conceptualisation, for example we can re-specify the above question as follows:

On a scale of 1 to 10, 1 being 'Very Dissatisfied' and 10 being 'Very Satisfied', how satisfied were you at the restaurant?

Very Dissatisfied   Very Satisfied

| 1 | 2 | 3 | 4 | 5 | 6 | 7 | 8 | 9 | 10 |

The scale 'captures the intensity, direction, level, or potency of a variable construct along a continuum' (Neuman, 2006). Assigning the numbers helps respondents to think about quantities rather than trying to explain the 'level of satisfaction' in words, for example, which is complicated. The conceptualisation and operationalisation of 'satisfaction' becomes clearer when using such a scale. The scale can be quantified to test hypotheses.

Likert scales are commonly used to collect attitude and opinion data. They were developed by Rensis Likert in the 1930s. In most research, a 5-point Likert Scale is used to add a neutral category for, for example, 'Strongly Agree', 'Agree', 'No Opinion', 'Disagree' and 'Strongly Disagree'. The responses can then be quantified, for example, 'Strongly Agree' can be given a score of 5 and 'Strongly Disagree' a score of 1.

Likert scales are called summated-ratings. You can combine several statements into a composite index if they all measure a single construct (Neuman, 2006). In our example of customer satisfaction, the scores on following statements may be summated to better understand customer satisfaction as in Figure 9.2.

Please circle your answer	Strongly disagree	Disagree	Neutral	Agree	Strongly agree
Employees provide prompt service	1	2	3	4	5
Employees handle complaints effectively	1	2	3	4	5
Service is on time	1	2	3	4	5
I will receive exactly what I will order	1	2	3	4	5
The food is well presented and cooked	1	2	3	4	5
The food is tasty	1	2	3	4	5
The food temperature is just right	1	2	3	4	5
A wide choice of menu is offered	1	2	3	4	5
The restaurant is clean and spacious	1	2	3	4	5
The restaurant is conveniently located	1	2	3	4	5
The restaurant has adequate parking	1	2	3	4	5
The restaurant's décor is appealing	1	2	3	4	5
The restaurant's facilities are up-to-date	1	2	3	4	5
The restaurant has a cheerful atmosphere	1	2	3	4	5

Figure 9.2 Example of summated-ratings

From the above statements, the highest possible index score will be 70 if the customer is very satisfied and 14 if he/she is not satisfied at all. How we use these data will be discussed in Chapters 17 and 18 where we show how to conduct data analysis.

In the above example, to ensure that the respondent is consistent in his/her responses that he/she, let's say, 'Strongly Agree[s]' with the statement, we need to ensure that he/she is not just ticking the boxes in a routine way or has tendency to keep ticking the boxes without reading the statements. To avoid such routine ticking, you can rephrase one or two statements in alternative directions to keep the respondent alert.

Wording

While designing the questions, there are certain aspects that need to be considered such as the wording of the questions. You need to ensure that the respondent understands your question if you want a valid response. To do so you should:

- Avoid words that are very complicated or technical; use everyday words or provide a definition if required.
- Use simple language.
- Be precise when setting a question – ask direct questions.
- Avoid leading questions, such as: 'Do you agree that tourists are driving up local prices?' If the local residents are responding to this question they are very likely to respond 'yes'. Reword the questions, for example: 'In your opinion, do tourists affect local prices?' 'Agree/Disagree'.
- Ask only one question at a time.
- Ask questions that relate to the present day rather than expecting the respondent to recall events dating back a couple of years.
- Avoid questions that will embarrass the respondent (especially if it is an interviewer-completed questionnaire) or sensitive questions like: 'What is your exact net income per month?'
- Avoid assessing the respondents, for example, when asking them to make certain calculations.

Questionnaire layout

To increase the response rate, attention to some details are essential in the layout of the questionnaire. Although you may have finalised the questions that will be included in the questionnaire, you do not necessarily need to start in the order we discussed above with a list of questions on 'who?', 'what?' and 'why?'. In fact, it is better to shuffle the questions and think of a structure to enable fluidity when the respondent is answering the questions.

Start by explaining the purpose of the survey and requesting assistance from the respondent. For example, at the top of the questionnaire, a few lines can be inserted. The title of the research can also be printed at the top of the questionnaire. In the case of a mail survey, a covering letter normally accompanies the questionnaire.

Always start with an easy question to get the respondent going. Get the attention of the respondent right at the beginning by asking relevant questions at the early stage of the questionnaire. Personal questions such as age, income and ethnic group are generally best left to the end. Sometimes it is better not to request too specific answers on personal matters, for example, age. It would be much better to either ask for date of birth or year born or specify age groups where the respondent can select.

The length of the questionnaire, font size and clear instructions will improve the response rate. The filters need to be clear so that the respondent does not skip relevant parts. Try to facilitate the task of the respondents to answer the questions by either circling numbers/options or ticking boxes.

Coding

With a range of computer software available, you are able to analyse the data from the questionnaire provided that you correctly code the responses. Numbers are best ways to code responses to enable data analysis. For instance, coding the responses in Figure 9.2, can easily aggregate the responses into an index and can also determine the level of satisfaction for each statement for the sample. Scaled answers are easy to code. Where numerical answers are provided, then there is no need to code, for example, when asking for the amount spent on a trip or respondent's age.

The complexity for coding responses arises when there are open ended questions. You will have to think of the possible responses that the question is likely to generate and code them accordingly. For example, if you are asking the following question:

What is your favourite sport? _____

You are likely to have a long list of responses for this type of question. In such a case, you may select, say, four of the most relevant sports to your study and code them from 1 to 4 and then code other responses as 5.

It is advisable to establish the coding scheme before you finalise your questionnaire and collect data. The coding will help you to refine your questions and the possible responses that you provide.

9.3 Reliability and validity

You must address the issues of reliability and validity when using a particular methodology. In a questionnaire, for example, the questions and measures that are being used to gather data must be checked for reliability and validity. Babbie (1990) explains that 'reliability is a matter of whether a particular technique, applied repeatedly to the same object, would yield the same result each time', while 'validity refers to the extent to which an empirical measure adequately reflects the real meaning of the concept under consideration', as cited in Jennings (2001).

Reliability refers to the quality of the measurement and the consistency of the measure. Neuman (2006) uses the example of a bathroom scale to demonstrate what is meant by measurement reliability. He explains that if you get on the scale and read the weight and you get off and on again and again, you have a reliable scale if you get the same weight each time. One way to check the reliability of the results is to split the sample into two and check the consistency of the results (if the sample size is small, this may pose a problem).

Validity refers to accuracy and whether a study measures or examines what it claims to measure or examine. For example, if, in a study measuring the impact of tourists on a local community, you use visitors rather than tourists to assess the impact in your sample, the study will not be valid. The research will then not truly reflect what the 'real' impact of tourists is but rather it will be of 'visitors'. This is an example on internal validity. How far the generalisation of the results, from a sample to a wider population, can be relied on is an example of external validity. This will depend on the sample selection.

Careful questionnaire design, as discussed above, and proper sampling principles will minimise threats to validity. To check the validity of the responses of the respondents, you can use dummy questions; for example, if you wanted to know which attractions visitors enjoyed most at the zoo, you may wish to add a non-existent attraction at the zoo to check whether the respondent has really been to the zoo or is just routinely ticking the boxes, is tired or is trying to impress. Such questionnaires should be discarded from the analysis.

Chapter summary

- Data measurement is an integral part of quantitative method.
- Primary data can be collected through various types of surveys such as mail surveys, street surveys, telephone surveys, household surveys, on-site surveys and e-surveys.
- Surveys can include questionnaires, interviews, observations, reports or documentaries.
- Attention must be given to the design of the questionnaire to improve the response rate.
- The questions to be included in a questionnaire have to revolve around the aim and objectives of the study.
- There are many ways to ask a question – it can open or closed. The appropriateness of the design of the question will depend on how the responses will be used and for what purpose.
- Coding responses will also determine how the questions are set.
- Reliability refers to the quality of the measurement and the consistency of the measure.
- Validity refers to accuracy and whether a study measures or examines what it claims to measure or examine.
- Always check for the reliability and validity when using a particular methodology.

Discussion questions

9.1 You are conducting a study on shopping behaviour of teenagers.
   (a) What factors you would consider?
   (b) Explain how you would conduct a street survey if you are to collect 150 responses in one week.
   (c) Design a questionnaire for this survey.

9.2 What are the advantages of undertaking an interviewer-completion questionnaire?

9.3 How can you minimise the threats of validity in designing a questionnaire?

9.4 How would you increase the response rate when conducting:

(a) a mail survey?

(b) a street survey?

(c) a telephone survey?

Further reading

Jennings G. (2001). *Tourism Research*. Milton: John Wiley & Sons Australia Ltd. [Chapter 8.]

Neuman, W.L. (2006). *Social Research Methods: Qualitative and Quantitative Approaches*. Boston: Pearson, Allyn and Bacon.

Saunders, M.N.K., Lewis, P. and Thornhill, A. (2009). *Research Methods for Business Students*, 5th edition. Harlow: Pearson Education Ltd.

Veal, A.J. (2011). *Research Methods for Leisure and Tourism*, 4th edition. Harlow: Prentice Hall.

Chapter 10

Mixed methods and triangulation

*Prabha Ramseook-Munhurrun
and Ramesh Durbarry*

A student is conducting a study on tourist experience at an attraction park. He has decided to use an on-site survey and has designed a short questionnaire. However, he suspects that he will not get in-depth information from his respondents to assess their experience. He then decides to carry out some in-depth interviews with some tourists.

The questions which cropped up were:

- Can he use both quantitative and qualitative methods in the same study?

- What are the advantages to doing so?

10.0 Chapter objectives

The mixed methods approach has been gaining momentum in conducting research. This is due to the limitations from studies which have relied solely on either quantitative or qualitative methods. This chapter explains this rise in its application and when it is more appropriate to employ it.

After studying this chapter, you will be able to:

- understand the use of mixed methods as an alternative approach to collecting data;
- describe the characteristics of mixed research; and
- explain when the mixed methods approach is appropriate to use.

10.1 The debate between quantitative and qualitative methods

There have been constant disputes among proponents of the quantitative and qualitative paradigms over the superiority of their respective research method (Kuhn, 1977). Sieber (1973) points out that, while the quantitative method claims to be providing hard and generalisable data, the qualitative research culture emphasises deep, rich and observational data. Still, in spite of their massive contribution towards enhancing knowledge, both quantitative and qualitative methodologies are constrained by a number of disadvantages, and are not applicable to all settings. On one hand, quantitative researchers are very often criticised for their narrow and superficial way of collecting and analysing data, and for being generally numerical and descriptive in nature. This means that they are unable to take into account human perceptions and true feelings, and focus instead on the closest match to answers which have been pre-set, and whose questions might reflect the researcher's views rather than the views of the respondents (structural bias/false representation). On the other hand, the major criticism generally levelled against qualitative studies are their subjectivity, their limited scope (being constrained by the need for an in-depth approach to data gathering and analysis) and the difficulty in replicating the research carried out.

Over time, however, pragmatism has gained primacy over these philosophical disagreements, and has contributed significantly to shedding light on how research approaches can be mixed successfully so as to expand one's understanding of any specific issue being researched. This has led to the popularisation of the mixed methods research approach, which can be defined as 'the class of research where the researcher mixes or combines quantitative and qualitative research techniques, methods, approaches, concepts or language into a single study' (Johnson and Onwuegbuzie, 2004, p. 17).

This combination of methods provides for complementary strengths and non-overlapping weaknesses (Brewer and Hunter, 1989), makes a full understanding of the topic under study more likely (Ford, 1987), and offers the best opportunities for answering key research questions under investigation. Indeed, based on this approach, researchers are in a position to select the right dosage of qualitative and quantitative content so as to reach the appropriate mix needed to answer their research questions in the specific context in which they find themselves.

Figure 10.1 The research continuum

The continuum illustrated in Figure 10.1, shows that research can either be purely qualitative or purely quantitative or mixed with an equal emphasis on qualitative and quantitative approaches.

The mixed methods research design uses both quantitative and qualitative approaches in a single research study to gather and analyse data. Several mixed methods theorists have developed mixed methods typologies (Creswell, 2003; Creswell and Plano Clark, 2007; Tashakkori and Teddlie, 2003).

10.2 Mixed methods approach

Tashakkori and Teddlie (1998) have noted the limitations of using a single method approach in research and this weakens the link between paradigm and methods. In order to counter the paradigmatic differences, that is, the restrictions of single research method designs, a group of researchers sought a philosophy that does not limit methodological practice, and proposed that both the qualitative and quantitative approaches could be employed in the same investigation (Patton, 1990; Tashakkori and Teddlie, 1998; Creswell, 2003). When qualitative and quantitative research is used simultaneously, this is known as mixed methods research (Creswell, 2002). Mixed methods research is recognised as the third methodological approach or research paradigm, together with the qualitative and quantitative approaches (Tashakkori and Teddlie, 2003; Creswell and Plano Clark, 2007; Johnson et al., 2007; Leech and Onwuegbuzie, 2010). These researchers are called pragmatists and have argued that pragmatism is the philosophical paradigm for mixed methods, where the research questions guide the choice of the methodological approaches (Patton, 1990; Tashakkori and Teddlie, 2003; Onwuegbuzie and Leech, 2005). Instead of questioning ontology and epistemology, the pragmatists argue that it is important to focus on the research problems and then use the pluralistic approaches to acquire knowledge about the problem to determine the research framework. Through this integrative research approach, explanations about the 'real world' can be tested both theoretically and empirically (Wheeldon, 2010). Pragmatism enables researchers to mix research approaches successfully so that the research questions are appropriately addressed (Johnson and Onwuegbuzie, 2004), consequently enabling them to better understand social reality.

10.3 Mixed methods typologies

Typologies are the systematic classification of theoretical concepts in the research model (Creswell, 2003). In order to integrate both the qualitative and quantitative research methods in a single research project, the research designs have to be properly and thoughtfully planned to recognise the contributions of each approach (Creswell, 2003). Wheeldon (2010) further emphasises that the combination of qualitative and quantitative research methods requires new thinking about the theoretical support for integrative research.

The research designs and approaches required the consideration of an alternative epistemological framework (Wheeldon, 2010) and pragmatism has emerged as a common alternative to the choice of positivism and constructivism (Tashakkori and Teddlie, 1998, 2003; Creswell, 2002; Creswell and Plano Clark, 2007). According to Creswell (2003), pragmatism links the selection of the research method approaches to the purpose and the nature of the research questions proposed. Table 10.1 summarises the knowledge claims, strategy of inquiry and the methods of collecting data across the three approaches of research methods and these are the major contributors for selecting the appropriate method (Creswell, 2003).

10.4 The mixed methods matrix design

The literature reveals several types of mixed methods using the qualitative and quantitative research designs (Figure 10.2). The use of mixed methods in a single study considers data collection or analysis sequentially or concurrently as well as the way the data and results are integrated at one or more phases during the design in order to best answer the research questions (Tashakkorie and Teddlie, 1998; Creswell, 2003; Johnson and Onwuegbuzie, 2004; Creswell and Plano Clark, 2007). Four types of mixed methods approaches have been presented, including: triangulation, embedded design, explanatory design and exploratory design (Creswell and Plano Clark, 2007).

These methods can be used either with equal status or with one dominant approach. A sequential research design involves either the quantitative phase first being carried out then subsequently the qualitative phase, or vice versa (Tashakkorie and Teddlie, 1998; Creswell, 2003; Johnson and Onwuegbuzie, 2004). The authors further explain that a concurrent research design does not use data emerging from the sample selected from one phase in the other phase. Instead, data obtained from both samples are combined and interpreted at the data interpretation phase. For example, in the concurrent study, QUAL + QUAN, both qualitative and quantitative data are collected at the same time and are given equal status, while in the sequential study, qual → QUAN, the qualitative data are collected followed by the quantitative data,

Table 10.1 Combination of knowledge claim, strategy of inquiry and methods in research

Research approach	Knowledge claim	Strategy of inquiry	Methods
Qualitative	Constructivist assumption	Ethnographic and narrative design	Field observation; open-ended interviewing
Quantitative	Post-positive assumption	Experimental design; survey	Measuring attitudes, behaviours
Mixed methods	Pragmatic assumption	Mixed methods design	Close-ended measure; open-ended observation

Source: Adapted from Creswell (2003, p. 20)

	Concurrent	Sequential
Equal status	QUAL + QUAN	QUAL → QUAN QUAN → QUAL
Dominant status	QUAL + quan QUAN + qual	QUAL → quan quan → QUAL QUAN → qual qual → QUAN

Figure 10.2 Mixed methods design matrix

→ means sequential; capital letters 'QUAL' and 'QUAN' indicate high priority or weight; initial capital letter/lowercase 'Qual' and 'Quan' indicate lower priority or weight.

Source: Adapted from Tashakkorie and Teddlie (1998), Creswell (2003) and Johnson and Onwuegbuzie (2004).

Note: 'Qual' means qualitative; 'Quan' means quantitative ; + means concurrent.

showing a quantitative dominance. Thus mixed methods allow either the qualitative findings to explain the quantitative results or vice versa, thereby enhancing the validity and reliability of the study. The qualitative data are primarily used to enhance the quantitative approach. The use of a mixed methods design aims to capitalise on the strengths of both quantitative and qualitative approaches and thus the results of the study will be more credible and reliable (Leech and Onwuegbuzie, 2010).

Mixed methods is increasingly popular in social and behavioural sciences research (Tashakkori and Teddlie, 1998; Johnson et al., 2007) and researchers have argued that mixed methods should be used in the same investigation to yield better research outcomes (Tashakkori and Teddlie, 1998, 2003; Creswell, 2002, 2003). These researchers argue that mixed methods research can be utilised to:

(a) provide a rich understanding of a phenomenon by combining exploratory, descriptive and causal research designs;
(b) address research questions better than single method approaches; that is, mixed methods approach can simultaneously answer the confirmatory and exploratory questions; and
(c) allow the development and justification of the conceptual model within one study.

Thus, based on the divergent findings, mixed methods provide the opportunity for expressing different viewpoints and thereby providing rich data and stronger conclusions (Tashakkori and Teddlie, 1998; Johnson et al., 2007). Using both the qualitative and quantitative methods compensates for each method's weaknesses if used alone.

10.5 Triangulation

Triangulation is concerned with the application and combination of several research methodologies in one study (Denzin, 1970; Saunders et al., 2003). The concept of triangulation is classified into investigator, theory, data and methodology triangulation. Triangulation looks at the same phenomenon from more than one source of data to corroborate or elaborate the research problem. Triangulation, using the mixed methods approach, primarily attempts to claim knowledge based on pragmatic grounds (Creswell, 2003). Denzin (1970) distinguishes four types of triangulation and Table 10.2 summarises the classification of triangulation.

Furthermore, this approach minimises the personal and methodological biases and enriches the study generalisation (Tashakkori and Teddlie, 2003; Onwuegbuzie and Leech, 2005). For example, researchers seek to check the validity of their findings by cross-checking them with another method in order to increase the quality and depth of the results. Data triangulation is the most popular triangulation as it is the easiest to implement.

10.6 Establishing the validity and reliability of the research approach

10.6.1 Validity

Validity is established when the findings of the study accurately reflect the research situation and the findings are supported by evidence. According to Cohen et al. (2000, p. 254) triangulation refers to 'an attempt to map out, or explain more fully, the richness and complexity of human behaviour by studying it from more than one standpoint'. Triangulation aims at enhancing the credibility and validity of the results, as it gives a more detailed and balanced picture of the situation (Altrichter et al., 2006, p. 117).

10.6.2 Reliability

The use of different data collection methods (methods triangulation), and the collection of information at different times and from different people (sources triangulation),

Table 10.2 Classification of triangulation

Classification of triangulation	Definition
Investigator	Involves the use of several different researchers to examine and interpret the same collected data
Theoretical	Entails the use of multiple perspectives to interpret the same set of data
Data	Concerned with the use of a variety of data sources such as primary and secondary data
Methodological	Involves the use of different data collection methods, where both qualitative and quantitative research methods are combined in the study

Source: Adapted from Denzin (1970) and Saunders et al. (2003)

allow for the verification of the consistency of findings. By the use of different methods, the researcher can also take advantage of the strengths and offset the weakness of each. This contributes extensively to the reliability of data collected for analysis purposes.

Chapter summary

- Mixed methods involves combining qualitative and quantitative research in a single research study and is based on the philosophy of pragmatism.
- Mixed methods yields better research outcomes, as it provides a rich understanding of a phenomenon by combining exploratory, descriptive and causal research designs.
- Mixed methods also addresses research questions better than single method approaches – that is, it can simultaneously answer the confirmatory and exploratory questions.
- Mixed methods allows the development and justification of the conceptual model within one study.
- Triangulation looks at the same phenomenon from more than one source of data to corroborate or elaborate of the research problem.

Discussion questions

10.1 Is qualitative evidence superior to quantitative evidence, or vice versa? Why?
10.2 Choose a research topic and explain which research approach you will adopt for your study. You should also explain the mixed methods design matrix that you will use for the study.
10.3 Describe how you would use mixed methods in your study.
10.4 What is meant by 'triangulation'?
10.5 What are the different types of triangulation?

Further reading

Creswell, J. and Plano-Clark, V. (2007). *Designing and Conducting Mixed Methods Research*. Thousand Oaks, CA: Sage.
Greene, J. (2007). *Mixed Methods in Social Enquiry*. San Francisco, CA: Wiley.

Chapter 11

The internet as a research tool and e-method

Netnography

Hania Janta

Ria is conducting her research on the influence that the experiences of tourists who stayed in five-star hotels during their visit in a tourist destination have on potential visitors. With the advent of the internet, booking websites, such as TripAdvisor, offer opportunities for visitors to relate and post their experiences. Such reviews, however, do have an impact on potential visitors. To conduct her study, Ria decides to make use of such data.

The question is how to conduct this type of study? How to analyse such data? Are there other sources of data? What are the issues with this method?

11.0 Chapter objectives

The internet has become a significant source in data collection and it has changed the ways we conduct research. Although the internet offers numerous opportunities for researchers, it also changes quickly, evolves and may complicate the research process. It wasn't long ago that Twitter did not even exist, while now researchers may use those short messages written in 140 signs as a source of data. Clearly, the internet provides a wealth of opportunities and researchers need to embrace them. The objective of this chapter is to introduce to you the use of the internet as a tool to engage in research.

The chapter focuses specifically on an overview of netnography and the usefulness of this method in conducting qualitative research online. This innovative method has large potential, as it uses rich data available online such as blogs, discussion fora or comments posted on social networking sites that occur 'naturally' – data that are not 'fabricated'. In other words, a netnographic approach can be used to study online communities and cultures including social networking sites interest groups from Facebook or WeChat (used extensively in China). We will show various types of research that most benefit this method to gather qualitative data. Examples of students' topics to which this research approach can be applied as well as case studies are shown. Detailed procedures are listed for performing a netnographic analysis in a rigorous way. As with other types of research, there are challenges and limitations that need to be considered.

In this chapter we look at the following questions:

- What is netnography?
- How do we use netnography?
- What types of netnographic research exist?
- What are the sources of netnographic data?
- How do we conduct a netnographic study?

After studying this chapter, you will be able to:

- understand what netnography is and how it can be used in (tourism) research;
- assess both the advantages and disadvantages of the netnographic approach;
- assess how to select appropriate sites for analysis; and
- perform a netnographic analysis in a rigorous way.

11.1 What is netnography?

Netnography uses original downloads (posts) from publicly available online discussion groups. It is derived from *ethnography*, adapted to the study of online communities and cultures. Netnography can be based on observations only – when you do not interact with the online users but just observe their online discussions. It can also be done with your participation. Netnography is also defined as an *approach* or a *multimethod* that combines various techniques including content analysis, historical analysis, semiotics, hermeneutics, narrative analysis and thematic analysis, among others. Robert Kozinets was the first to try to conceptualise the approach and he coined the term *netnography*, nevertheless, many others have also attempted to transfer ethnographic principles to online environments, using, for example: 'net ethnography' or 'multi-sited ethnography' (Wittel, 2000), 'virtual ethnography' (Hine 2000, 2005), 'ethnography online' (Gatson and Zweerink, 2004) or 'digital ethnography' (Murthy, 2008). As can be seen, many terms are used to define research in a virtual environment.

In this chapter we use the procedures proposed by Kozinets and modified by other researchers who use the term 'netnography' rather than other terms. This *netnographic approach* developed by Kozinets is considered as one of the 'innovations' in qualitative research methods (see Bengry-Howell et al., 2011, from the ESRC National Centre for Research Methods for a detailed discussion of the approach). The importance of understanding the approach is justified by the widespread use of the method. Netnography, which was originally developed for marketing and consumer research, is a popular approach used in research, increasingly being applied to the study of hospitality (Watson et al., 2008), leisure (Beaven and Laws, 2007), events (Morgan, 2009) and tourism (Martin et al., 2007; Mkono, 2012).

It should be noted, however, that some researchers do not employ netnography when analysing the content of blogs or other social media. For example, Enoch and Grossmann (2010) conducted an analysis of the blogs of Israeli and Dutch tourists. In their case, less attention was given to the actual methodology of the study. Others try to conceptualise netnography in tourism research. For example, Lugosi et al. (2012) provided a detailed exploration of how this method can be conceptualised and used in hospitality studies. In this chapter we refer to the studies that state specifically the use of netnography.

11.2 Who are the participants/fora users?

Those who actively participate in online discussions can be classified based on their level of involvement within the online community they belong to. Kozinets (1999) categorised them as 'tourists', 'minglers', 'devotees' and 'insiders'. The first of these, 'tourists', only post causal questions, while the latter two categories of users represent the most important data sources. Different typologies also exist (see for example, O'Reilly et al., 2007). Table 11.1 list the sources of data which can be used for netnographic study.

Table 11.1 Sources of netnographic data

What sources of data can be used for a netnographic study?	
Fora/message boards	Enable users to engage in asynchronous exchanges (not at the same time) or postings on a different topic thread
Blogs	Written by individuals, to which others may respond. They also provoke ongoing asynchronous exchanges
microblogs	Enable users to post 140-character status messages (Twitter)
Websites	Provided by commercial and non-commercial organisations or individuals
Review sites	Enable users to post comments about destinations (TripAdvisor)
Social networking sites	Focus on facilitating the building of social relations among people who may share interests or real-life connections (Facebook)

11.3 Two ways of data collection

11.3.1 Netnography with active research – overt research

Netnographic data can be also collected when the researcher is *overt* and he/she posts a message to the users. Once the message has been posted on a forum, the users may react in various ways. The reactions from the users can be divided into three types:

- users offering their help and replying positive comments;
- users not participating in the discussion; and
- users expressing their dissatisfaction with the topic or researcher.

Access issues

In the online environment the last of behaviours listed above is not uncommon. Sometimes, the community moderator may delete an unwanted post. Increasingly, a form of aggressive behaviour online called *flaming* is taking place in the context of new media (Thompsen and Foulger, 1996; O'Sullivan and Flanagin, 2003). Flaming is defined as comments that are perceived by other users to be hostile, and can be of different degrees of hostility, from tension to antagonism. As researchers, we need to remember to remain professional and that the tone and style of language used by us when entering an online forum is key. After all, the researcher is only 'a guest' and does not belong to the group. While re-posting is recommended, particularly when using those very active fora with numerous users and posts, it is also important not to post persistent messages which may be mistaken for 'spam', and to respect the online community.

Potential challenges of conducting online research in an overt way

- Moderators might deny access to their groups because they treat the researcher's post as a 'spam'.
- Reaction to a researcher's request may become a target of abusive comments and turned into *flaming*.
- An influential user/users may advise other members to boycott the research, by referring to the researcher's study as spamming, or replying with insulting remarks (Hudson and Bruckman, 2004). One explanation for such online behaviours is a possibility that the same online group may be a subject of study multiple times and be asked to participate in research by various researchers. Clearly, this leads to an interruption of community life.

11.3.2 Netnography based upon observation/passive netnography

Observing online users' discussions is a popular technique used by researchers. Indeed, observations rather than the researcher's involvement in the group's interactions do not disrupt community life. This chapter will focus mainly on this approach.

Box 11.1: data collection using Twitter and a #hashtag tool

Twitter, founded in 2006, is a microblogging service that allows users to post 140-character status messages (*tweets*). They can be about the poster's current mood, location or events. Because of their length, the language used in tweets differs from that on websites or fora; twitters need to be creative in putting their information in a short message.

A usual tool that can be used in research is a *hashtag* – a special 'tag', originally invented by Twitter users mark *keywords* or *topics* in tweets. They are composed of a single word or phrase beginning with a '#' (with no spaces or punctuation). The hashtag lets users search the subject of a tweet. For example, a search for #tourism should reveal tweets where users chose to use tourism in their subjects. Hashtags are commonly used at conferences or in discussions of major events. The use of hashtags in research can be particularly valuable in allowing real-time searching (Ovadia, 2009).

11.4 Why are we using netnography?

The main reason to apply netnography in the age of Web 2.0 is simply due to the amount of data available in social media. Fora now consist of large amounts of rich anonymous data. This may be important if we try to explore a sensitive topic. The data is collected in a manner that is entirely unobtrusive, convenient, accessible and economical (Kozinets, 2002). You do not direct the topics discussed by users; therefore, there is no impact of a third person as there is in case of interviewing. Obtaining 'not fabricated', 'naturally' occurred data is one of the main advantages of this approach. Additionally, there is no need to transcribe responses, as the data is ready to download in its existing form. Clearly saving time is one of the advantages of this approach. You are also able to revisit the original data whenever necessary, as the rich source remains available (O'Reilly et al., 2007). Credibility of the data can be checked by others.

Key questions

- Do we use netnography as a sole method/approach or as one of the methods?
- When can we use netnography as a primary data collection method in research?

It can be seen from the case studies in Boxes 11.2 to 11.4, netnographic research can be used as a first phase of data collection when two or more methods are involved or it can be used as a sole method. It is advisable to use this approach to conduct *an exploratory study*. Netnography is often used when the research concerns a particular community online, i.e. Watson et al. (2008) discuss blogs of 'foodie' community, while Podoshen (2013) analyses large online black metal communities based in Europe, in the United States, and a variety of black metal groups on Facebook and other social media sites.

Box 11.2: student research *topic 1*

Title: The effects of on the day service at weddings on the overall event experience

Research questions:

Which tangible and intangible elements are the most important for the customers at weddings?

How did the service providers respond to a service failure during the wedding function?

Research design: There is a growing number of wedding venue review sites offering brides the chance to share their experiences. Using the existing data on the review sites key themes were identified and used to form the interview questions for the main data collection. The interviewees were approached online from the existing active users. Six interviews were conducted via phone.

Box 11.3: student research *topic 2*

Title: Hotel Managers' responses to TripAdvisor comments

Research questions:

How do managers choose to which reviews respond to?

What type of language do they use?

Which hotel owners respond to TripAdvisor comments – do SMEs (small and medium-sized enterprises) or large hotels respond to reviews?

Research design: The aim of the research concerns managers' online behaviour and their views, therefore two phases of research collection were chosen. The first consisted of a netnographic study of the TripAdvisor website and the second was interviews with hotel managers. In order to narrow down the research one location was chosen: Bournemouth – an English seaside destination. In the first stage the researcher looked for reviews of hotels in Bournemouth. For the second stage of data collection, six interviews with actively responding hotel managers were conducted. Interviews allowed the researcher to get an insight into why managers respond to reviews and the impact this may have.

11.5 Issues with using netnography

The disadvantage of undertaking research online is that the identity of the informant cannot be verified and the accuracy of information that relies on the informant's trustworthiness cannot be guaranteed (Wittel, 2000). In practice, it is extremely difficult to measure how many distinct participants are involved in one exchange (Kozinets, 2002). There is also the difficulty in deciding what to include and what to exclude from the wealth of information. Furthermore, a disadvantage of employing netnography is not being able to direct online exchanges, for example when a researcher would like to clarify something or ask about a detail. Netnography that is based upon observation does not allow this. Ethical issues in netnographic studies can be a potential limitation of conducting research online as the monitoring of internet fora raises a number of ethical questions concerning privacy and informed consent.

Table 11.2 Advantages and disadvantages of using netnography

Advantages	Disadvantages
• Rich data ready available online • Data come from a wide range of geographically dispersed people/communities • Data collection is unobtrusive, accessible, free and time saving • Data is downloadable, no need to transcribe the data • Ability to revisit the data when needed • Useful in exploring sensitive topics	• The identity of the online users cannot be verified • Difficulty in selecting what to choose for the analysis because of the amount of data • The respondents are not directed • Ethical issues – online users do not know that they are being studied

11.6 Collecting data – step by step

Robert Kozinets developed a detailed procedure for how a netnographic study should be conducted. The guidance suggests the following steps: entrée, data collection, analysis and interpretation, as well as ethics and member feedback.

If you are staying for a while and have time to spare than I would recommend taking the 50 bus from accross the road to Swanage. Its brilliant value and if you get a day ticket you can hop on and off when you want. We got a day ticket for £18 for 4 adults, the kids were free. The ferry alone would have cost us £14 for 2 cars and then there would have been parking and petrol. We stopped off at Sandbanks and then continued to Swanage which is a lovely little place. All in all we had a brilliant holiday and were lucky with the weather. A few relatively minor changes could turn this good hotel into an excellent one.

Stayed August 2011, travelled with family

Value   Cleanliness
Sleep Quality   Service

Helpful?   1   Thank dancinqueen0   Report

Ask dancinqueen0 about Hotel Collingwood

This review is the subjective opinion of a TripAdvisor member and not of TripAdvisor LLC

barryclarke, Owner at Hotel Collingwood, responded to this review, 13 August 2011

Our reception staff are friendly and recieve many compliments. At times they are busy with work load.
The menu changes daily over 7days with completely diferent choices of starters, soups and 5 main courses each day. Chef makes a daily hot sweet.
The doorlock had to be changed due to a problem with the barrel, it is true that the cause was not ascertainable.
Thank you for the kind and constructive comments.

Barry Clarke

Report response as inappropriate

This response is the subjective opinion of the management representative and not of

Figure 11.1 An example of a message posted on TripAdvisor and the manager's response

11.6.1 Entrée

First, the research questions need to be identified. For example, the purpose of the study might be to gain some insights from Polish migrant workers on their attitudes, perceptions and feelings towards their experience in the hospitality sector (Janta and Ladkin, 2009; Janta, 2011). Another research question related to managers' comments posted on TripAdvisor are shown in Figure 11.1.

11.6.2 Data collection

The first step is to choose fora that have high traffic. As suggested by Kozinets (2002), the highest amount of traffic (the number of messages) posted daily can be an indicator of the website's popularity among internet users. It is important to select a number of active sites for analysis. Box 11.5 suggests some criteria for selecting sites. Relevant message boards can be found by examining headings or by using the search engines in those sites and searching for specific words. The elements visible on a discussion forum are: *Topic title*, *Replies* – the number of messages replying to the thread (defined as a 'hierarchically organised collection of notes in which all notes are written as "replies" to earlier note' (Hewitt, 2005, p. 568); *Topic starter* – the nickname of the user who started the topic; *Views* – the number of viewings (in other words, traffic on the website); and *Last Action* – the last message displayed underneath the post.

Box 11.5: criteria for selecting sites (Kozinets, 2010, p. 89)

1)	**relevant**	to the research focus and questions
2)	**active**	with recent and regular communications
3)	**interactive**	having flows of communication between participants
4)	**substantial**	in terms of numbers of users
5)	**heterogeneous**	involving different participants
6)	**data-rich**	with substantial and insightful discussions

Case study 1: Watson et al. (2008) – examines 'foodie culture' through an analysis of an active and rich *blog* called *Grab Your Fork* (grabyourfork.blogspot.com/). Helen Yee's blog, established in 2004, won a number of prestigious for food blog awards.

Case study 2: Janta et al. (2012) – explores migrant workers' language learning mediated through hospitality work on- and offline. The *discussion fora* selected for analysis are those with the biggest traffic:

gazeta.pl – with more than 102 million posts written with 7474 different fora including a forum called 'Work in Great Britain and Ireland' with 152,000 posts

mojawyspa.co.uk (my island) – has 23,000 threads

ang.pl (dedicated to those who learn English) – has more than 72,000 threads

---

Second, the researcher needs to identify the threads that are of relevance of the study. The investigation needs to be limited to a number of selected threads, as it is usually unmanageable to analyse all discussions on a specific site. For example, approximately 100 existing threads can be downloaded (printed, if needed) and analysed. Threads should be chosen for their rich content, relevant topic matter and active participation (Kozinets, 2002).

11.6.3 Analysis and interpretation

Threads relevant to the study must be extracted from the material, copied and can be printed also. Common themes are recognised at this stage, taking into account the name of the thread. The length of the debates usually varies, some of them may have more than 100 postings. At this stage, it is important to decide on the type of data analysis. There are a number of ways to analyse qualitative data. One of them is 'thematic analysis' consisting of reading, re-reading and identifying themes.

11.6.4 Ethics and member feedback

The last steps of Kozinet's (2002) guidance for conducting netnographic studies concern the full disclosure of the researcher, who should seek permission from the members of community sites. This part of the methodological procedures has been modified by Langer and Beckman, who argue that it is worth contacting members of fora when collecting the data on those sites that are not entirely public (2005, p. 194). Thus, obtaining consent for publicly available fora is not necessary and this view is shared by other internet researchers (Ess and The AoIR Ethics Working Committee, 2002; Madge, 2006; Beaven and Laws, 2007).

We suggest following the modified guidance and not informing the participants or asking for their permission when discussion fora used for the netnographic study are publicly available. Further suggestions of Kozinets (2002) include ensuring the confidentiality and anonymity of informants. Thus, it is recommended to delete the names of participants and other information that could potentially identify the users, such as their emails and phone numbers. For example, in their study, Xun and Reynolds (2010) did not disclose users' pseudonyms or avatars in order to protect their identities; instead the users were distinguished as 'Participant x, y, z'.

Case study 1: online tourist reviews of restaurant experiences

A netnographic examination of constructive authenticity in Victoria Falls tourist (restaurant) experiences (Mkono, 2012)

Aim: to examine how authenticity is projected onto cultural objects.

Method: netnographic analysis of online tourist reviews on TripAdvisor of two popular Victoria Falls restaurants: 'Mama Africa Eating House' and 'The Boma – Place of Eating'. The reviews were accessed 17 March 2011 and analysed using Thematic analysis.

Analysis:

1   The reviews were read and re-read a few times.
2   Manual coding included: identifying, marking out and making notes on interesting and recurrent ideas.
3   Illustrative quotes were highlighted for reference and evidence in the discussion of findings.

Presentation of findings: names of the participants are not revealed. Quotations are not edited for typographical or grammatical errors in order to prevent misrepresenting the postings. An example of a quote:

I thought it would be was just a buffet restaurant but there is an interactive drumming session as well as.

(Mkono, 2012, p. 390)

Case study 2: hospitality workers' perceptions

Polish migrant labour in the hospitality workforce: implications for recruitment and retention (Janta and Ladkin, 2009)

Aim: to explore the implications for recruitment and retention in the hospitality industry as a result of the increasing involvement of Polish migrants in the workforce.

Method: a netnographic approach is used. The threads analysed were launched after 2005 and lasted between a few days and/or until the time of writing (2008). Approximately 100 threads for Polish migrants in the UK, are analysed.

Analysis: using thematic analysis.

Presentation of findings: quotations are translated from Polish into English by one of the researchers. The names of the participants are excluded, site's name and the date are displayed.

I am currently living in the UK and have been leaning over backwards trying to find a job, at the moment I am living by doing waitressing in a cafe and I have sent a few CV's, we will see how it goes, but fingers crossed. (gazeta.pl, 2/13/07)
(Janta and Ladkin, 2009, p. 9)

Chapter summary

- Netnography makes use of rich data available online such as blogs, discussion fora or comments posted on social networking sites.
- Netnography is defined as an *approach* or a *multimethod* that combines various techniques including content analysis, historical analysis, semiotics, hermeneutics, narrative analysis and thematic analysis, among others.

Hania Janta

- Netnographic data can be collected when the researcher is overt and he/she posts a message to the users and may react to the posts.
- The style of language used by the researcher when posting messages and requesting access to the online community needs to be considerate and well thought-out.
- Observing online users' discussions is a popular technique used by researchers.
- The availability of the amount of data in social media make netnography a very popular technique. It is also very accessible and economical.
- The disadvantage of undertaking research online is that the identity of the informant cannot be identified and the accuracy of information that relies on the informant's trustworthiness cannot be guaranteed.
- Threads are analysed using thematic analysis.

Discussion questions

11.1 Think of three different research topics that can include:

(a) netnography as the main and only research method used to collect the data.
(b) netnography as the first stage of data collection.

11.2 Think of three topics where you would not recommend selecting netnography as the data collection approach.

11.3 Some students choose the netnographic approach because they consider it 'an easy' research method. Do you agree with that statement?

11.4 Should we or should we not ask online users for permission to study their community?

11.5 What challenges can you think of when analysing the content of tweets?

Further reading

Netnography used in tourism research

Beaven, Z. and Laws, C. (2007). '"Never Let Me Down Again": Loyal customer attitudes towards ticket distribution channels for live music events: A netnographic exploration of the US leg of the Depeche Mode 2005–2006 World Tour', *Managing Leisure*, 12, 120–142.

Janta H. and Ladkin, A. (2009). 'Polish migrant labour in the hospitality workforce: Implications for recruitment and retention', *Tourism, Culture and Communications*, 9 (1–2), 5–15.

[*An exploratory study on the experiences of Polish migrant workers in the UK hospitality industry. Key themes are identified and recommendations on the recruitment and retention of staff for the hospitality industry are made.*]

Lugosi, P., Janta, H. and Watson, P. (2012). 'Investigative management and consumer research on the internet', *International Journal of Contemporary Hospitality Management*, 24 (6), 838–854.

[*Netnography is conceptualised as a form of 'streaming'. Three international empirical cases are used to illustrate the application of Investigative Research on the Internet (IRI) and streaming in research on international workers, consumer cultures and on emerging business phenomena.*]

Mkono, M. (2012). 'A netnographic examination of constructive authenticity in Victoria Falls tourist (restaurant) experiences', *International Journal of Hospitality Management*, 31 (2), 387–394.

[*A study of Trip Advisor online reviews of two restaurants in Zimbabwe.*]

Podoshen, J.S. (2013). 'Dark tourism motivations: Simulation, emotional contagion and topographic comparison', *Tourism Management*, 35, 263–271.

[*A study on dark tourism motivations related to 'blackpackers' and fans of the musical performance art known as black metal using netnography as one of the research methods.*]

Watson, P., Morgan, M. and Hemmington, N. (2008). 'Online communities and the sharing of extraordinary restaurant experiences', *Journal of Foodservice*, 19, 289–302.

[*A study on the experiences of 'foodies' with an analysis of blogs.*]

General literature on netnography

Bengry-Howell, A., Wiles, R., Nind, R. and Crow, G. (2011). *A Review of the Academic Impact of Three Methodological Innovations: Netnography, Child-Led Research and Creative Research Methods*. ESRC National Centre for Research Methods, NCRM Working Paper Series, 01/2011. Swindon: ESRC. Available at: http://eprints.ncrm.ac.uk/1844/1/Review_of_methodological_innovations.pdf (accessed 30 January 2013).

Dholakia, N. and Zhang, D. (2004). 'Online qualitative research in the age of e-commerce: Data sources and approaches', *Forum: Qualitative Social Research*, 5 (2), Art. 29. Available at: http://nbn-resolving.de/urn:nbn:de:0114-fqs0402299 (accessed 30 January 2013).

Enoch, Y., and Grossman, R. (2010). 'Blogs of Israeli and Danish backpackers to India', *Annals of Tourism Research*, 37 (2), 520–536.

Ess, C. and The AoIR Ethics Working Committee (2002). Ethical decision-making and internet research: Recommendations from the AoIR Ethics Working Committee. Available at: www.aoir.org/reports/ethics.pdf (accessed 9 May 2011).

Gatson, S.N. and Zweerink, A. (2004). 'Ethnography online: "Natives" practicing and inscribing community', *Qualitative Research*, 4 (2), 179–200.

Hewitt, J. (2005). 'Toward an understanding of how threads die in asynchronous computer conferences', *Journal of Notes the Learning Sciences*, 14 (4), 567–589.

Hewson, C., Yule, P., Laurent, D. and Vogel, C. (2003). *Internet Research Methods: A Practical Guide for the Social and Behavioural Sciences*. London: Sage.

Hine, C. (2000). *Virtual Ethnography*. London: Sage.

Hine, C. (ed.) (2005). *Virtual Methods: Issues in Social Research on the Internet*. Oxford: Berg.

Hudson, J.M. and Bruckman, A. (2004). '"Go Away": Participant objections to being studied and the ethics of chatroom research', *The Information Society*, 20 (2), 127–139.

Kozinets, R.V. (1999). 'E-tribalized marketing? The strategic implications of virtual communities of consumption', *European Management Journal*, 17 (3), 252–264.

Kozinets, R.V. (2002). 'The field behind the screen: Using netnography for marketing research in online communities', *Journal of Marketing Research*, 39, 61–72.

Kozinets, R.V. (2010). *Netnography: Doing Ethnographic Research Online*. London: Sage.

Langer, R. and Beckman, S.C. (2005). 'Sensitive research topics: Netnography revisited', *Qualitative Market Research: An International Journal*, 8, 189–203.

Madge, C. (2006). Online research ethics module. Leicester University. Available at: www.geog.le.ac.uk/orm/ethics/ethprint3.pdf (accessed 30 January 2013).

Martin, D., Woodside, A.G. and Dehuang, N. (2007). 'E'tic interpreting of naïve subjective personal introspections of tourism behavior: Analyzing visitors' stories about experiencing Mumbai, Seoul, Singapore, and Tokyo', *International Journal of Culture, Tourism and Hospitality Research*, 1 (1), 14–44.

Morgan, M. (2009). 'What makes a good festival? Understanding the event experience', *Event Management*, 12 (2), 81–93.

Murthy, D. (2008). 'Digital ethnography: An examination of the use of new technologies for social research', *Sociology*, 42 (5), 837–855.

O'Reilly, N.J., Rahinel, R., Foster K. and Peterson, M. (2007). 'Connecting the megaclasses: The netnographic advantage', *Journal of Marketing Education*, 29 (1), 69–84.

O'Sullivan, P.B. and Flanagin, A.J. (2003). 'Reconceptualizing "flaming" and other problematic messages', *New Media & Society*, 5 (1), 69–94.

Ovadia, S. (2009). 'Exploring the potential of Twitter as a research tool', *Behavioral & Social Sciences Librarian*, 28 (4), 202–205.

Stebbins, R.A. (2010). 'The Internet as a scientific tool for studying leisure activities: Exploratory Internet data collection', *Leisure Studies*, 29, 469–475.

Thompsen, P.A. and Foulger, D.A. (1996). 'Effects of pictographs and quoting on flaming in electronic mail', *Computers in Human Behavior*, 12 (2), 225–243.

Wittel, A. (2000). 'Ethnography on the move: From field to net to internet', *Forum: Qualitative Social Research*, 1 (1), Art. 21. Available at: http://nbn-resolving.de/urn:nbn:de:0114-fqs0001213 (accessed 30 January 2013).

Xun, J. and Reynolds, J. (2010). 'Applying netnography to market research: The case of the online forum', *Journal of Targeting, Measurement and Analysis for Marketing*, 18, 17–31.

Chapter 12

Online surveys

Hania Janta

Ria, a Mauritian researcher, is a conducting her research to determine the attributes that tourists with children consider before selecting a destination for their holidays. Having carefully designed a conceptual framework, she embarks on the stage to design a method to collect her data. However, she faces a bigger challenge: how to select the respondents? In fact, if she conducts an on-site survey she will only be able to interview tourists who have already made their decision to visit Mauritius based on attributes which only Mauritius has. Alternatively, she will have to travel to a few destinations and interview tourists with children, which will be very costly indeed and will take a lot of time. Accordingly, with the on-site survey she will never be able to determine all the possible factors which led tourists to choose alternative destinations. She decides, then, to use an online survey.

These are some of the questions which arise:

- What are the advantages and disadvantages of online surveys?
- How does she distribute the online survey?
- What are the challenges in accessing online groups when distributing the survey?
- How does she increase the response rate?
- What online surveys can she use?
- What type of sampling does she employ when using an online survey?

12.0 Chapter objectives

With the growth of the internet, conducting research online has become exceptionally popular. Not surprisingly, it offers a range of opportunities – opportunities that evolve as access to the internet and e-communication expand. Wide access to the internet facilitates collecting data in a way that is quicker and cheaper than conventional surveys. Online surveys can be easily implemented by researchers with a variety of free survey tools available on the internet. They can be posted on social networking sites such as Facebook where users of particular communities complete it in timely manner on their machine, their smartphone or other devices (i.e. tablets). In this chapter we focus on overviewing online surveys by discussing basic surveys tools that can be used in research. We look at different distribution channels: discussion fora, mailing lists, social networking sites as well as emails, and assess their usefulness. We also examine the challenges that researchers face relating to accessing various types of online communities when administering the survey. As with other types of research, we discuss challenges and limitations that need to be considered when using online surveys.

By the end of the chapter, you will be able to:

● understand how online surveys can be used in tourism research;
● assess both advantages and disadvantages of online surveys; and
● identify distribution modes such as mailing lists, emails, discussion fora and social networking sites as well as challenges that you may face when accessing them as a researcher.

12.1 Types of online surveys

There are three types of surveys that can be used on the internet:

● an email survey
● a questionnaire sent as an attachment
● a web-based questionnaire

(Denscombe, 2007)

While a questionnaire sent as an attachment or an email survey were used in the past, nowadays it has become common for researchers and students to use a web-based questionnaire/an online survey to collect data. There are numerous providers that offer free or affordable access to surveys, for example *SurveyMonkey* or *SurveyGizmo*, where the data can be exported to excel or Statistical Package for the Social Sciences (SPSS) software and some basic statistics are also available online. These surveys can be defined as: 'a web page and located on a host site where visitors to the site can access it' (Denscombe, 2007, p. 160). Box 12.1 lists some of the survey tools available online.

12.1.1 Design and implementation

The web-based questionnaire should be designed and implemented according to a set of recommendations and tested thoroughly before it is launched. More specifically, researchers recommend listing only a few questions per screen, ensuring respondents' privacy and providing some indication of the progress in completing the question-naire (Schonlau et al., 2002). Allowing respondents to interrupt and finish the survey later could be beneficial. Additionally, the use of the graphics should be limited.

Box 12.1: basic survey tools available online

A number of free or low-cost online tools are available which are very good for smaller scale students' surveys. Some new features introduced more recently include responses collection offline using apps or provision of access to a group of panellists from which representative samples can be drawn.

- **SurveyMonkey** (www.surveymonkey.com): the free version may be useful for small surveys, as it can collect 10 questions and 100 responses per survey. Data can be collected via weblink, email, Facebook, or a site or blog. However, it allows little customisation of the look of the survey, no downloads of reports or data.
- **Zoomerang** (www.zoomerang.com): this is similar to SurveyMonkey in many respects including its web design (and now part of SurveyMonkey). It can collect 10 questions and 100 responses per survey.
- **PollDaddy** (https://polldaddy.com): this free package offers a maximum of 10 questions per survey and 200 responses per month, plus basic reporting.
- **SurveyGizmo** (www.surveygizmo.com): this free package includes 25 question types and provides reporting.

12.1.2 Sampling

It is often difficult for students to justify their sampling well when using online sur-veys. Non-probability sampling is common for internet surveys (Schonlau et al., 2002; Sue and Ritter, 2012). As pointed out by Hewson: '[t]he main concern with the Web-based procedure is non-response bias and lack of a sampling frame' (2000, p. 82). The sampling chosen in online surveys is similar to *volunteer opt-in panels*, as respond-ents are recruited via some form of online advertising (Sue and Ritter, 2012). In other words, internet surveys employ self-selection into the sample. The main issue is that in most cases it is impossible to assess how many respondents are reached.

12.1.3 Representativeness – a limitation of online surveys

A principal limitation of all internet surveys is the difficulty in claiming the repre-sentativeness of the sample. Thus, the main limitation of the online surveys is that it excludes those who do not have access to the internet. Furthermore, internet users can choose whether they want to take part in the study or not, which makes self-selection bias another limitation. Finally, respondents may start filling in the survey but not complete it. Bias occurs on these three levels.

12.1.4 Distribution/outlets selected for distributing online surveys

The following can be used to distribute online surveys:

- discussion fora (see Case study 1: Janta, 2011)
- social networking sites such as Facebook (see Case study 2: Paris, 2012)
- mailing lists (see Illum et al., 2010)
- emails (see Case study 3: Murdy and Pike, 2012)

From the case studies presented in this chapter, it can be seen that social networking sites and discussion fora may have much higher response rate that mailing lists or emails. A pilot study can be always a good test to assess whether the particular mode of survey distribution online is going to produce an appropriate response rate.

12.1.5 Pilot questionnaire

In order to validate the survey instrument, a pilot study is always recommended. Other aims of the pilot study are to assess:

- the mode of distribution;
- the length of the questionnaire; and
- the feasibility of conducting a survey online: its response rate, dropout rate and perception of the survey.

The results from the pilot survey allow eliminating and rephrasing unclear questions and sometimes adding some new ones in order to achieve the research objectives.

12.1.6 Access issues/challenges

With internet fora, social networking sites and mailing lists access issues may create a potential challenge. One of the ways of accessing the sites is to *contact the administrator* of each group. For example, the administrators of Facebook groups may allow access to the group or even direct messages to be sent to members of the Facebook groups requesting help with completion of a questionnaire (see Paris, 2012 for details). A link to the survey and a short message explaining the purpose can be sent to group members. However, instead of contacting each group/site/discussion forum administrator, the researcher may just post a message with a link to their survey *without contacting the administrator*. It is necessary to observe these sites and make sure that the community moderator does not delete an unwanted post as he or she may treat it as 'spam'. When this happens, the researcher usually is not able to repost a message on the same website.

Second, the distribution of the questionnaires in public fora may result in the researcher *losing control* over how the study is perceived by internet users and they may even become the target of abusive comments. Such messages posted by other users may turn into *flaming* – defined as aggressive, abusive or insulting comments with different degrees of hostility (see i.e. O'Sullivan and Flanagin, 2003). It is easy to become a target of hostile comments, usually initiated by an influential user who may advise other members to boycott the research. Flaming has recently been recognised as a worsening problem and is being researched in the context of the new media, popular social networking sites and YouTube. Indeed, Hudson and Bruckman (2004) revealed that researchers disclosing information about conducting research in a chatroom were kicked out of 63 per cent of discussion groups. References to their study as spamming or insulting remarks were common among group users. For that reason, bearing in mind that the anti-social use of the sites is not uncommon, the language used by the researcher when posting a message and requesting access to the online community is crucial and needs to be carefully thought-out.

12.1.7 Reposting – increasing response rate

With some very active fora, posts can move down the list of posts quickly, and will eventually become invisible to the users. In order to increase the response rate, reposting is essential. However, it is also important not to attack users with persistent messages as this can lead to being excluded by the moderator or treated as 'spam'.

12.2 Advantages of online surveys

There is a common agreement among researchers that an internet survey when compared to postal surveys, face-to-face surveys and telephone surveys is cheaper, quicker and easier to conduct (Schonlau et al., 2002; Sue and Ritter, 2012; Denscombe, 2007). One of the major advantages of this type of internet survey is that the responses can be seen automatically and they can be exported to SPSS or Microsoft Excel, which also increases the accuracy of the data. Other advantages include efficiency and access to individuals in distant locations (Schonlau et al., 2002; Wright, 2005; Sue and Ritter, 2012; Denscombe, 2007). Bryman (2008) adds some other qualities such as: better response to open questions and fewer unanswered questions. What is more, the use of software enables participants to respond more quickly because they type their answers. A comparison between a paper-based survey and an online survey for a tourism subject was conducted in Switzerland and the results showed that the dropout quota and the number of omissions in the questionnaire were lower for online than for paper respondents (see Dolnicar et al., 2009). Finally, respondents are able to start filling out the survey, then stop and come back again when it is convenient for them.

12.3 Disadvantages of online surveys

The disadvantages of using web-based questionnaires include coverage bias, lack of knowledge of who is responding to the questions and reliance on software (Sue and Ritter, 2012). For example, it may be challenging to design a survey in another language when a specific alphabet is not available. Also, it may not be possible to replace some specific jargon (for example the instructions 'please specify') because of the incompatibility of the software, which may have had a negative effect on the professional image of the survey. The control and selection of the sample remains a challenge as does the exclusion of individuals who do not have internet access. Self-selection bias and non-response bias is a limitation of online surveys (Wright, 2005; Hewson, 2002). If an online survey features a prize for participants responding, this may induce false or incomplete responses.

Table 12.1 Advantages and disadvantages of online questionnaires

Advantages	Disadvantages
• Low-cost or free • Can be administered faster than ordinary mail surveys • The researcher can trace the number of responses in real-time • Has the potential to generate more responses, which can be geographically dispersed, or access specific group of panellists • Provides the ability to refine surveys • Offers flexibility due to the variety of options available during the construction • Can be visually attractive with colours, shapes, use of logo or drop-down boxes • Is flexible in the sense that participants are able to complete the survey in their own time. This means an online questionnaire has the potential to be less disruptive than other methods • Allows the data to be easily analysed and the information is already on a computer so that data do not need to be input into an analysis tool	• Self-selection bias and non-response bias/representativeness of the sample • Lacks knowledge about who is responding to the questions • Lacks information about the exact number of questionnaires distributed • Relies on software • May create potential technological problems • Relies on groups' administrators or members who are the gate-keepers in terms of accessing the community • If an online survey features a prize for participants responding then this may produce incomplete responses • Excludes or reduces the chances of certain groups to complete an online survey (i.e. reluctance of older people or non-computer literate) • Motivating respondents to complete the survey can be challenging

Sources: author's experience; Schonlau et al. (2002); Sue and Ritter (2012); Denscombe (2007); Wright (2005)

Case study 1: profiles of migrant workers in the UK hospitality industry

Polish migrant workers in the UK hospitality industry: profiles, work experience and methods for accessing employment (Janta, 2011)

Aim: to reveal the profile of Polish migrant workers and the methods used for accessing employment.

Method: an online survey was distributed via online discussion fora across the UK dedicated to Polish migrants and the two social networking sites most popular among Poles: Facebook.com and Nasza-klasa.pl ('Our class'). The online survey was distributed via 45 websites and it remained open for a period of seven weeks. Two other methods were used in this study to collect data.

Pilot study: six websites were chosen for the pilot study with an average traffic of about 2,000–7,000 posts in order to understand the perceptions of the survey, response and dropout rate.

Justification for using an online survey:

- the absence of reliable population frames for Polish hospitality workers in the UK
- wide use of the internet among the Polish community in the UK
- past research on migrant employees using purposive sampling

Case study 2: backpacking culture

Flashbackers: an emerging sub-culture? (Paris, 2012)

Aim: an examination of the contemporary backpacker culture and the apparent emergence of a flashpacker sub-culture with a particular focus on the differences between flashpackers and non-flashpackers.

Method: surveys were administered through Facebook backpacker groups and in hostels in Cairns, Australia. To select the Facebook backpacker groups, a search was conducted using the internal Facebook search engine. The first 25 backpacker groups showing recent activity among members were selected. Administrators were contacted for a permission to post the link to the survey. Fifteen agreed to do so.

Pilot Study: the survey was pre-tested with a small group of individuals through a Facebook backpacker group and ten graduate and undergraduate students.

Justification for using an online survey: combining the two modes allowed for a diverse sample of backpackers that included travellers from many different nationalities, individuals at home or travelling and not in a backpacker enclave, older backpackers and those travelling for an extended period of time.

Case study 3: DMOs and a visitor relationship marketing (VRM) orientation

Perceptions of visitor relationship marketing opportunities by destination marketers: an importance-performance analysis (Murdy and Pike, 2012)

Aim: to examine the extent to which destination marketing organisations (DMOs) around the world have developed a VRM orientation.

Method: the database of participants was created first from online searching, including representation of DMOs at different levels. DMOs were emailed the link to the questionnaire, which was hosted online by the university. From the 1,435 emails sent, 174 were returned without reaching the intended participant

(continued)

> *(continued)*
>
> due to out-of-date email addresses and spam filters. From the 1,265 believed to have reached the intended participant, 65 responses were received, representing a response rate of 5.2 per cent. As an incentive, participants were offered a prize draw.
>
> **Justification for using an online survey**: researchers attempted to reach DMOs from around the world.

Chapter summary

- Conducting research online has become very popular with the advent of the internet.
- Online surveys can be easily implemented by researchers with a variety of free survey tools on the internet.
- A web-based questionnaire is far more efficient than an email survey or questionnaire sent as an attachment.
- Attention should be paid to the design and implementation of the online survey, such as allowing respondents to break off and finish the survey later.
- With internet surveys, the representativeness of the sample is difficult to ascertain.
- As researcher you need to seek access to social networking sites and keep an eye on posts.
- Online surveys are cheaper, quicker and easier to conduct than other forms of survey.
- The limitations of an online survey include coverage bias, lack of knowledge of who is responding to the questions and designing the questionnaire in a language where a specific alphabet is not available.
- Potential technology problems may also limit its use.

Discussion questions

12.1 Think of three different research topics that can include:
   (a) An online survey as the main and only research method used to collect the data. Justify why this is the best research method to be used in those cases.
   (b) An online survey as the first stage of data collection. What could be the second stage of data collection in each of those cases?

12.2 Think of three topics where you would not recommend selecting an online survey as the data collection method.

12.3 Should we or should we not ask online group administrators for permission to enter their community? Give reasons.

12.4 How would you form a question that will be posted on a forum or Facebook group requesting that users help you to complete your survey?

12.5 Does a smartphone as a device for self-administered surveys create any challenges for the researcher?

Further reading

Hung, K. and Law, R. (2011). 'An overview of Internet-based surveys in hospitality and tourism journals', *Tourism Management,* 32, 717–724.

Illum, S.F., Ivanov, S.H. and Liang, Y. (2010). 'Using virtual communities in tourism research', *Tourism Management*, 31 (3), 335–340.

Sue, V.M. and Ritter, L.A. (2012). *Conducting Online Surveys*, 2nd edition. Los Angeles: Sage.

Toepoel, V. (2016). *Doing Surveys Online*. London: Sage.

Chapter 13

Sampling

Ramesh Durbarry and Anjusha Durbarry

Mary has already selected her research method and is now at the stage of collecting data. She is well aware that the results she will obtain should reflect the point of view of all the subjects. However, she is confronted with the issue of how many subjects to include in her study, that is, what should be the sample size? Will the sample reflect the opinion of all the subjects? How should the subjects be selected?, and so on.

These are questions that Mary is asking. What would be your advice?

13.0 Chapter objectives

This chapter is an introduction to sampling techniques used in quantitative and qualitative research. The key areas that are addressed are samples and population, probability and non-probability sampling and selecting the sample size.

After studying this chapter, you will be able to:

- understand the significance of sampling;
- understand the span of probability and non-probability sampling techniques; and
- choose the appropriate sampling technique.

13.1 Population and sample

Whether you are using primary or secondary data, sampling forms an integral part of the study. Although you would like to include all the subjects under consideration in your study, it is not always possible for a variety of reasons, such as time and costs. When all subjects are being considered a lot of resources are involved, for example, when conducting a census – a count of all people. This exercise, for example, is carried out every ten years in the United Kingdom (www.ons.gov.uk) and in some countries every five years (e.g. Austria, Canada, Japan and Mauritius).

For a research study involving collection of primary data, you have to, first, identify the population under study and then choose an appropriate sampling technique to select the sample, if necessary. If the population is small (depending what we mean by *small*), there is no need to select a sample. Let us first define what we mean by a population.

A *population*, in research terms, does not necessarily comprise of people. A population can also refer to products, companies, events or generally a collection of related elements sharing common characteristics. All elements within a population are known as the *sample frame*.

A *sample* is a portion of the overall population that the researcher wishes to study. This is illustrated in Figure 13.1. A population is a collection of related elements; a sample is a portion of the population.

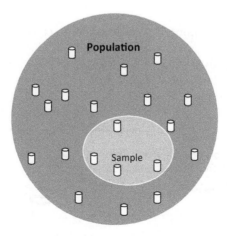

Figure 13.1 Population and sample

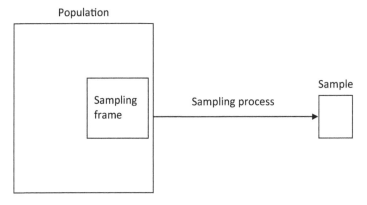

Figure 13.2 Drawing of a sample from the population

For some research questions, you may be collecting and analysing data from every possible subject especially when the population is small, for example, all the students in your class. However, in certain cases you cannot perform observations on every individual in the population you are studying. Instead, you can get access to only a subset of individuals or subjects and in such a case you draw a sample from the population as illustrated in Figure 13.2. It is from these observations that you will conduct your study and later on we will see how you can make use of data analysis to offer conclusions for the entire population (see Chapters 17 to 18).

For many researchers sampling is an alternative to census because it is:

- less time-consuming than surveying the entire population;
- less costly to administer than a census; and
- less cumbersome and more practical.

To know if you have chosen the right sample it must be representative of the population. From Figure 13.1, the more subjects that are selected, the higher the chance of it being representative. Samples which are not representative of the population are said to be biased and will lead to biased conclusions about the population. For this reason, there are a series of sampling techniques which you can use in either qualitative or quantitative research.

13.2 Sampling techniques

Sampling techniques provide a span of methods that allow you to reduce the amount of data required by considering only data from a subset rather than from the entire population.

The sampling techniques can be broadly divided into two main types:

- Probability sampling: in this approach, each element of the population has a known and usually equal chance of being chosen for inclusion in the sample.
- Non-probability sampling: this sampling method provides a range of alternative techniques based on subjective judgement.

Figure 13.3 illustrated the range of sampling techniques which can be used by a researcher.

13.2.1 Probability sampling

Many strategies can be utilised to create a probability sample. The probability sampling is commonly linked to survey-based research whereby inferences are made from a sample about a population to answer the research question. It is important to define a *sampling frame*, which can be regarded as a list of all elements in the population of interest (e.g. *tourists or visitors*). The sampling frame operationally defines

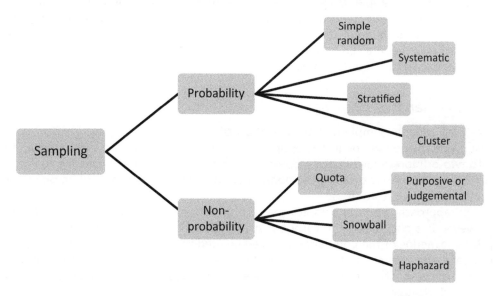

Figure 13.3 Probability and non-probability sampling techniques

the target population from which the sample is drawn and to which the sample data will be generalised for the population.

The main probability-based sampling methods are:

- simple random
- systematic random
- stratified random
- cluster

Simple random sampling

Simple random sampling is a simple method to identify an element from the population, which can be combined with other methods such as cluster sampling. In simple random sampling, you must ensure that the sampling frame is defined and each element in the frame is numbered or coded. Each element from the frame has an equal chance of being selected according to a mathematically random procedure. A table of random numbers or computer random number generator (e.g. using Microsoft Excel) can be used for this to select the element for inclusion in the sample.

Systematic random sampling

The systematic random sampling is basically simple random sampling with a short cut for the random selection. This sampling is carried out by selecting the elements for inclusion in the sample at regular interval using a randomised starting point. The following procedure is used:

1. Define the sampling frame, number or code of each element of the sampling frame.
2. Select the first element using a random number.
3. Calculate the sampling interval. For example, if the sampling frame is 1,200 and the required sample size is 300 then the sampling interval will be 4 (1200/300).
4. After the random starting point, choose the fourth element from the sampling frame. For example, if the randomised starting number is 2 then the fourth element must be selected each time, that is second, sixth, tenth, fourteenth . . . until a sample size of 300 is reached.

Stratified random sampling

Stratified random sampling is an alteration of the random sampling in which you first divide the population into subpopulations or strata. The population is subdivided into two or more relevant strata based on some common characteristic e.g. gender, nationality, etc. After dividing the population into strata, a simple random sample is drawn from each stratum.

This approach produces samples that are more representative of the population. However, it is only feasible to carry out stratified random sampling if you have some prior knowledge of the population that can be used to separate it into distinct groups or strata. For example, if you are conducting a study on gender differences, you can stratify the population into male and female and then use an equal number of subjects from each stratum.

Cluster sampling

Cluster sampling is used to compile an exhaustive list of the elements that make up the target population. Usually, the population elements are already grouped into subsets (e.g. by geographic regions) and records of those subpopulations may already exist or can be created. Cluster sampling may be useful if the sample has the same variability and characteristics of the population, then the sample will be representative.

Box 13.1: choosing a sampling method

The guide below will help to choose some of the relevant sampling methods.

Method	Attributes
Simple random sampling	Entire population is available/presented
Stratified sampling	There are defined subgroups to investigate
Systematic sampling	A stream of representative elements is available
Cluster sampling	The population group are distinct and separated, e.g. *distant towns*

13.2.2 Non-probability sampling

As the term indicates, with non-probability sampling each element of the population being studied does not have an equal chance of being included in the study. It is commonly used by qualitative researchers and the sample size is not determined in advance. This method provides an alternative way of selecting the sample based on subjective judgement.

There are a number of non-probability sampling approaches such as:

- quota
- purposive
- snowball
- haphazard

Quota sampling

Quota sampling is normally used for interview surveys and is entirely non-random. You normally determine a set number of participants for inclusion in the sample on the basis of pre-determined characteristics inherent in the overall study population. The difference between quota sampling and stratified random sampling is that the latter separates the population into strata and may then select participants by random selection, while the former determines the number in each stratum and then follows up with *convenience sampling*.

> ## Definition: convenience sampling
>
> Convenience sampling is selecting subjects which are accessible and easy to include in the study. Such examples are volunteers or the first five customers entering a hotel.

Purposive sampling

Purposive sampling is also known as judgemental sampling. You make a decision about who or what subjects will be included in the study and the logic used to select the subjects because a purposive sample should be dependent on the research question(s) and objectives. This sampling method is used in case study research, especially when working with small samples and you select cases that are particularly informative for your study.

Snowball sampling

Snowball sampling is also referred to as network, chain referral or reputation sampling. It is commonly used where there are difficulties reaching members of a desired population and it is a method for selecting cases in a network. Once you identify one member of the target population, the other members are identified by this member who then identifies further members and, thereafter, the sample snowballs. Snowball sampling therefore starts with one or a few people or cases, and expands on the basis of links to the initial cases (Neuman, 2006).

Haphazard sampling

Haphazard sampling is also known as convenience, accidental, chunk and grab sampling – all suggesting the focus is not a systematic selection process. You select the cases based on convenience but you can easily get a sample which is highly unrepresentative of the population. The sample displays those study units convenient to you at the time the study was carried out and such sampling does not have the ability to reflect other time periods (Sarantakos, 1998, p. 151).

13.3 How large should a sample be?

'How large should a sample be?' is a common question among students and novice researchers. A larger sample can produce more accurate results – but excessive responses can be costly. It is important to consider the following points when determining the sample size:

- characteristics of the population
- overall size of the population
- accessibility of the population

A rule of thumb which is widely accepted by researchers (as cited in Neuman, 2006, p. 241) is as follow:

● For populations under 1,000 a researcher requires a large sampling ratio (about 30 per cent), that is, a sample size of 300 is required for a high level of accuracy.
● For populations under 10,000, a smaller sampling ratio of about 10 per cent is needed to be equally accurate, that is, a sample size of about 1,000.
● For populations over 150,000, smaller sampling ratios of 1 per cent are possible and samples of about 1,500 can be accurate.
● For very large populations of over 10 million, a minor sampling ratio of 0.025 per cent can be used and samples of about 2,500 can generate the accuracy required.
● For populations over 200 million the size of the population is no longer relevant once the sampling ratio is very small.

That the size of the sample bears some link to the overall size of the study population, such as, a sample being 10 per cent or 20 per cent of the population, is disputed by Veal (2011, p. 362). He emphasises that it is the absolute size of the sample which is important, not its size relative to the population and this rule applies to all situations, except when the population is small.

On the other hand, the sample size can also be calculated (see Box 13.2); you need to determine a few points about the target population and the sample you need:

1 **Population size**: it is important to know the population size. It is common for the population to be unknown or approximated.
2 **Confidence interval**: you must decide how much error to allow because no sample will be perfect. The confidence interval determines how much higher or lower than the population mean you are willing to let your sample mean fall.
3 **Confidence level**: you must also decide how confident you are that the actual mean falls within a certain interval. The most common confidence intervals are 90 per cent, 95 per cent and 99 per cent.
4 **Standard deviation**: determines the amount of variation in the data. Given that the survey has not been administered, the safe decision is to use 0.5 – this is the most tolerant number and ensures that the sample will be large enough.

Box 13.2: calculating sample size (for an unknown population size or a very large population size)

Confidence level corresponds to a Z-score. This is a constant value needed for this equation. The Z-scores for the most common confidence levels are:

● 90% – Z-score = 1.645
● 95% – Z-score = 1.96
● 99% – Z-score = 2.326

(continued)

(continued)

If a different confidence level is selected, use the Z-score table to find the score.
  Next, insert in your Z-score, standard deviation and confidence interval into this equation:

Required Sample Size = (Z-score)² × Std Dev × (1-StdDev)/(margin of error)²

Assuming 90% confidence level, 0.5 standard deviation and confidence interval of ± 5%, we get:

((1.645)² × .5(.5)) / (.05)²

(2.706 × .25) / .0025

0.6765 / .0025 = 270.6

271 respondents are needed

Alternatively, you can visit: www.research-advisors.com/tools/SampleSize.htm

13.4 Sampling for qualitative research

Qualitative research does not entail statistical calculation and generally does not require quantitative representativeness. In fact, non-probability sampling is more commonly used in such research. The researcher using a qualitative method is more concerned to get in-depth and richer information from the subjects than about the sample size or random section (Henderson, 1991). Depending on your aims and objectives, generalisation may not be required and hence sampling does not become an issue. Validity and significance of qualitative research most of the time owe everything to the richness of the data derived from the subject selected, rather than the size of the sample.

Qualitative research most commonly will involve some form of purposive sampling. Patton (2002) and Miles and Huberman (1994) suggest a series of strategies for sampling in qualitative research. Some of these commonly used strategies are listed below:

Method	Characteristics
Convenience	Use of easily accessible persons or organisations, e.g. colleagues, friends, local
Purposive	Selection is randomised and is based on some typical criterion to maximise credibility
Stratified purposeful sampling	Selection of a variety of cases based on defined criteria
Opportunistic sampling	Taking advantage of opportunities that occur, e.g. sample during a holidaying period

Homogeneous sampling	A well-defined subset studied in depth
Maximum variation sampling	Studying a varied group which cuts across most of the variation
Snowball sampling	Continuous recommendation from one subject to the next

Chapter summary

- Define the population which you are studying and appropriately draw the sample using a sampling technique.
- It is important that the sample is representative of the population, particularly in quantitative research.
- There are various sampling methods which can be used to draw a sample. These are divided into two main types: probability and non-probability sampling.
- Probability sampling is more commonly applied in quantitative research, while non-probability sampling methods are very popular in qualitative research.

Discussion questions

13.1 What is a sample?
13.2 What would you consider to draw your sample? Justify your answer.
13.3 What is probability sampling? Is it always appropriate? Why or why not?
13.4 Explain a situation where you would combine two sampling methods.

Further reading

Levine, D.M., Stephan, D.F. and Szabat, K.A. (2017). *Statistics for Managers Using Microsoft Excel*, 8th edition. New York: Pearson Education.
Sharpe, N.D., De Veaux, R.D. and Velleman, P.F. (2015). *Business Statistics*, 3rd edition. Harlow: Pearson Education.

PART III

Analysing data, research writing and presentation

Chapter 14

Analysing qualitative data

Sally Everett and Areej Shabib Aloudat

Real-life scenario

Mark Littleton (a pseudonym) was undertaking his MSc in International Tourism Management and loved art and museums. Consequently, he decided to undertake his dissertation exploring the motivations of people visiting art galleries and their emotional experiences. In seeking to understand the nature of art tourism and visitors engaging in art-related touristic activities, qualitative data were generated using in-depth semi-structured interviews with visitors, members and visitor assistants at three art galleries in London. Mark spent weeks generating data and ended up with 60 interview transcripts which once transcribed, totalled over 300,000 words. He panicked! How could he write about all of this? Mark had mountains of data, but no idea how to organise it, use it and condense it down into a 20,000-word dissertation. His supervisor had to step in with some helpful tips and advice on how to make it manageable and how to get the most from his qualitative data. With a mature and methodical approach, he made sense of his data . . .

Mark achieved top marks for his dissertation and secured a Distinction in his master's degree.

14.0 Chapter objectives

This chapter focuses on analysing qualitative data and looks at the key principles of qualitative data storage, coding and analysis. It discusses the ways in which qualitative data can be securely retained, analysed and interpreted – both manually and with the help of computer software. Given that qualitative data can be generated in many different ways and takes different forms which range from detailed focus group transcriptions, to recorded interviews to the content in marketing materials, the chapter provides an outline of how to make sense of your data. Unlike quantitative data which use more established analytical processes to analyse numerical and statistical information, qualitative data is extremely diverse and can vary from extensive interview transcripts to pictures to observational notes and even videos and films. There are no set and accepted set of conventions for qualitative analysis and it has often been regarded as more of an art than a science (Patton, 2002). Given the complex nature of qualitative data and the numerous options available, this chapter particularly focuses on grounded theory and provides detailed case studies into how this approach to qualitative data generation and data analysis works in practice.

After studying this chapter, you will be able to:

- organise and effectively store your qualitative data;
- summarise your data for different audiences;
- undertake different practical and theoretical approaches to coding your data;
- understand your role as a data analyst;
- analyse and interpret visual images and film; and
- confidently undertake your own qualitative data analysis.

The following key areas are covered in this chapter:

1   organising and storing your qualitative data;
2   coding and approaches to qualitative data analysis;
3   different types of data analysis: content, doman and discourse; and
4   interpreting visual images and film.

14.1 Organising and storing your qualitative data

Key questions

- How do I ensure my data are stored securely, safely and ethically?
- Transcriptions: to transcribe myself, or not?

Above all else, you should ensure that your data are stored securely and confidentially. Where transcripts and digital files have been generated, it is important that consideration is given to their safe storage and, where sensitive data may have been generated, you have the responsibility of ensuring that no one else is able to access the material.

Real-life scenario: lost data and disaster!

Sarah was in her in final year of the BA International Tourism Management course. Her final project (due in April) was examining the effectiveness of staff training programmes for airline staff. She had secured access to a major airline and was invited to talk to its employees during the course of one week in early February at their Head Office. They insisted that her reports should be anonymous, as much of the material would be personal and confidential and she had secured their consent to undertake interviews and gain ethical approval from the university. Sarah decided to digitally record all of the interviews (six with top managers, 20 with staff) on a new Dictaphone. It allowed her to concentrate on the interview without needing to write notes. She was not staying at home so had decided not to download the files and she had not written up the transcripts of the interviews yet so kept all of the recordings on the Dictaphone until she got back home at the end of the sixth day of recording. By the fifth day she had recorded 19 interviews and she was delighted by the depth and insight of her respondents' interviews. She put the recorder in her bag, set off for the hotel and as she was nearing the hotel someone came up behind her, grabbed her bag and snatched it away from her and ran off. She screamed, but she saw her bag, purse and 19 recorded unique interviews (stored on the Dictaphone) lost in the distance . . . the interview data was not only lost, but the personal experiences of her respondents was now out there, open to abuse . . .

Don't let this scenario happen to you. Ensure you keep copies of your data and keep them safe. It is recommended that all of your respondents are given *pseudonyms* (fictitious names) to ensure that they remain anonymous and, unless participants explicitly agree to being named (by means of a consent form and information sheet), this can be done through numbers, or simple codes such as 'tourist1', 'tourist2', 'manager2', and so on. If respondents refer to the names of others in their transcripts, it may also be necessary to code these names and provide pseudonyms. Ensure you keep a separate list of real names against the pseudonyms, as you may wish to check the final transcriptions or discuss themes with your original respondents at a later date.

Sometimes, you may find yourself in a situation where it is necessary to name key informants due to the aims and focus of the project, or it may be obvious if there is only one director of a certain company in a region, but this is where you need to make a judgement and ensure your respondents are aware of the disclosure (and have completed the consent form). It is also recommended that, if you use computer software (such as Microsoft Word, Excel or NVivo), you ensure the files are password protected to minimise security risks.

It is usually preferable to digitally record the conversations of interviews (Riley, 1996). Data recording reflects that the interviews are serious enough to warrant exact reproduction. Furthermore, the benefits of audio taping can minimise disturbance that would happen if you took hand notes – it also allows you to concentrate more fully on your participant and the conversation. The selected note taking may bias informants' conversations and direct their responses to what they may think the investigator wants. Additionally, the importance of the information cannot often be recognised until it is analysed.

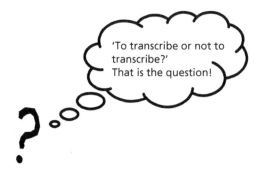

'To transcribe or not to transcribe?'
That is the question!

There is ongoing debate about whether you should type up your own digital recordings of interviews and focus groups. One of the arguments for transcribing your own interviews is that there may be ethical issues involved where sensitive data have been generated and should not be heard by a third (external) party. Furthermore, in undertaking your own transcriptions will allow you to get much closer to your data. Although it is a labour intensive task, often taking 3-5 hours per hour of digitally recorded interview (depending on your typing speed!), it is often an invaluable process that allows you to identify early emergent themes and patterns. It also allows you to make some early assessments of the data and can provide an indication of the likely direction and form your analysis will take. You should also ensure that you write up notes and observations immediately after an interview because often it may be days or weeks before you get an opportunity to type up the audio files. Field notes will prove invaluable when you come to analysing your data.

There are plenty of companies who offer transcription services and, if you decide to go down this route, ensure you keep password protected copies of all of the audio files in case they go missing or are corrupted. You often only get one chance to conduct an interview or focus group, so don't take any chances.

Practical tips

Immediately after you have conducted an interview, take a few minutes to jot down some important points (although bullet wise) and observations that took place during the interview. Often, we tend to say 'I'll do it tomorrow', and we know what probably happens then!

14.2 Approaches to coding qualitative data

Key questions

- What approaches are there to make sense of my data?
- What do I need to do *before* the final analysis?
- What is my role?
- How do I start coding my data?
- How can I ensure my interpretations are valid?
- Do I have to use computer software to code my data?

As alluded to in the introduction, there are numerous possible approaches to analysing qualitative data. Depending on your basic philosophical approach, many methods exist for analysing data. In general, these range from quasi-statistical methods, with structure and formulaic structure, to the more fluid, reflective and immersive approaches. The approach really depends on what you are interested in and should be considered early on in your research project. If you are interested in the type of language and words used, you may wish to adopt a quasi-statistical approach; however, if you are more interested in researcher reflection, insight and a more creative interpretation then you may wish to consider more immersive, more fluid and less

Table 14.1 Different approaches to qualitative analysis

Different approaches to qualitative analysis	Characteristics
Quasi-statistical approaches (e.g. content analysis)	Quasi-quantitative approach Themes often present in several transcripts, not just one Content analysis where words or phrases are counted. Frequencies and inter-correlations are key ways of determining the importance of certain terms and concepts This is the most 'scientific' approach, which Patton might describe as: 'The scientific part is systematic, analytical, rigorous, disciplined, and critical in perspective'
Template approaches	Key codes might have already been established before the data generation (a priori) as they may have emerged from your literature review. These have emerged in a *deductive* way Or such codes may emerge from your initial read of your data These codes provide templates (or bins) for your analysis and can be developed and edited as you progress Text segments which highlight and support key codes are identified Adopt the use of matrices, models, network maps, flowcharts and similar diagrams
Editing approaches	A more interpretative and flexible approach to the template approach Very few (or no) a priori codes Codes are based on the researcher's interpretation This is the grounded theory approach, which is addressed in Chapter 15
Immersion approaches	Reliant on the researcher's interpretations, creativity, intuition and insight. Methods are fluid and open to change The most artistic side of interpretation, as Patton (1988) describes: 'The artistic part is exploring, playful, metaphorical, insightful, and creative'. Miles and Huberman (1994) note that the interpretive approach might be used by qualitative researchers in semiotics, deconstructivism, aesthetic criticism, ethnomethodology and hermeneutics Examples might include discourse analysis

Source: based in part on Drisko (2000); Robson (2002, p. 458)

Sally Everett and Areej Shabib Aloudat

scientific approaches. For example, Crabtree and Miller (1999) looked at the different methods to produce a simple typology which ranges from quasi-statistical, template approaches, to editing approaches to immersion approaches.

14.2.1 Your role as the analyst

As outlined in the approaches above, particularly the 'immersion' and 'editing' approaches, the human element of qualitative data inquiry is both its strength and weakness (and thus where it comes under criticism from the more traditional, quantitative school of thought). Its strength is fully using human insight and experience, its weakness is being so heavily dependent on the researcher's skill, training, intellect, discipline and creativity. It is not the 'easy' option as it demands thoughtfulness, time, persistence and perseverance. The researcher is the instrument of qualitative inquiry, so the quality of the research depends heavily on the qualities of that human being (Patton, 1988).

Fetterman (1989, p. 88) further suggests that, 'first and foremost, analysis is a test of the ability to think – to process information in a meaningful and useful manner'.

Figure 14.1 Example of field notes – ensure they are detailed but leave room for notes

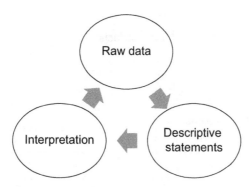

Figure 14.2 The analysis continuum

As outlined above, some qualitative analysis is akin to art and intuition rather than a rigid statistical process, which is why it is important to recognise human deficiencies and develop strategies to ensure the reliability of the data and the findings. Qualitative approaches emphasise interpretation and, thus, the onus is on you to be the interpreter and ensure the story being told is the story actually within the data. To overcome some of these issues, it is advisable to reduce the risk of deficiencies and biases by mapping the evolution of your analysis, by keeping memos, and returning to your original respondents (where possible) to ensure your respondents recognise your interpretation.

It is generally agreed that you should keep field notes and memos as you generate data. Bogdan and Biklen (1992) describe the practical approaches to writing up field notes. They recommend writing field notes with large margins in which to write later notes as data are later analysed, as well as in which to write codes for these data. They also advise that text be written in blocks with room left for headings, notes and codes. This is discussed further in Chapter 15 on grounded theory.

You need to consider qualitative data analysis as inductive and iterative, where you are constantly re-visiting your raw data as you develop codes and identify emergent themes (Figure 14.2).

Similarly, Miles and Huberman state that qualitative data analysis consists of 'three concurrent flows of activity: data reduction, data display, and conclusion drawing/verification' (1994, p. 10) (see Figure 14.3).

Miles and Huberman (1994, p. 15) ask: 'How can we draw valid meaning from qualitative data? What methods of analysis can we employ that are practical, communicable, and non-self-deluding – in short, scientific in the best sense of that word?' As alluded to above, in Table 14.1, there are different approaches to coding which include:

- a priori (pre-determined) or grounded (emergent)
- coding, sorting and categorising into 'bins' (Miles and Huberman, 1994, p. 245)
- different levels: 'open', 'axial' and 'selective' as used in grounded theory (Chapter 15)
- constant comparison (Glaser, 1978) and counter discourses: continuous and iterative
- Strauss and Corbin (1998) suggested 'microscopic examination' (line by line) of data

Miles and Huberman (1994, p. 9) outline some key steps (analytic moves) which have been translated into Figure 14.4.

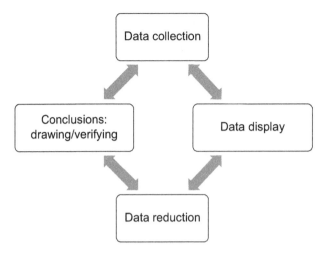

Figure 14.3 Adapted from Miles and Huberman's (1994) components of data analysis

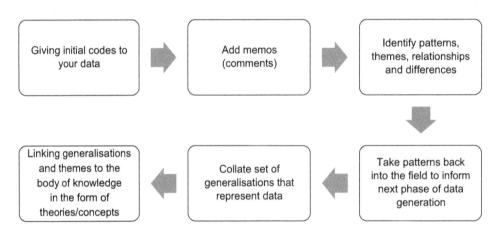

Figure 14.4 Key steps (analytic moves) for qualitative analysis

14.2.2 Coding

As Miles and Huberman (1994, p. 56) note:

> Codes are tags or labels for assigning units of meaning to the descriptive or inferential information compiled during a study. Codes are usually attached to 'chunks' of varying size – words, phrases, sentences or whole paragraphs.

The first step of giving codes to your data and a number of different coding schemes have been presented which you may wish to consider. Overall, the schemes help to focus attention on key aspects. These aspects will be heavily influenced by your research aim and objectives, but provide a useful starting point as you think about analysing your own data. Lofland's scheme from 1971 provides six key areas with which to frame your analysis, Bogdan and Biklen's (1992) scheme adds to this and provides ten:

Lofland's coding scheme (1971)	Example notes from interview data (taken from a study on food tourism)
I. Acts – temporary and brief action	'I had to run to the cake stall and grab one of the locally made cakes . . .'
II. Activities – actions of longer duration	'We tend to spend a week in this area, five days at the food festival and then another two visiting local producers'
III. Meanings – verbal production of participants	'The smell of the fish makes me remember my childhood and there is something quite nostalgic about this place for me'
IV. Participation – people's involvement in study setting	'Yes, I do think tourists buying these products keeps these small businesses alive'
V. Relationships – interrelationships among several people	'I always come with my husband, but he is so fussy, so often I will leave him at the guesthouse and find something to eat myself!'
VI. Settings – the entire setting as unit of analysis	'I love it here, the landscape is so beautiful and green. It is quiet and rural. It is a wonderful backdrop for this food trip'

Furthermore, you may wish to use more coding headings and the same study on food and tourism can be further organised with Bogdan and Biklen's ten areas:

Bogdan and Biklen (1992)	Example (quotes from data)
I. Setting/context	'I love it here, the landscape is so beautiful and green. It is quiet and rural. It is a wonderful backdrop for this food trip'
II. Definition of the situation	'We are food tourists and what we do is inspired by our love of food – so here we are at this festival'
III. Perspectives	'It is important to support these events and not just go to McDonalds or a large supermarket'
IV. Ways of thinking about people and objects	'I have great respect for these fishermen – they work very hard and get less and less money'
V. Process and sequence of events	'We always visit the festival first to get ideas and then go onto visit producers'
VI. Activities	'We tend to spend a week in this area, five days at the food festival and then another two visiting local producers'
VII. Events	'It was wonderful to see a cooking demonstration . . .'
VIII. Strategies	'I will purposely avoid supermarkets and always go to farmers' markets and local places to buy food – it is political and economic'
IX. Relationships and social structures	'I always come with my husband, but he is so fussy, so often I will leave him at the guesthouse and find something to eat myself!'
X. Methods	'I do a lot of research before the trip, especially on the internet . . .'

A further version which is adapted from Bogdan and Biklen (1992), Strauss (1987), Mason (1996) and Gibbs (2007) is presented here. Think of brief examples yourself now which might populate in the 'your data' column. Reflect on what elements you are including for each code and why?

Coding heading	Your data?
I. Behaviours, specific acts	
II. Events – short once in a lifetime events or things people have done that are often told as a story	
III. Activities – these are of a longer duration, involve other people within a particular setting	
IV. Strategies, practice or tactics	
V. States – conditions experienced by people	
VI. Meanings – a wide range of phenomena at the core of much qualitative analysis	
VII. Participation – adaptation to a new setting or involvement	
VIII. Relationships or interaction	
IX. Conditions or constraints	
X. Consequences	
XI. Settings – the entire context of the events under study	
XII. Reflexive – researcher's role in the process	

Perhaps more simply, Frankfort-Nachimas and Nachimas (1996) suggest that you ask yourself a number of questions to assist in your analysis:

1 What type of behaviour is being demonstrated?
2 What is its structure?
3 How frequent is it?
4 What are its causes?
5 What are its processes?
6 What are its consequences?
7 What are people's strategies for dealing with the behaviour?

The important thing is you should look for patterns or regularities that occur and for examples that illustrate or describe the aspect under focus. Try to identify key words or phrases to make sense of the data. Look for statements that not only support your theories, but also refute them and this way you can build a comprehensive response to your research aim.

14.2.3 Techniques for coding

There are three main approaches to the technical and mechanical side of qualitative data coding:

- manual: coloured pens, paper, cutting and pasting, numbering
- computer-aided: Excel spreadsheet or MS Word grids

- qualitative data analysis software packages: for example, NVivo (this will be discussed in the Chapter 16)

Manual coding

This method can be very effective with small amounts of data. A variety of approaches can be used here, ranging from using hard-copy transcripts with a wide margin to make notes of themes, to literally cutting out sections from the transcripts and placing them into bins/piles, to using the computer and colour coding/highlighting key areas of text.

It is often very useful to use coloured pens to highlight key areas of text and allocate a different colour for each code or theme. The colour coding makes it much easier to identify all the relevant data for each theme/code as it is visually attractive and clear. For example, part of your transcript might be similar to this (used for manual and computer-aided example below):

Interviewee 1: 'I think the main thing is about escape and getting away from it all, it's something different isn't it? Sometimes there are good deals and although I don't have that much money, there are airlines that do some good deals and it's a good opportunity. I feel different.

I enjoy meeting new people and experiencing new cultures and places – it's an adventure really isn't it, something out of the ordinary. You see things that you wouldn't normally see like temples, unusual buildings.

I also like to try new food and drink. I like to go to restaurants, but also just try local food in some lovely locations. However, my husband stops me from spending too much!'

The manual coding of this transcript example might look something like Figure 14.5.

Code/Theme	Transcript 1
Escape **Economic factors** Increased opportunities *The 'Other'* **New experiences** *Relationships*	I think the main thing is about escape and getting away from it all, it's something different isn't it? Sometimes there are **good deals and although I don't have that much money**, there are airlines that do some good deals and it's a good opportunity. I feel different. *I enjoy meeting new people and experiencing new cultures and places – it's an adventure really isn't it, something out of the ordinary.* You see things that you wouldn't normally see like *temples, unusual buildings.* **I also like to try new food and drink. I like to go to restaurants, but also just try local food in some lovely locations.** <u>*However, my husband stops me from spending too much! ...*</u>

Figure 14.5 Simple example of a coded transcript

Note: for illustration purposes, we have used grey shading, bold, underline and italics. However, using colour pens/highlighters might be a better option for visual illustrations.

Practical tips for manual coding

- Read through all of your data without colouring it – this will help you get a good overview of your data sets.
- Only use one or two colours at a time to represent one theme/code – using several all at once will be confusing.
- Ensure you write down what each colour represents and signifies in a clear key.
- Leave a lot of time to undertake your coding – it will take much longer than you think!

14.2.4 Computer-aided coding

Word processing packages such as Microsoft Word and spreadsheet packages such as Microsoft Excel can be very effective in storing data as well as helping you analyse them. Such packages allow you to use the types transcripts from your interviews immediately and allow you to store them and back them up safely (unlike the dangers of keeping paper copies). Word or Excel allow you to add comments, colour code sections, cut and paste sections into different places, produce tables of words, search for key words and phrases, provide line numbering and cross referencing, produce simple diagrams (flowcharts, hierarchies, and so on) and save elements in different files and formats.

For example, Word or Excel can be used to produce a simple matrix in which to place notes and data against emergent codes. The empty sheet might look like:

THEME /CODES	Interviewee 1	Interviewee 2	Interviewee 3	Interviewee 4 ...

The emergent Excel sheet for the same section of interview transcript presented above might look like the following:

THEME /CODES	Interviewee 1 (transcript from above)	Interviewee 2 (next transcript)
Escape	I think the main thing is about escape and getting away from it all, it's something different isn't it?	I like to get away and escape
Increased opportunities	. . . there are airlines that do some good deals and it's a good opportunity.	There are far more places to go and I want to see a lot more of the world . . .
Economic factors	Sometimes there are good deals and although I don't have that much money . . .	Memo and quotes here

The 'Other'	I enjoy meeting new people and experiencing new cultures and places	Memo and quotes here
Relationships	Husband and wide dynamics, 'However, my husband stops me from spending too much!'	My family stop me
NEXT CODE . . .		

14.3 Different types of data analysis: content, domain and discourse analysis

Key questions

- What types of data analysis are there?
- What are the differences between the different data analysis approaches?
- Which one fits my theoretical approach?

14.3.1 Content analysis

Content analysis has been described by Mayring (2000, p. 2) as:

> an approach of empirical, methodological controlled analysis of texts within their context of communication, following content analytic rules and step by step models, without rash quantification.

Content analysis looks at the presence, placement and frequency of certain words or phrases within texts or documents. It is the most quasi-statistical approach which has a history in more positivistic approaches to research. This method of analysis allows researchers to quantify and analyse the presence, meanings and relationships of different key words and concepts. In essentially counting words and developing frequencies, you are then able to make inferences about what the key themes are in the transcriptions and thus what are the dominant issues being faced by the respondents or destinations under scrutiny. It is used to determine the presence of certain words, concepts, themes, phrases, characters or sentences within texts or sets of texts and to quantify this presence in an objective manner. Zhang and Wildemuth (2017, p. 318) claim that:

> qualitative content analysis goes beyond merely counting words or extracting objective content from texts to examine meanings, themes and patterns that may be manifest or latent in a particular text. It allows researchers to understand social reality in a subjective but scientific manner.

It can be used in a number of tourism contexts, such as analysing marketing material for certain discourses or ideas, government policy documents, films and interview transcripts.

There are two general categories of content analysis: *conceptual analysis* and *relational analysis*. Conceptual analysis is looking at the existence and frequency of concepts in a text. Relational analysis is about relationships and builds on conceptual analysis by examining the relationships among concepts in a text.

Case study: 'destination image representation on the web: content analysis of Macau travel related websites'

This study looks at the image representations of Macau on the internet by analysing the contents of a variety of web information sources – the Macau official tourism website, tour operators and travel agents' websites, online travel magazine and guide websites, and online travel 'blogs'. Both qualitative (text mining and expert judgement) and quantitative approaches (correspondence analysis) were used to content-analyse the narrative and visual information on the sampled websites.

The full article can be found at: Choi, S., Lehto, Z. and Morrison, A. (2007). 'Destination image representation on the web: Content analysis of Macau travel related websites', *Tourism Management*, 28 (1), 118–129.

Practical tips

- Keep detailed notes on everything you do.
- Leave twice as much time to undertake the analysis than you think it might take.
- Gather as many all of your sources as you can (newspapers, transcripts, media files, brochures) before you start the process.

Of course, content analysis has its critics. As Krane et al. suggest:

Placing a frequency count after a category of experiences is tantamount to saying how important it is; thus value is derived by number. In many cases, rare experiences are no less meaningful, useful, or important than common ones. In some cases, the rare experience may be the most enlightening one.

(1997, p. 214)

Box 14.1 lists some advantages and disadvantages of content analysis. You might prefer to undertake a form of analysis which considers cultural settings, such as domain analysis.

Box 14.1: advantages and disadvantages of content analysis

Advantages

- Allows a closeness to the text which can alternate between specific categories and relationships.
- Provides a statistical analysis of the text.
- Looks directly at the messages in transcripts in a simple and organised way.
- Can allow for both quantitative and qualitative operations.
- Can provide valuable historical/cultural insights.
- Can identify clear relationships which can be mapped and networked.
- Provides an unobtrusive means of analysing interactions.
- Provides insight into complex models of human thought.
- Considered as a relatively 'exact' research method and is thus more recognised by 'traditional positivistic' researchers (uses hard facts, as opposed to discourse analysis).

Disadvantages

- Very time consuming.
- Is subject to increased error, particularly when relational analysis is used.
- Often fails to have a theoretical base.
- Attempts to simplify and draw meaningful inferences which may be more subtle.
- Inherently reductive, particularly when dealing with complex texts.
- Tends too often to simply consist of word counts and frequencies.
- Often disregards the context that produced the text, as well as the state of things after the text is produced.
- Can be difficult to automate or computerise.

14.3.2 Domain analysis

Another lesser-known form of qualitative data analysis has been most associated with the work of James Spradley and is about using domains as the main way of conceptualising and understanding cultural settings, which makes it appropriate for tourism research. These domains are categories of meaning and allow for the researcher to identify relationships and connections (Spradley, 1980, 2016; Jennings, 2010; Neuman, 2006) and there are three key components: *cover term* (name); *included terms* (subcategories); and *semantic relationship* (is a kind of . . .).

Cultural domain's components		Example
Cover term	Name	Holiday
Included terms	Subcategories of the name	Food and drink
Semantic relationship (see below)	'is a kind of . . .'	Food tourism is a kind of holiday

Jennings (2010, p. 214) offers a useful table which takes Spradley's (1980) ideas. For this chapter, the example of food and drink tourism is used to provide examples. It is still worthwhile looking at Jennings (2010, Table 7.5) which builds on the work of Spradley where she explains semantic relationships. An example of a table which builds on this work for food and drink tourism (for example) is below.

Relationship	Semantic relationship	Example from food tourism project
Strict inclusion	A is a kind of B	A food festival is a type of food tourism offer.
Spatial	A is a place in B	The market is a place in the town centre.
Cause-effect	A is a part of B	Eating local food is a result of buying it straight from the local producer.
Rationale	A is a result of B	Supporting local businesses is a reason for buying direct from the producer.
Location for action	A is the reason for doing B	The restaurant is a place to try new foods.
Function	A is used by B	A fork is used to eat food.
Means-end	A is the way to do B	Trying new foods is a way to develop greater cultural capital.
Sequence	A is a step and stage in B	Walking into a food festival is a stage in the food tourism experience.
Attribution	A is a characteristic of B	Better tasting food is generally a characteristic of locally purchased and made food.

There are several steps involved in conducting domain analysis which are primarily outlined in Jennings (2010, p. 215):

(i) Choose a semantic relationship (as above).
(ii) Produce a domain analysis worksheet which has the included terms, the semantic relationship and then the cover terms.
(iii) Choose the empirical materials.
(iv) Examine the materials for cover terms and included terms that match the semantic relationship.
(v) Re-examine the materials for other semantic relationships.
(vi) Produce list of domains (or *taxonomies*).

Case study: domain analysis

Domain analysis is not a commonly adopted approach to tourism research. One example is a study of the Florida manatee as a tourism attraction. Data was generated from participant observation notes, interviews and documentary analysis (newspapers and promotional material). A preliminary domain search was undertaken to create categories which provided a systematic way to analyse the terms and ideas used by subjects to describe their world. From domain analysis, they constructed taxonomies, categories organised on the basis of semantic relationships. They used the software ATLAS.ti to code the data (see Chapter 16).

Issues identified from field notes and interviews were grouped into encounter-specific and non-encounter-specific categories. The latter comprised general concerns such as boating-related mortality and random events. Encounter-specific issues were defined as those that related directly to the manatee encounter experience. Five issues were identified: water quality, harassment, density and crowding, enforcement and education. These concerns were expressed in relation to both visitor experiences and manatee welfare. After close domain analysis, it was found that:

> Where endangered species are concerned, when mechanisms are not in place to control the tourism component, there is greater potential for negative impacts to the target species as the setting evolves. In this case, the salient issues identified by stakeholders were related to controlling visitor use and behavior more so than the management of the manatees themselves.
>
> (Sorice, 2006, p. 81)

Source: Sorice, M., Shafer, C. and Ditton, R. (2006). 'Managing endangered species within the use–preservation paradox: The Florida manatee as a tourism attraction', *Environmental Management*, 37 (1), pp. 69–83.

14.3.3 Discourse analysis

Discourse analysis is a part of the linguistic turn in the social sciences and the humanities which emphasises the role of language in the construction of social reality, and how people make sense of their own world. It is one of the dominant or mainstream research approaches in communication, sociology, social psychology and psychology and is only a relative new-comer to tourism research (Hannam and Knox, 2005). Discourse analysis can be undertaken with any type of written or spoken language, such as a conversation transcript, policy document or a newspaper article. Generally, discourse analysis is a method that has been adopted and developed by social constructionists.

Discourse analysis can be characterised as a way of approaching and thinking about a problem. The focus is identifying underlying social structures, which may be assumed or played out within the conversation or text. It concerns the sorts of tools and strategies people use when engaged in communication, such as slowing one's speech for emphasis, use of metaphors, choice of particular words to display affect, and so on. Discourse analysis will make it possible to reveal hidden motivations or what lies behind the choice of a particular method of research to interpret that text.

Discourse analysis is generally perceived as the product of the postmodern period. The reason for this is that while other periods or philosophies are generally character- ised by a belief-system or meaningful interpretation of the world, postmodern theories do not provide a particular view of the world, other than that there is no one true view or interpretation of the world. Key influences have been Michel Foucault, Jacques Derrida (who coined the term 'deconstruction'), Julia Kristeva, Jean-Francois Lyotard and Fredric Jameson. In qualitative discourse analysis your role as researcher is to iden- tify categories, themes, ideas and views in your data. The aim is to identify commonly shared discursive resources (shared patterns of expressing ideas and talking). You need to think about how the discourse helps you understand the issue under study, how people construct their own version of an event and how people use discourse to main- tain or construct their own/others identity.

In tourism, Hannam and Knox (2005) argue that discourse analysis should look at the things that are not said which may lead to a more critical approach to tourism studies:

> Discourse analysis should proceed by recognizing that all texts are produced inter- textually in relation to other texts, which are in turn embedded within power relations that give degrees of authority. Discourse analysis should thus treat texts as mediated cultural products which are part of wider systems of knowledge.

Some examples of tourism studies using discourse analysis

Pritchard, A. and Morgan, N. (2001). 'Culture, identity and tourism representation: marketing Cymru or Wales?', *Tourism Management*, 22 (2), 167–179.
Stamou, A.G. and Paraskevopoulos, S. (2004). 'Images of nature by tourism and environmentalist discourses in visitors books: A critical discourse analysis of ecotourism', *Discourse & Society*, 15, 105–129.
Thurlow, C. and Jaworski, A. (2003). 'Communicating a global reach: Inflight maga- zines as a globalizing genre in tourism', *Journal of Sociolinguistics*, 7 (4), 579–606.
Xiao, H. (2006). 'The discourse of power: Deng Xiaoping and tourism develop- ment in China', *Tourism Management*, 27 (5), 803–814.

14.4 Interpreting visual images and film

Key questions

- How do I analyse photos and still images?
- How can I analyse films and moving images?
- Are there any examples of studies I can reference?

Wileman (1993, p. 114) suggests that visual interpretation is about the 'ability to read, interpret and understand information presented in pictorial or graphical image'. It seems rather surprising that given the nature and importance of the visual in tourism, there is surprising little on how to analyse, interpret and make sense of visual data. However, the tourism industry is characterised by a plethora of visual forms (postcards, brochures, advertisements, and photographs, travel programmes and films).

Early pioneers of visual analysis were Chalfen (1979) on photographic behaviour, Uzzell (1984) who looked at holiday brochures, and Dann (1996) who undertook content analysis of holiday advertising in Cyprus. Film analysis remains relatively limited, although examples include an analysis of *Captain Correlli's Mandolin* by Tzanelli (2003) and Winter's (2003) analysis of *Tomb Raider* in relation to Cambodia and how it encourages tourists to re-enact the scenes, against the conservation message being promoted at the site. It is impossible to discuss how to interpret images in a short chapter such as this, but the following sections, first on still images (photos) and then moving images (film) should give you a starting point if you are considering using images as part of your research.

14.4.1 Analysing still images

Researchers must provide their own interpretative narrative on their visual data, it is a subjective process and needs very careful attention. You must ensure you produce detailed notes, follow a framework which explains your approach and seek to support findings with literature and theoretical support.

Gillian Rose (2016) has written what is considered the seminal text on visual methodologies (*Visual Methodologies: An Introduction to the Interpretation of Visual Materials* – now in its fourth edition). Tourism scholars have built on this work, Rakić and Chambers (2011) offer *An Introduction to Visual Research Methods in Tourism*. A simple framework to help analysis visual data (photos, postcards, and so on) is included below.

Try to write notes on the following aspects:

Elements to consider	Description – aspects to make notes on
Personal reaction to the image	Do you like it? Why? Emotional impact?
Background to the image	Who produced the image? Date of production? Where was it produced? Why was it produced originally?
Overall content	What and who is featured?
Subject, concept and mood	What features in the image? What mood is created? What kind of messages are relayed in the message and how?
Background, surroundings and the overall scene	What has been chosen as the background? Why? Impact and meaning of this? Use of perspective?
Colour	What colours have been used? Is it colour or black and white? Peaceful and calm colours or bold and dramatic? What mood is created?

(continued)

(continued)

Elements to consider	Description – aspects to make notes on
Composition and placement of the objects	Where are the subjects placed in the frame in relation to each other? Foreground and background placement?
Text	Is there any text in the image – what does it say? Is there any text explaining the image – what does it say?
Technical aspects	Exposure, depth of field, lighting? Frame size? Blurred or sharp images?
Tourism theory and literature	Give examples of literature or studies that have written about these subjects or places? These will help you when you write up your findings

Some researchers have undertaken a *semiotic analysis*, which is not just looking at the image but takes into consideration the context and history behind its production (can also apply to texts). Semiotics is the study of signs and stems from the early work of Saussure (1857–1913) and Pierce (1839–1914). It can be applied to virtually any sign that signifies a meaning, or concept as a means of communication in the outside world. Rose refers to this as the 'social effects of meaning'. The process occurring between signs, objects (signified) and the interpretants (signifiers) are how viewers make sense of an image, though these meanings are not fixed, i.e. visuals can have multiple meanings and uses and this should be considered when analysing texts.

Further reading on visual methods in tourism and research examples

Amsden, B., Stedman, R. and Kruger, L. (2011). 'The creation and maintenance of sense of place in a tourism-dependent community', *Leisure Sciences*, 33 (1), 32–51.

Burns, P., Palmer, P. and Lester, J. (2010). *Tourism and Visual Culture*. Wallingford, Oxon: CABI.

Garrod, B. (2008). 'Exploring place perception a photo-based analysis', *Annals Of Tourism Research*, 35 (2), 381–401.

Sather-Wagstaff, J. (2008). 'Picturing experience: A tourist-centered perspective on commemorative historical sites', *Tourist Studies*, 8 (1), 77–103.

Tuohino, A. and Pitkdnen, K. (2004). 'The transformation of a neutral lake landscape into a meaningful experience – interpreting tourist photos', *Journal Of Tourism & Cultural Change*, 2 (1), 77–93.

14.4.2 Analysing moving images (film)

One good example to read is Burns and Lester (2005) in their chapter in Ritchie on visual methods in a case study of Dennis O'Rourke's 1987 film *Cannibal Tours*, which discusses the idea of 'visual literacy'. They argue every single shot in a film is a conscious choice by the director and, in analysing film, one needs to go simple beyond what is presented and look at how each element is presented to the audience and why. They present a very useful table outlining an approach to critical film analysis which has been simplified and reduced here to give you an idea of how to approach it (Table 14.2 below). Their chapter is a useful one in describing how they wrote up the film scenes and outlines the practical approach to film analysis.

Practical tips for analysing moving images

- You will need to view each film under analysis at least 5–7 times to be able to get a real sense of the film.
- View the film several times all the way through and then view the film in close detail, scene by scene, sometimes frame by frame if necessary.
- Take very detailed notes which will help you when you write up your findings.
- You must read widely and draw on literature that discusses emergent themes, as well as work on visual interpretation.
- Film analysis takes a long time, so ensure you start early and leave enough time for several viewings.

Table 14.2 Structure for critical film analysis

Parameter	Description – aspects to make notes on
Bibliographic information	Title, director, length, date of film, distributor
Type of film (and genre)	Fiction, historical fiction, documentary
Literary analysis	What are the messages in the film? What points are being made? What is the storyline? Significant turning points? Who are the characters? Their role in the film?
Aesthetic analysis	What is the mood created and how? Perspectives of each character? Relationship of characters to each other? What role do light, colour and shadow play in the film? Types of shot? – distance (short/long), focus, angle (deep/sharp), point of view, pans, tilts, zooms, rolls,
Editing	Assess the scenes in terms (long/short) of their length, speed and rhythm. How are images and scenes cut together and what meanings does this impose? Is the narrative clear? How does the film flow? How does it begin (this is crucial for a film)? Type of cuts (fade, jump, unmarked, dissolve)
Soundtrack	Sound can be divided into environmental, speech and music. What emotions do the sounds suggest? Is silence used? Is voice over used and to what effect?

Source: adapted from Burns and Lester (2005, p. 54)

Chapter summary

- Qualitative data are data that describes meaning and experiences though words.
- You should ensure that your data are stored securely and confidentially.
- Transcribe your data yourself as much as possible, as data may be sensitive, but also you tend to get closer to the data and you have an opportunity to review or make an early assessment of the data, your observation, interaction, the conversation and the arguments.
- There are numerous possible approaches to analysing qualitative data: from quasi-statistical, template approaches, to editing approaches to immersion approaches.
- You need to consider qualitative data analysis as inductive and iterative, where you are constantly re-visiting your raw data as you develop codes and identify emergent themes.
- Code your data manually or using computer-aided software.
- The data analysis can be conducted using content, domain and discourse analysis.
- Visual interpretation can be very useful in tourism.

Discussion questions

14.1 Should you type up your own interview transcripts?
14.2 What are the reasons for undertaking an iterative process when conducting qualitative research?
14.3 What is coding? What types are available to use?
14.4 What are the key aspects you should consider when analysing visual data?

Further reading

Ateljevic, I., Pritchard, A. and Morgan, N. (eds) (2007). *The Critical Turn in Tourism Studies: Innovative Research Methodologies*. Oxford: Elsevier.

Coffey, A. and Atkinson, P. (1996). *Making Sense of Qualitative Data*. Thousand Oaks, CA: Sage.

Denscombe, M. (1998). *The Good Research Guide: For Small-Scale Social Research Projects*. Buckingham: Open University Press.

Denzin, N. and Lincoln, Y. (eds) (2000). *Handbook of Qualitative Research*, 2nd edition. Thousand Oaks, CA: Sage.

Glaser, B. and Strauss, A. (1967). *The Discovery of Grounded Theory*. Chicago: Aldine.

Jennings, G. (2010). *Tourism Research*, 2nd edition. Milton: John Wiley & Sons Australia Ltd.

Miles, M.B. and Huberman, A.M. (1994). *Qualitative Data Analysis: A Sourcebook of New Methods*, 2nd edition. London: Sage.

Patton, M.Q. (2002). *Qualitative Research and Evaluation Methods*, 3rd edition. London: Sage.

Phillimore, J. and Goodson, L. (eds) (2004). *Qualitative Research in Tourism: Ontologies, Epistemologies and Methodologies*. London: Routledge.

Ritchie, J., Spencer, L. and O'Connor, W. (2003). 'Carrying out qualitative analysis'. In J. Ritchie and J. Lewis (eds), *Qualitative Research Practice: A Guide for Social Science Students and Researchers*. Thousand Oaks, CA: Sage, pp. 219–263.

Robson, C. (2002). *Real World Research*, 2nd edition. Oxford: Blackwell.

Veal, A.J. (2011). *Research Methods for Leisure and Tourism: A Practical Guide*, 4th edition. Harlow: Pearson Education.

Walle, A. (1997). 'Quantitative verses qualitative tourism research', *Annals of Tourism Research*, 24 (3), 524–536.

Yin, R. (1994). *Case Study Research: Design and Methods*, 2nd edition. London: Sage.

Chapter 15

Grounded theory and data analysis

Sally Everett, Areej Shabib Aloudat and Ramesh Durbarry

Jenny has been reviewing the literature on her topic and does not seem to be quite satisfied on the explanation given about the interaction of tourists with tour guides and how this interaction enhances the tourists' experience. To better understand her topic, Jenny decides to 'wipe the slate' and start afresh to offer an explanation.

For such type of research, her supervisor recommends that she uses the grounded theory.

So Jenny has been asking: What is grounded theory? How is this method applied and how can she code her data?

15.0 Chapter objectives

Given the complex nature of qualitative data and the numerous options available, this chapter particularly focuses on grounded theory and provides detailed case studies into how this approach is used to generate qualitative data. Grounded theory is an inductive methodology and is particularly used to offer explanation on the topic you are researching or in the construction of a theory through data analysis, as if to say that the theory is grounded in the data. How the data analysis works in practice is further discussed using a case study.

By the end of this chapter, you will be able to:

- understand what is grounded theory;
- when to use grounded theory;
- appreciate the different approaches of grounded theory; and
- understand how to analyse data using grounded theory.

15.1 Grounded theory and comparative analysis

A very good definition of grounded theory (GT) is provided by Charmaz (2006):

> A method of conducting qualitative research that focuses on creating conceptual frameworks or theories through building inductive analysis from the data. Hence the analytic categories are directly 'grounded' in the data. The method favours analysis over description, fresh categories over preconceived ideas and extant theories, and systematically focused sequential data collection over large initial samples. This method is distinguished from others since it involves the researcher in data analysis while collecting data – we use this data analysis to inform and shape further data collection. Thus, the sharp distinction between data collection and analysis phases of traditional research is intentionally blurred in GT studies.
>
> (p. 187)

GT methodology is traced back to Barney Glaser and Anselm Strauss (1967). The two authors published *The Discovery of Grounded Theory*, which introduced GT as a challenge to the quantitative research paradigm. This book was a 'revolutionary' work because it challenged:

> (a) arbitrary divisions between theory and research, (b) views of qualitative research as primarily a precursor to more 'rigorous' quantitative methods, (c) claims that the quest for rigor made qualitative research illegitimate, (d) beliefs that qualitative methods are impressionistic and unsystematic, (e) separation between data collection and analysis, and (f) assumptions that qualitative research could produce only descriptive case studies rather than theory development.
>
> (Charmaz, 2000, p. 511)

The function of GT methodology is to generate or develop a theory. The theory is grounded in data systematically gathered and analysed through the research process.

During actual research there is a successive interplay between the collection and analysis of data that moves towards constructing the theory (Strauss and Corbin, 1998).

15.2 Different versions of grounded theory

After the publication of *The Discovery of Grounded Theory*, the approach has fractured into two ways. Glaser, in *Theoretical Sensitivity* (1978) and *Emergence vs. Forcing* (1992a), asserted that verification has no place in GT, whose purpose is to generate hypotheses, not to test them. On the other hand, Strauss and Corbin, in *Basics of Qualitative Research: Grounded Theory Procedures and Techniques* (1990) and the improved second edition (1998), suggested that the theory should and could be developed and verified through the research process within the systematic process of data collection and analysis, and not only through follow-up quantitative research (Strauss and Corbin, 1998).

The divergence between the perspectives of the original authors resulted in two different GT approaches: Glaser's approach and Strauss and Corbin's approach. The major differences between the two approaches are that Glaser (1978) advocates that you should enter the research area with no prior defined research problem, and the problem will emerge from the area to be investigated. Conversely, Strauss and Corbin (1990) believe that you should formulate the research questions from the beginning of the research even if very broadly (Lye et al., 2006). Glaser critiques this process and considers it as a way to force data. Glaser's view is that reality is out there and you should have trust and patience that the conceptual framework will emerge from the research process (Glaser, 1978); the theory is melted in data and your function is to discover it (Glaser, 1992a). By contrast Strauss and Corbin emphasise the step-by-step research process and the application of the analytical techniques they propose (Strauss and Corbin, 1990, 1998).

Departing from these two approaches, Charmaz has added a third position to GT, that is constructivist GT. For Charmaz, there are two types of GT, *objectivist* GT and the *constructivist* GT (Charmaz, 2000, 2006). She criticised Glaser's and Strauss and Corbin's approaches as they remain instilled with positivism with its objectivist underpinnings. Likewise, Denzin and Lincoln (1994) categorised GT under the post-positivistic paradigm. Charmaz argues that Glaser's (1978, 1992a) position is close to positivism because of its beliefs in an objective, external reality, and the need for a neutral observer to discover the data. Strauss and Corbin's (1990, 1998) point of view, Charmaz suggests, also supposes an objective external reality, and the possibility of unbiased data collection and analysis, achieved by technical procedures, in support of verification through research. However, their position developed towards post-positivism because of the emphasis they gave to the 'voice' of their respondents and the need to represent them as fully as possible (Charmaz, 2000, p. 510).

The approach of Charmaz is based on the notion of constructivism that 'assumes the relativism of multiple realities, recognises the mutual creation of knowledge by the viewer and the viewed' (Charmaz, 2000, p. 510). A constructivist approach 'adopts GT guidelines as tools but does not subscribe to the objectivist, positivist assumptions in its earlier formulations. A constructivist approach emphasises the studied phenomenon rather than the methods of studying it (Charmaz, 2000, p. 509). It does not assume that data is out there waiting to be discovered and studied, nor does it suppose that you enter the research area without an interpretative frame of reference. Instead, what observers see and hear depends upon their prior 'interpretive frames, biographies, and interests as well as the research contexts, their relationships with research participants, concrete field experiences, and modes of generating and recording empirical materials' (Charmaz, 2005, p. 509). Constructivism means seeking meanings of both the respondents' and the researchers' meanings. By contrast objectivism assumes that 'the world is composed of facts and the goal of knowledge is to provide a literal account of what the world is like' (Karin Knorr-Cetina, 1981, cited in Schwandt, 1994, p. 125).

To summarise, constructivist GT emphasises building an analysis, studying process, and attending to how people create and view their worlds. Objectivist GT assumes a single reality that a passive, neutral observer discovers through value-free inquiry (Charmaz, 2006, p. 401).

15.3 The process of a grounded theory research

The research process starts with the identification of a research area. GT as other qualitative research is used to research topics that have been ignored in the literature or where little is known about them, or to provide new insights into a previously researched area (Strauss and Corbin, 1997; Goulding, 2002).

It is important to clarify further some of the key principles you should adhere to in a study that uses the GT methodology. This involves: theoretical sensitivity, theoretical sampling, theoretical saturation and the constant comparison method.

15.3.1 Theoretical sensitivity

Researchers in a GT study do not come to the research problem with preconceptions and propositions. However, you have to possess the ability to give meanings to theorise data (Glaser and Strauss, 1967). Strauss and Corbin (1998) argue that theoretical sensitivity implies 'the ability to give meaning to data, the capacity to understand, and capability to separate the pertinent from that which isn't' (Strauss and Corbin, 1998, p. 42). Glaser (1978) illustrates the importance of the sensitivity by titling one of his books on GT *Theoretical Sensitivity* (Locke, 2001). Sampling in GT is tied to your theoretical sensitivity. You can have varying degrees of sensitivity. The ability to be sensitive or to conceptualise data is gained from different sources. This includes the disciplinary literature, and your professional and personal experience.

Using the literature carefully can provide a rich source of ideas that stimulate your thinking and suggest possible questions (Strauss and Corbin, 1998). It also serves to highlight important issues to be researched (Gray, 2004). In this regard, it is important to clarify the function and the place of the literature review in a GT study. A typical research practice is to comprehensively review the literature relevant to the study before starting fieldwork. In the grounded approach it is not necessary to conduct an exhaustive review of literature in advance. This is to avoid bringing into the study preconceptions and ideas that already exist in other work and then being biased by them (Glaser and Strauss, 1967; Glaser, 1978; Strauss, 1987; Goulding, 2002; Charmaz, 2005).

However, you do not enter the field with a totally blank sheet, as 'we all bring to the inquiry a considerable background in professional and disciplinary literature'

(Strauss and Corbin, 1990, p. 48). You can conduct general disciplinary literature in order to 'construct possible conceptual framework' (Goulding, 2002, p. 71), and to know 'more theoretical codes in order to be sensitive to rendering in explicitly the subtleties of the relationships in this data' (Glaser, 1978, p. 78). Therefore, the first stage in reviewing the literature should be a broad one in order to understand key concepts involved in the study area and to locate the research among previous studies and to hint at the paucity of knowledge in the area under study. The literature that is reviewed at this stage helps you to enhance your theoretical sensitivity to be able to give meaning to data (Glaser, 1978; Strauss and Corbin, 1998).

The next step in examining the literature is during the data collection and analysis where at this time the review is driven by the concepts that emerged from the data analysis. The literature in this phase is also compared with the emergent accounts, therefore, to validate and refine the emerged knowledge. During a GT study 'progressive accessing and reading relevant literature can become a part of data collection procedures' (Strauss and Corbin, 1998, p. 49). Therefore, the second stage of the literature review is undertaken after the findings (concepts and categories) start to emerge and shape. To conclude, the literature review comprises two types: first, an inductive review that is a general disciplinary review, and, second, a deductive review that is a review oriented by emergent categories.

Your experience is another source that enhances the theoretical sensitivity. This includes your professional experience, for example, a nurse investigating the experience of other nurses in a particular setting. Your professional experience helps you to be familiar with the research area without the need to spend more time (Strauss and Corbin, 1998). However, Strauss and Corbin warned that this sort of experience may freeze perception if depending heavily on it. Therefore, in order to use this source to support your sensitivity, it is important to continue comparing what you know with what others see. In addition, you should be aware that the participants' perceptions have priority over your own (Strauss and Corbin, 1998).

Personal experience is an additional source that increases the sensitivity. This refers to your experience in the research problem, for instance, a researcher experiencing divorce examining the life of divorced people, or experiencing a fatal disease and researching those who have the same illness.

15.3.2 Theoretical sampling

This sort of sampling is one of the distinguishing features of GT. Theoretical sampling is a method for collecting data based on concepts derived from the research process. It is defined as:

> Data gathering driven by concepts derived from the evolving theory and based on the concept of "making comparisons", whose purpose is to go to places, people, or events that will maximize opportunities to discover variations among concepts and to densify categories in terms of their properties and dimensions.
>
> (Strauss and Corbin, 1998, p. 201)

Theoretical sampling is defined as 'sampling on the basis of emerging concepts, with the aim being to explore the dimensional range or varied conditions along which the properties of concepts vary' (Strauss and Corbin, 1998, p. 73). Theoretical sampling's basic principle is that the emerging theory governs the data collection. Its purpose is to research further the emergent categories rather than replicating existing categories. Therefore, 'the rationale for theoretical sampling is to direct the data gathering efforts towards gathering information that will best support development of the theoretical frameworks' (Locke, 2001, p. 55). Its aim is to refine ideas, not to increase the size of the original sample (Charmaz, 2000, p. 519). You continue the sampling process depending on the emergent concepts. This is to seek more data to explore the different dimensions of the concepts and to fill any gaps in the analysis. This can be done through different strategies such as conducting more interviews or observations, re-interviewing the research participants, or studying documents (Charmaz, 2006). As codes and memos accumulate, you will begin to perceive relationships between them. The end-result of this analytic process is *axial coding*. It is termed 'axial' because 'coding occurs around the axis of a category, linking categories at the level of properties and dimensions' (Creswell, 2007, p. 123). The concepts are then reduced and abstracted to a higher level, to construct the major categories which reflect the main themes revealed from the analysis. The comparison process continues until the saturation point is reached and you are able to distinguish the basic categories that are the basic elements of the theoretical formulation.

15.3.3 Theoretical saturation

The next step is to select a core category that all major categories can be fitted into as if under an umbrella. This is referred to the *selective coding*, 'the process of integrating and refining categories' (Strauss and Corbin, 1998). In this stage you may specify possible relationships or linkages between categories, 'alternatively, propositions or hypothesis may be specified' (Creswell, 2007, p. 67). The result of data collection and analysis is substantive-level theory that interprets or explains problems or issues in particular areas.

The process of data collecting and analysis continues until no further evidence emerges and therefore *theoretical saturation* has been achieved (Glaser and Strauss, 1967; Strauss and Corbin, 1990, 1998). Generally, when you get involved in theory developing, gather data until you reach the saturation point (Glaser and Strauss, 1967; Glaser, 1978; Strauss and Corbin, 1998). Strauss and Corbin (1998) clarified this point as the stage when (a) no new or relevant ideas are emerging in the data; (b) the category is well developed in terms of its dimensions and properties; and (c) the relationships between categories are well established and validated (Strauss and Corbin, 1998, p. 212). However, reaching the point where no new data found is a relative matter. You may, even in the final stages of the research, still find that potential new concepts could be deduced. This problem disappears once you find that the new data does not add much more to the ideas and concepts that have already been inventoried. The progression of data collection and analysis continues, as described by Creswell (2007) in a zig-zagging process because of the continuous interplay between data collection and analysis. This strategy of simultaneous data collecting and analysing offers you the opportunity to learn about gaps in the data from the earliest stages of research.

15.3.4 Constant comparative method

Typically, data are collected through interviews, as well as other methods such as: direct observations, focus groups, and life histories (Goulding, 2002). As the data starts to accumulate, the analysis takes place simultaneously using the *constant comparative method*. Constant comparison is the method used to generate theory. This method entails comparing like with like, and looking for similarities and differences within the data and among the concepts and categories emerging. This process continues until you reach the final findings. The constant comparative method involves different stages of comparisons at the different levels of coding (open, axial and selective). Its principle is based on an axial question that is: whether more data analysis provides similar concepts and categories to previously constructed concepts and categories, or whether other new patterns emerge. It is a comparison between data and data, data and concepts, concepts and categories, and categories and categories. The comparison process continues until the saturation point is reached and you are able to distinguish the basic categories that are the basic elements of the theoretical formulation. Figure 15.1 illustrates these.

The analysis of data initiates with *open coding*, which begins with first interviews or observations. This primary type of coding is done by scanning the full transcription gathered from interviews, field notes, observations or other documents. The elicited texts are analysed (coding) line by line and sometimes world by world. Strauss and Corbin (1998) refer to this as the microscopic analysis. The aim is to 'open up' the inquiry in an attempt to identify key words or sentences which relate the participants' perspectives to the situation under investigation. The result will be identification of concepts which are used as a basis for further data collection. In addition to open coding, you should be involved, according to precept, in writing memos. These are the notes taken by you immediately after data collection; they are used as means of reminding and documenting your 'thoughts, interpretations, questions and direction for further data collection' (Strauss and Corbin, 1998, p. 110). They are the ideas revisited by you to direct you during the data analysis.

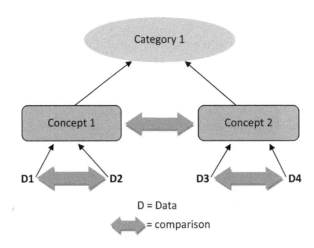

Figure 15.1 The constant comparative method

15.4 Grounded theory in tourism research

GT was first applied in the field of health sciences and has been widely used in a variety of disciplines, such as psychology, anthropology, education, social work and nursing. It was employed to investigate different socially situated, problematic topics, including: relations between service providers and their clients; the phenomenological experiences and conditions of people seen as social problems, or requiring public policy initiatives (e.g. being single mothers); and issues and conflicts in managerial situations (e.g. scientist-supervisor relationships).

In the context of tourism research, although there still many untapped areas in the tourism subject, GT remains relatively uncommon and slightly used by tourism researchers (Hobson, 2003). However, GT was employed to investigate a number of tourism issues, for instance: the travel experience of cruisers (Jennings, 1997); the leisure activity of visiting heritage sites by visitors (Goulding, 1999); the emic perspective of tourists' interpretations of authentic and inauthentic experiences (Mehmetoglu and Olsen, 2003); and the analysis of stakeholder facilitation of sustainable tourism (Hardy, 2005).

15.5 Coding data with a grounded theory approach

As mentioned above, the GT research process is characterised as an iterative process. This means that the findings of each stage in the research process guide the next stage (Hardy, 2005). Additionally, based on the principles of theoretical sampling and the constant comparisons method, the GT research path is a non-linear path (Glaser and Strauss, 1967). You do not collect all your raw data and then start the analysis. The data collection and analysis processes are done in parallel.

Strauss and Corbin's (1990) advice for beginners in GT research is to record and transcribe all materials especially those in the early stage of the research because coding these provide guidance for the next field observations and/or interviews (Strauss and Corbin, 1990, p. 30). By following this recommendation, the researcher has limitless opportunities to return to the original audio tape or/and to the transcriptions to redefine his/her interpretation.

The analysis of data is performed by going back and forth between the different levels of coding. According to Strauss and Corbin (1998), detailed analysis is necessary at the beginning of the research. This is referred to as the microanalysis. Microanalysis serves to generate initial categories and to discover the relationships among concepts. The concepts are the building blocks of theory, while the categories are the concepts that stand for phenomena (Strauss and Corbin, 1998, p. 101). This analysis may involve every word, phrase, line or paragraph. Narrowly examining the data 'compels the analyst to listen closely to what the interviewees are saying and how they are saying it [In addition, this may help the researcher to notice], in vivo concepts that will further stimulate our analyses' (Strauss and Corbin, 1998, p. 65). Two levels of analysis are involved in this type of analysis – open and axial coding. After generating categories in the open coding, then relating those categories to their subcategories in the axial coding, the researcher then turns to the process of integrating and refining the theory through the selective coding method.

15.5.1 Open coding

Open coding is the first step in breaking down the data into smaller analytic pieces (Glaser, 1978). It refers to the process in which the researcher begins to identify the concepts, their properties and dimensions (Strauss and Corbin, 1998). The properties are the characteristics of a category, the delineation of which defines and gives meaning. The dimensions are the range along which general properties of a category vary (Strauss and Corbin, 1998, p. 101). Open coding is governed by making comparisons and asking questions. The analysis starts once an interview is transcribed. This procedural analysis is line by line and sometimes word by word. The aim in this process is to identify potential categories. These categories are then labelled with names to express the meaning extrapolated from them. Once the category is found, it is then compared with previous data. If the new data does not fit the category the interpretation is adjusted, or a new category is created. The categories of this stage are considered first-order categories. The close inspection of data in the beginning of the research is necessary to build a dense and tightly integrated theory (Strauss and Corbin, 1998, p. 281).

15.5.2 Axial coding

After defining the categories in open coding, the researcher then turns towards making connections between the categories and subcategories. This process is called axial coding. Strauss (1987, p. 64) stated that axial coding involves several tasks, including: laying out the properties of a category and their dimensions; identifying the variety of conditions, actions/interactions, and consequences associated with the appearance of the phenomenon referenced by the category; and relating a category to its subcategories through statements.

15.5.3 Selective coding

After the microscopic analysis illustrated in the open and axial coding, a skeleton of the theoretical structure starts to emerge. This skeleton is extended and further refined through a higher level of coding, which is selective coding (Strauss and Corbin, 1998). In this rank of coding higher levels of conceptual categories are identified. They are called core categories. This process is no different from axial coding but it is done at a higher level of abstraction. This process of identifying the core category or categories makes possible the narrative through which a story can be told (Gray, 2004). To be chosen as a core category the category should fulfil, as Strauss (1987) clarifies, the following requirements. It must: be central, and be related to as many lower level categories as possible; appear frequently in the data; relate easily to subcategories; have implications for a more general theory; and be broad enough to allow for building in the maximum variation to the analysis.

Coding type	Nature of coding
Open	Emergent codes and first-order categories
Axial	Making connections between the categories and subcategories
Selective	Core categories – conceptually and theoretically-led codes

Case study: the worldview of tour guides

This research aimed at developing a framework that theorises the worldview of tour guides using the GT approach. Strauss and Corbin's (1990, 1998) version was employed because this path offers for beginners in GT a set of guidelines to conduct a study. Moreover, based on Glaser's approach, the researcher should enter the research area with no predefined problem and the problem will emerge from the area to be investigated. By contrast, Strauss and Corbin advocate that a research question should be formulated, even if very broadly (Hoque, 2006, p. 145). Accordingly, the selection of Strauss and Corbin's approach was appropriate because it met the administrative requirements of the researcher while presenting her proposal with a predefined research problem. *The theoretical sensitivity* of the researcher during this study was gained from different sources, including: the professional and personal background and the knowledge of the general concepts and perspectives of tourism literature. The data collection process in this research was accomplished through three phases.

The first phase was the pilot study. The data was collected to explore and bring out themes that may be used as the main areas to be further explored. Consequently, purposive sampling was used in this stage. A focus group interview was conducted with seven tour guides. Their selection was based on their experience and the recommendation of an experienced tour guide known to the researcher whom she used as key informant. Thereafter, the *theoretical sampling* technique was used. Two other tour guides and two tour operators were interviewed in an effort to discover more themes and new perspectives on the early concepts emerging from perceptions of the performance of Jordanian tourism. The bulk of the themes explored in this stage were related to *the tourism performance of Jordan*. In addition, other themes were revealed relating to *socio-cultural issues* that arose in the guiding process. The outcomes of this stage represented the basic leads that directed the researcher in the main fieldwork of the investigation.

The second phase was the start of the main fieldwork. The data collection was driven by the early analysis of data. The researcher started to collect the data relevant to the early categories that had begun to emerge through the pilot study. The collection and analysis of data were interrelated. The sampling technique at this stage remained purposive. More interviews were carried out and analysed. The data analysis of this stage involved a comparison between data and data, between data and concepts, and between concepts and categories. This technique is called *systematic constant comparison*. The sampling process thereafter was theoretical sampling. It was driven by the emergent concepts and the need to clarify the data, and to compare and verify the research categories. Therefore, the rest of the interviews in this stage were conducted to confirm previously emerging categories, to fill gaps and to gather the necessary data. At the end of this stage, the basic categories of the research were identified. These include three pillars relating to: *the ability of tour guides to*

(continued)

(continued)

inform on the tourism performance of a destination; their self view on their industry role; and the occupational career structure of tour guiding and its relative status.

In the third phase, the data collection was more focused and targeted. Follow-up semi-structured personal and telephone interviews were used to ask special focused questions. The researcher in the final stage continually sought to determine whether the research schedule had reached that point where conducting more interviews and performing more analysis was only generating the same concepts and categories that had already been revealed. The aim of this stage was to reach saturation point where no new data was emerging in any further interviews. This point was the beginning of abstracting the substantive theory from the findings. The sample size in this research was 29 interviews. The total number of the interviews was thus within the indicative range of 20 to 30 suggested by Charmaz (2006) and Creswell (2007). Finally, the research findings were conceptualised through three major categories namely: *Destination-based knowledge*; *Role-based knowledge*; and *Career-based knowledge.* These categories represented the knowledge constructed from the empirical materials gathered from the tour guides. The three major categories were linked to a core category that was labelled *Occupational knowledge of tour guides.* The core category and its related major categories provided understandings on the lived experience of the research participants in being tour guides.

It is important to note that the GT research process is an iterative process. This means that the findings of each stage in the research process guide the next stage (Hardy, 2005). Additionally, based on the principles of theoretical sampling and the constant comparisons method, the GT research path is a non-linear path (Glaser and Strauss, 1967). The researcher does not collect all his/her raw data and then start the analysis. The data collection and analysis processes are done in parallel. The analysis is performed by going back and forth between the different levels of coding. An example of the GT analysis is explained in the next section.

Some of the respondents' excerpts elicited from the interviews conducted in the case study are represented below. The analysis is related to the first major category that emerged in this research, *Destination-based knowledge*.

Interview with Guide (1)

Guide (1), in describing the performance of Jordanian tourism, said:

> What is obviously seen by all, and the size of work shows that tourism in Jordan is growing in a big way, especially in this year 2008, but we can say that four years ago after the end of Iraqi war, it is seen that there is an increase in numbers of tourists but this year there is a huge increase compared to last year, a growing more than what normally happened every year, and this can be attributed to Petra and gaining accreditation as one of the Seven Wonders of the World; I think that it is the major reason of the increase in this year . . . Petra is a major reason, but Jordan as a

destination becomes preferred or wanted, why? Because it is a secure country and the reputation of Jordan is good . . . The place most developed and promoted is Petra wherever you go . . . from the plan and even before when the tourist buy the trip the first thing he reads is about Petra even the pictures in the brochure, the majority of them are for Petra and the websites are almost all for Petra but . . . there are a lot of other sites and the tourist discovers these when he comes to the country like Jerash . . . The tourist itinerary normally is seven days but if it is more, it will cover all parts of Jordan from the North to the South. There are more important sites. These seven days cover the top sites in Jordan, but there are different things such as the Dana nature reserve that could be visited and not all tourists visit it and it is ignored.

The above interview gave rise to a number of open general codes. The codes that are related to the first major category of this study (*destination-based knowledge*) are: working size; years' comparison; identifying core attractions; strength points; observing the infrastructure; ignoring other sites; lacking promotion; tourism distribution; tourism itinerary description.

Interview with Guide (6)

Guide (6) described the tourism performance of Jordan as:

I have worked as a tour guide since 2003. Tourism in Jordan is developing; as long as Jordan is a stable and safe destination the tourists' numbers are increasing . . . We were working successively in spring in April and May and June but in summer the numbers decrease so it is the low season. In September, October, and November we work very hard but in the last 2 years 2006–2007 even in the low season we had plenty of work . . . in the 1990s in 1993, 1994 I was still in the school . . . I remember that my Uncle who is a tour guide was talking about tourism and from his talking about this period it was a flourishing period.

The open codes raised from this expert in relation to the first major category are: tourism seasonality; political stability and tourism performance; telling about the past and the present, tour guiding and peer groups.

Interview with Guide (14)

Guide (14) said:

When I started to work in 1987 the number of tour guides was countable, you could count them on your fingers . . . My licence's number was 152, and the total number was 300 guides but now the number is increased to reach around 700 in 2008 . . . [There] was one bus company, sometimes we had to use the public buses but now there are about six transportation companies . . . The hotels, I remember that in Petra in the 1980s there were two . . . we used to put five or six tourists in the same room . . . Now Petra is full of hotels, Aqaba, and Amman as well . . . the numbers of tourists were not like today, now an increase and the nationalities of tourists now are various, before that we depended on German, Italian and French but now there are Japanese, Spanish now all nationalities from all over the world . . . In 2001, the tourists become scared from coming to

Sally Everett, Areej Shabib Aloudat and Ramesh Durbarry

this area because once you say Palestine it means Jordan as well, because of that there was no work for the tour guides. They started to search for other work some of them left the tourism sector and went abroad to work or found a job.

The open codes revealed from the previous quotation in relation to the first major category were: development of tourism services; tourism trend changes; unstable career; lack of tourism services; and political instability.

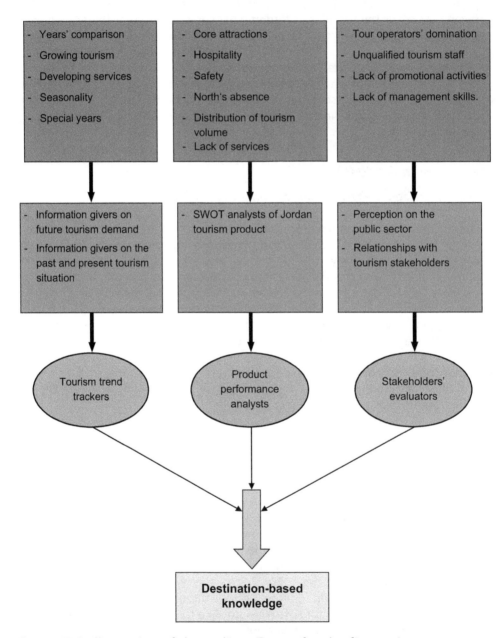

Figure 15.2 Illustration of the coding process for the first major category (*Destination-based knowledge*)

By continuing to examine the open codes and the comparison between incidents through the constant comparison method, more dimensions were revealed. Then, connections and relationships between the concepts started to take place in order to group them in higher level categories. This is the axial coding, the next coding step, where the descriptive concepts were raised to categories. Some of the labels given at this stage were: telling about the past, present and future performance; telling about other stakeholders; and observing tourism product.

The coding process then was continued with a selection of labels for the subcategories. The subcategories were given the labels of: tourism trends trackers; stakeholders' critical evaluators; and tourism product analysts. Those subcategories emerged from examining all the interviews and comparing data with data, data with concepts, and concepts with categories. Then the researcher started to find a label that would fit all the subcategories. This was the first major category that was named *Destination-based knowledge* of the tour guides. Figure 15.2 on the illustrates the first major category, its subcategories and concepts.

Chapter summary

- Grounded theory is a methodology employed to generate or develop a theory.
- It is a method which conceptualises data.
- The theory is grounded in data systematically gathered and analysed through the research process.
- Using the literature review provides a rich source of ideas that stimulate your thinking and suggest possible questions to conduct your research.
- Two main divergent perspectives have resulted in two different grounded theory approaches. One advocates that you should enter the research area with no prior defined research problem, and the problem will emerge from the area to be investigated, and the other that you should formulate the research questions from the beginning of the research, even if very broadly.
- A third notion is a constructionist view which recognises the mutual creation of knowledge by the viewer and the viewed.
- During data collection and analysis concepts will emerge from data analysis.
- Professional and personal experience may affect the theoretical sensitivity to provide meaning to the data collected.
- When you get involved in theory developing, gather data until you reach the saturation point.
- Generated theory or explanations can be verified through systematic data collection to revisit the theory.

Discussion questions

15.1 What are the basic principles of grounded theory?
15.2 Discuss the various approaches of grounded theory?
15.3 Using a research problem, discuss how you will use grounded theory.
15.4 What do you understand by the term *theoretical saturation*?

Further reading

Allan, G. (2003). 'A critique of using grounded theory as a research method', *Electronic Journal of Business Research Methods*, 2 (1), 1–10.

Bernard, H.R. and Ryan, G.W. (2010). *Analyzing Qualitative Data: Systematic Approaches*. Thousand Oaks, CA: Sage.

Bryant, A. (2002). 'Re-grounding grounded theory', *Journal of Information Technology Theory and Application*, 4, 25–42.

Charmaz, K. (2000). 'Grounded theory: Objectivist and constructivist methods'. In N.K. Denzin and Y.S. Lincoln (eds), *Handbook of Qualitative Research*, 2nd edition. Thousand Oaks, CA: Sage, pp. 509–535.

Charmaz, K. (2006). *Constructing Grounded Theory*, 2nd edition. London: Sage.

Strauss, A. and Corbin, J. (1994). 'Grounded theory methodology: An overview'. In N. Denzin and Y.S. Lincoln (eds), *Handbook of Qualitative Research*, 1st edition. Thousand Oaks, CA: Sage, pp. 273–284.

Thornberg, R. and Charmaz, K. (2012). 'Grounded theory'. In S.D. Lapan, M. Quartaroli and F. Reimer (eds), *Qualitative Research: An Introduction to Methods and Designs*. San Francisco, CA: John Wiley/Jossey–Bass, pp. 41–68.

Chapter 16

Analysing qualitative data using NVivo

Sally Everett and Areej Shabib Aloudat

Key questions

- Should I use computer software to analyse my data?
- Where do I start? Which one should I use?
- How does it work?
- Where can I go for help?

16.0 Chapter objectives

After studying this chapter, you will be able to:

- identify and understand which computer software for coding is appropriate or not;
- understand how qualitative data analysis software works;
- use software to analyse data; and
- confidently undertake qualitative data analysis.

16.1 Analysing qualitative data

It is important to give some attention to the emergence of new technology-informed ways of analysing data. There are a number of different computer programs that can help you analyse qualitative data. The most common are: ATLAS.ti, HyperRESEARCH and QSR NVivo (see Table 16.1). These are often referred to as 'computer-aided qualitative data analysis software' packages (CAQDAS) and are useful if you have a

Table 16.1 Types of qualitative analysis software package

Name	Functions and use	Further details
Word processor (MS Word)	Writing, note-making, transcriptions, annotations, memos, searches, managing multiple and long documents and formats, linking, hypertext.	www.microsoft.com
ATLAS.ti	Theory building using VISE – Visualisation, Integration, Serendipity, Exploration. Managing a wide range of materials, generating texts and memos, building codes. Creating visual representations. Building theories. Hypertext linkages, geo-coding, multimedia files, pdf support available.	www.atlasti.com
HyperRESEARCH	Managing multimedia materials and text. Use for code and retrieval operations, theory building, generating text files, memos and annotations. Hyperlink linkages available and work sharing with team members.	www.researchware. com
QSR NVivo	Works with all sorts of materials that can be stored, coded and linked using 'nodes'. Allows deep analysis of data using powerful search, query and visualisation tools. Uncover subtle connections, add your insights and ideas as you work, rigorously justify findings, and share work. (The software is regularly updated.)	www.qsrinternational. com/products_nvivo

lot of data and a large number of documents (and even images and film these days) to analyse. But, be aware that it will take you time to learn how to effectively use the software and often projects do not have enough time set aside for this kind of training and learning. However, once you have set up your project in the software and uploaded the documents, the process of analysis is often easier, quicker and more methodical.

The basic functions in most of the programs outlined include storage of all relevant data, importing files, text editing, note and memo taking, coding, text retrieval and code (node)/category manipulation. Increasingly, the software allows the researcher to create visual diagrams, models and presentations so relationships are easy to present and articulate.

16.2 Using QSR NVivo

Although there is some variation among the software packages available, the principles are very similar, therefore QSR NVivo is used as the example to outline how you might like to use software. It is recommended that you obtain the official manual for the software and attend a training workshop if you are planning to use it. A useful outline of NVivo is presented in Veal (2011, Chapter 16).

It is a very complex and sophisticated package, so this section will just outline the components and hopefully give you an idea whether it is appropriate for you to use. Useful texts to refer to are Bazeley (2007) and the guide to NVivo 11 (latest version at the time of writing) at www.qsrinternational.com/nvivo-training. Brief notes about how to get started and use NVivo are offered here, and a breadcrumb line (> >) is provided to give you the key steps to get started and perform the basic functions.

16.2.1 Starting a project in NVivo – first steps

- You must install NVivo on your computer. To launch it, click on the icon and give the project a title (the title of your research project). You should then see the NVivo workspace (see Figure 16.1).
- Download a copy of the *Getting Started Guide* for your version of NVivo. There is also an example project which will help you familiarise yourself with the software.
- Format all of your documents (transcripts, etc.) using consistent paragraph styles to support auto coding. You can do the formatting in Microsoft Word before import, or in NVivo after import.
- With audio, video or picture data, consider any editing requirements before import. Try to avoid uploading large media files.
- Upload all relevant documents (transcripts, proposals, interview guides, pictures and field notes) by clicking on *Import Internals* and browse and click all of your primary sources (documents in text (.txt), rich text (.rtf), portable document format (.pdf) or Word (.doc), image formats, and so on).
- Create *Import Externals* for links to files that you cannot import – handwritten diaries, books, PowerPoint presentations, and so on. You can provide a description of the file, or provide a link to a file on your computer or link to a web page.
- *Create* or *Import Memos* to record your thoughts and observations. It is important to keep research and field notes.

Title bar

Menu

Folders

List of all imported
documents

Navigation view

Status bar

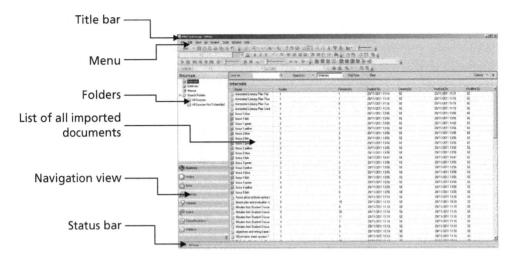

Figure 16.1 The NVivo workspace (example student project)

Source: Herman (2012)

You can create new folders to arrange and organise your work. You are also able to 'import internals' (documents/files) at any time during your project. Double-click to open the file from the document list.

To add notes to videos or pictures (media files) double-click to bring up *Detail View* and notes can be made by the side and you can highlight parts of the image to link memos and notes to in this same view.

16.2.2 Memos

Memos are imported or created in the same way as documents and are stored in the *Memos* folder. A memo may be about your project as a whole or it could be 'linked' to a particular project item. They are important aspects of your research process, especially with a grounded theory approach. To create a linked memo while working in a source in NVivo go to the *Links* menu, click the *Memo Link* option > Click the *Link to New Memo* option > The *New Memo* dialog box is displayed > Enter a name and description, then click *OK*.

16.2.3 Coding in NVivo (using nodes)

To make sense of your data, you need to set up a coding system. NVivo allows you to create and use nodes as part of 'tree nodes'. You should click on the *Node* tab in the navigation bar and this allows you to create new nodes or code your data with existing nodes (or codes/themes/categories). You can also add 'child nodes' to the main tree node by returning to the list of nodes and creating a new node under the main 'parent' node. Free floating concepts not linked to a tree structure are called 'free nodes'.

The *Attributes* folder will allow you to sort and add values. You can create a case to gather all the information related to a particular research participant, site, institution or other object of your focus. Unlike other nodes, cases can have attributes such as 'gender', 'age', 'location'. Attributes enable you to compare cases using demographic variables. For example, you could create a case for 'Bob' and assign the attributes 'male' and 'urban'. In a focus group interview, you could code everything Bob said at the case called 'Bob'. If you do this for all focus group participants, you can use queries to ask questions such as: what did the men say? Was there a difference between urban or rural participants?

To code document content you need to drag and drop. Open the document you want to code (*Detail View*) > open the required node folder to display the nodes in *List View* > if required, re-arrange the views for easy coding on the *View* menu, click *Detail View* > *Right*: select the content you want to code and drag it to the required node (see Figure 16.2).

To code at a new node you need to go to the *Coding* toolbar, select the *Name* option from the *Code At* drop-down list > enter a name for the new node > from the drop-down list, select the location for the node > click the *Code* button. The content is coded at the node. If you open the node, you can see coded content. For multimedia files and images, you can select a section in detail view and assign codes in the same way.

Coding strips are often useful to see how documents have been coded. Often the same data can be assigned a number of different codes. In NVivo, coding stripes are coloured bars that enable you to see the nodes for documents, the attributes of content coded at a case (gender, age, and so on), and coding by different researchers. To display these useful coding stripes you need to open the required source > under the *View* menu, click *Coding Stripes* > click the *Selected Items* option to choose specific nodes, attribute values or users. You can also choose a pre-defined selection such as *Nodes Most Coding* or *Nodes Recently Coding*.

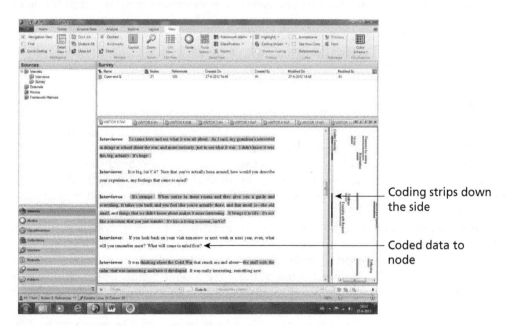

Figure 16.2 Coding data and coding strips

Source: Hermann (2012)

To open a node and see all the references that have been coded there, go to *Navigation View* and click on *Nodes* > click the required node type > in *List View*, double-click the required node > it is opened in *Detail View* with the *Reference* tab displayed.

If you wish to interrogate your data, you need to set up and save queries. There are a few types that are reached by going to *Navigation View*, click the *Queries* button > click the *New* toolbar button > select the *Query Type*. This allows you to undertake content, discourse or domain analysis.

Query	Function
Text search query	Lists all sources that contain specified text. This can provide a quick way of coding your sources – you can search for words and code the occurrences at a particular node.
Word frequency query	Lists words and the number of times they occur in selected items.
	Seeing which words appear most frequently can help you to identify themes and concepts. This is content analysis at the most basic level.
Coding query	Gathers content based on how it was coded. For example, show me all the content where 'women' talked about 'personal goals'.
Matrix coding query	Creates a matrix of nodes based on search criteria. For example, show me 'attitudes about volunteering by age group'.
Compound query	Combines text and coding queries – searches for specified text in or near coded content.
Coding comparison query	Compares the coding of two researchers or two groups of researchers.

16.2.4 Displaying your data

Whether you are using software or not, it is very important that you display and present your data and findings clearly and effectively. Often this is done with charts, graphs, tables, model diagrams, as well as clearly displayed quotations. The final presentation of your work is often an indication of the quality of the final piece of work. Charts also allow you to test hypotheses, assess relationships and look at patterns.

NVivo allows you to display your data in numerous ways with models and charts. All of these can be printed or exported. To create a model, go to *Navigation View* and click the *Models* button > on the *Main* toolbar, click the *New* button > click the *Dynamic Model in This Folder* button > the *New Model* dialog box is displayed > enter a name in the *Name* field > if required, enter a description in the *Description* field > click *OK*.

The example model shows how much data have been coded to which nodes (see Figures 16.3 and 16.4).

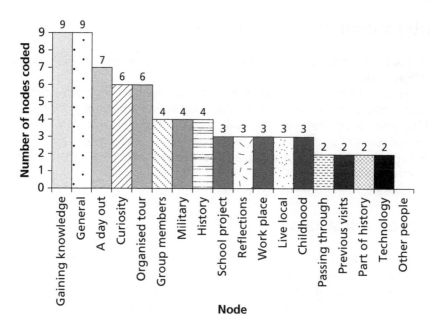

Figure 16.3 Model of nodes, from a project looking at the purposes of visiting Cold War tourism sites

Source: Hermann (2012)

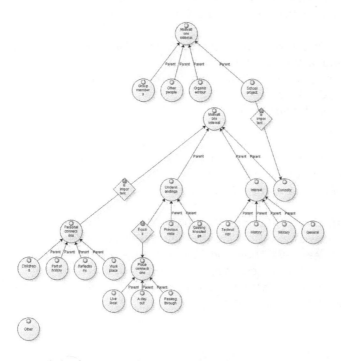

Figure 16.4 Model of tree and child nodes, from a project looking at the purposes of visiting Cold War tourism sites

Source: Hermann (2012)

Chapter summary

- There are a number of different computer programs that can help you analyse qualitative data.
- The basic functions in most of the programs used in qualitative data analysis include storage of relevant data, importing files, text editing, note and memo taking, coding, text retrieval and code (node)/category manipulation.
- To make sense of your data, you need to set up a coding system.
- It is very important that you display and present your data and findings clearly and effectively.

Discussion questions

16.1 What are the advantages and disadvantages of using computer software for qualitative data analysis?
16.2 What is the difference between a tree node and a free node in NVivo?
16.3 What are the best ways of presenting qualitative data?

Further reading

Bazeley, P. (2007). *Qualitative Data Analysis Using NVivo*. London: Sage.

Coffey, A. and Atkinson, P. (1996). *Making Sense of Qualitative Data.* Thousand Oaks, CA: Sage.

Denscombe, M. (1998). *The Good Research Guide: For Small-Scale Social Research Projects*. Buckingham: Open University Press.

Denzin, N. and Lincoln, Y.S. (eds) (2000). *Handbook of Qualitative Research*, 2nd edition. Thousand Oaks, CA: Sage.

Fisher, M. (1997). *Qualitative Computing: Using Software for Qualitative Data Analysis*. Aldershot: Ashgate.

Gibbs, G.R. (2007). *Analysing Qualitative Data*. London: Sage.

Miles, M.B and Huberman, M.A. (1994). *Qualitative Data Analysis: An Expanded Sourcebook*, 2nd edition. London: Sage.

Patton, M.Q. (2002). *Qualitative Research and Evaluation Methods*, 3rd edition. London: Sage.

Ritchie, J., Spencer, L. and O'Connor, W. (2003). 'Carrying out qualitative analysis'. In J. Ritchie and J. Lewis (eds), *Qualitative Research Practice: A Guide for Social Science Students and Researchers*. Thousand Oaks, CA: Sage, pp. 219–263.

Robson, C. (2002). *Real World Research*, 2nd edition. Oxford: Blackwell.

Veal, A.J. (2011). *Research Methods for Leisure and Tourism: A Practical Guide*, 4th edition. Harlow: Pearson Education.

Chapter 17

Analysing quantitative data

Ramesh Durbarry

Rushie, a final year student, came to see me with her end of year results and showing her disappointment at the grade she obtained for her dissertation. She had with her a copy of the dissertation and insisted that I have a look, questioning why my colleague had given her an average mark despite the fact that she had collected her data using an onsite administered questionnaire, analysed the data and interpreted it using bar charts, pie charts, histograms and scatter plot diagrams.

I then asked her whether her findings were for the sample she selected or for the whole population. I also asked her what the implications of her results were. She hesitated to answer. She then replied that she did not give that much consideration to the implications and to generalising the results for the population.

Can you advise her about what she should have done?

17.0 Chapter objectives

In Chapter 9 we looked at how primary data can be collected using various surveys and questionnaire-based surveys. In this chapter we now introduce statistical tools that can be used to analyse raw data collected. Application of statistical analysis enables us to 'make sense of the data'. For instance, we can summarise the data in such a way that the reader can get a first glimpse of the phenomenon under study and paint a brief picture.

A common mistake by students is that they often rush to test the hypotheses that have been specified without having a feel for the data. It is perhaps more important to use simple *descriptive statistics* to simply check whether the data have correctly been entered or whether some patterns or trends can be seen emerging from the data.

Another mistake which students tend to do is deriving conclusions based on the descriptive statistics from the sample. Remember that the primary purpose of using samples was because of time and cost that the whole population could not be included in the study. However, any analysis should shed light on the phenomenon for the population. It is this reason that we make use of *inferential statistics* to make inferences for the population.

Many studies are also conducted using secondary data. In this chapter we present an elementary regression analysis to show how we can test hypotheses and associations between variables using time-series, cross-section and panel data.

After studying this chapter, you will be able to:

- use descriptive statistics on the data collected;
- analyse relationships between variables;
- use inferential statistics and conduct hypothesis testing; and
- introduce regression analysis and data reduction techniques for further analysis.

17.1 Descriptive analysis

Data that have been coded and entered into a spreadsheet, such as in Excel or SPSS, are in raw form. They can be summarised visually (by using graphs) or using statistical measures such as averages to get a first feel of the data. We use a hypothetical dataset generated from an onsite survey at *The Resto* restaurant for the following questions:

1 **Gender:** $\square_1$ **Male** $\square_2$ **Female**
2 **How old are you? Tick the appropriate box.**

    $\square_1$ **15–24** $\square_2$ **25–34** $\square_3$ **35–44** $\square_4$ **45+**

3 **What is your monthly income? £_____**
4 **How satisfied are you with the dining experience at The Resto today? Please circle your answer.**

Very dissatisfied	Dissatisfied	Neutral	Satisfied	Very satisfied
1	2	3	4	5

(Note the coding of the responses.)

The hypothetical data are illustrated in Figure 17.1. Notice the variables created in the first row:

Respondent: there are 30 respondents, numbered 1 to 30.

AgeGroup: 1 for age group 15–24, 2 for age group 25–34, and so on.

Income: the monthly income in pounds.

Satisfaction: the level of satisfaction selected by the respondent.

Let's say from the data we want to get an overview of the age composition of the respondents in the sample. If we just plot the data as they are by using a bar chart, we will get an illustration as shown in Figure 17.2. But what can you deduce?

From Figure 17.2 very little can be concluded. In fact, the best we can do is to count the bars, for example, we can see that there are five respondents who are in the age group 45+. Hence, in its present form, the visual representation is not helpful at all and this becomes meaningless and cumbersome if we have, let say, over 1,000 respondents.

Microsoft Excel - Data1

	A	B	C	D	E	F	G
1	Respondent	AgeGroup	Gender	Income	Satisfaction		
2	1	1	1	3000	3		
3	2	2	1	4500	4		
4	3	3	2	2200	2		
5	4	2	1	5000	3		
6	5	1	2	3000	2		
7	6	3	2	5500	3		
8	7	4	2	2700	4		
9	8	1	1	3200	4		
10	9	2	1	4100	3		
11	10	2	2	2800	3		
12	11	3	2	3100	4		
13	12	3	1	2600	4		
14	13	2	2	4000	4		
15	14	2	2	3000	4		
16	15	3	1	2000	5		
17	16	3	2	1800	4		
18	17	3	2	7000	5		
19	18	2	2	5000	5		
20	19	4	1	6500	4		
21	20	4	1	3200	3		
22	21	4	1	4000	4		
23	22	2	1	2500	4		
24	23	3	2	2400	3		
25	24	3	2	2700	5		
26	25	2	2	2800	4		
27	26	3	1	3000	5		
28	27	4	1	3100	4		
29	28	3	1	3300	5		
30	29	2	1	3500	3		
31	30	2	2	2400	5		
32							

Sheet1 / Sheet2 / Sheet3

Figure 17.1 A hypothetical dataset on dining experience

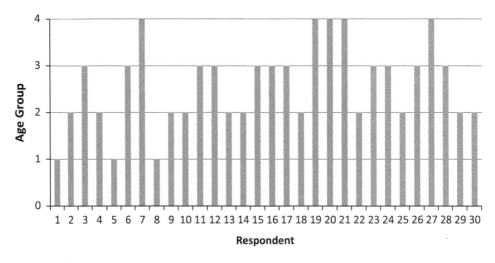

Figure 17.2 A bar chart for age group

Such data representation is better depicted when on the x-axis we have the age group and on the y-axis the number of respondents (frequency) in each age group. This is done by counting the number of respondents in each age group. The final outcome then gives use the distribution of the data. This is called the frequency distribution of the variable, for example, as shown in Table 17.1.

From this summarised data we can then produce a more meaningful bar chart, as illustrated in Figure 17.3.

To learn how to produce such bar chart in Excel, refer to Levine et al. (2017). With SPSS, the production of the bar chart is simpler, as illustrated in the next chapter. From Figure 17.3, it is much easier to describe the age profile of the respondents: for instance, we can infer that most of the respondents are from the two age groups 25–34 and 35–44. This graph has substance in it. You can also use a pie chart to illustrate the data. The type of visual illustration you select should be able to communicate a clear picture of the data. To do so you need to present the data in such a way that the graph provides substance and statistics. Clarity and precision will help to paint a picture of the data.

Table 17.1 Frequency distribution of age group

Age group	Frequency
1	3
2	11
3	11
4	5

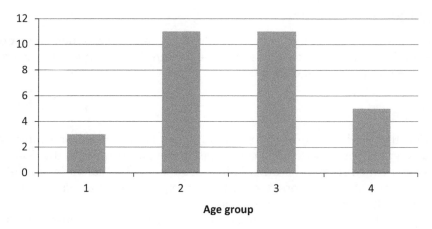

Figure 17.3 Frequency distribution of age group

Practical tips

Always use several dimensions when illustrating your data, such as bar chart, pie chart and stack bar chart.

17.2 Measures of central tendency

To better summarise the information on one variable into a single number, the three measures of central tendency – mean, mode and median – are very practical to use (they are often called *measures of location*).

17.2.1 Mean

The mean, also called arithmetic average, is the most widely used measure of central tendency. It is computed by adding up all the scores then dividing by the number of scores. The formula is given by:

$$\bar{X} = \frac{\sum_{i=1}^{n} X_i}{n}$$

Where $\bar{X}$ (pronounced X bar), X_i is the ith score for the variable X and n is the number of scores. Mean is affected by extreme values.

Can you calculate the mean monthly income in above hypothetical example? You should get $\bar{X}$ = £3,463.33

17.2.2 Mode

Mode is the value that occurs most frequently. There can be more than one mode for a variable: for instance, in the above example we can find that there are two modes for the age groups 25–34 and 35–44.

17.2.3 Median

Median is the middle point of the distribution and is the fiftieth percentile. When re-arranging the data in ascending order, half of the observations in the distribution fall below the median and the other half above the median. For variables that have an even number of observations, the median is computed as the average of the values associated with the two middle observations.

In normal distributions (observed as a bell-shaped curve), the mean, mode and median are clustered around the same point (see Figure 17.4).

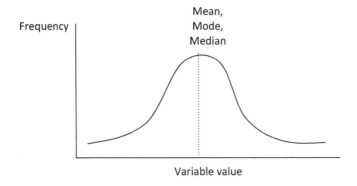

Figure 17.4 Normal distribution curve

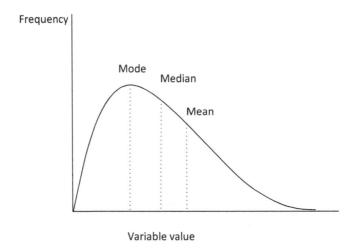

Figure 17.5 Positively skewed distribution

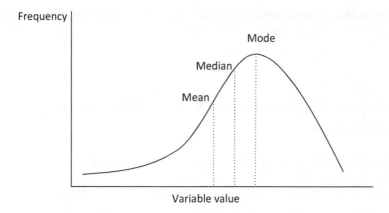

Figure 17.6 Negatively skewed distribution

The distribution can be skewed when the frequencies are not evenly distributed about the central point. If the mode is less than the median which is less than the mean, the distribution is said to be *positively skewed* (values are clustered around the lower values, see Figure 17.5). When the mode is greater than the median which is greater than the mean, the distribution is said to be *negatively skewed* (values are clustered around the upper values, see Figure 17.6). The variability within the data can be examined by looking at the dispersion of the data. This leads to the discussion on measures of variation.

17.3 Measures of variation

The measures of variation are commonly known as the measures of spread and consider the dispersion or variability in the variable; they are the variance, standard deviation, range, lower quartile, upper quartile and interquartile.

The range is a very simple statistic – it is the difference between the smallest and largest value in the dataset. The range can be influenced by a single extreme value in the set and can be misleading in analysing the distribution of the data. A better measure is the interquartile range, which is the difference between the lower quartile (first quartile) and the upper quartile (third quartile). It is called the midspread, as only the middle 50 per cent of the data is considered. This measure can also distort the picture depending on the degree of the clustering of the data, as the first quarter and fourth quarter of the data are ignored.

The variance is the average of the squared deviation from the mean. The variance for the sample is given by s^2 and computed as follows:

$$s^2 = \sum_{i}^{n} \frac{(X_i - \bar{X})^2}{n-1}$$

If all the values are identical, the variance will be zero; in fact, the greater the dispersion, the greater the variance. Variance has no unit.

A better measure of the spread in the data is the standard variation, which identifies the difference between the values of a variable and its mean. It is simply the square root of the variance and the obtained value is expressed in the original units. The standard deviation indicates by how much the value are dispersed from the mean.

$$s = \sqrt{s^2}$$

17.4 Relationship between two variables – cross-tabulation

Cross-tabulation can be used to observe any preliminary pattern or relationship. From the dataset, some preliminary investigation of the relationship between two or more variables can be performed. For example, a bivariate table can be constructed to cross-tabulate two variables. Using a hypothetical dataset, Table 17.4 shows the responses for 150 respondents who took part in an onsite survey at a restaurant where they were asked whether they were satisfied with their dining experience against the quality of the food.

From Table 17.2 we can observe that there is a positive relationship between respondents who agreed that they had a very satisfied dining experience with those who agreed that the quality of the food was value for money. There is a clear indication also that those respondents who disagreed that the quality of food was value for money also agreed that they had a unsatisfactory dining experience.

Cross-tabulation can also be carried out with three variables – for example, we can analyse the responses by gender as well – but the analysis becomes more tedious.

17.5 Inferential statistics

Descriptive statistics are used to describe the population or sample that is being studied. The summary statistics obtained from the group cannot be used to generalise to

Table 17.2 Dining experience satisfaction by the quality of food

		The quality of food was value for money					Total
		Strongly disagree	Disagree	Neutral	Agree	Strongly agree	
Overall, I was very satisfied with my dining experience	Strongly disagree	8	6	3	1	1	**19**
	Disagree	2	4	2	1	0	**9**
	Neutral	1	1	2	5	1	**10**
	Agree	2	3	3	14	43	**65**
	Strongly agree	0	4	1	12	30	**47**
	Total	**13**	**18**	**11**	**33**	**75**	**150**

any larger group. To be able to make inferences or predictions about a population, based on a sample, we make use of *inferential statistics*.

First, let us define what is meant by a population and a sample. A *population* is the total set of individuals or objects which is under consideration. We use parameters to describe the characteristics of the population – for example, the mean of the data is denoted by μ (Greek alphabet *mu*), and is computed as follows:

$$\mu = \frac{\Sigma_i^N X_i}{N} = \frac{X_1 + X_2 + \ldots\ldots\ldots + X_N}{N}$$

where N is the population size and *i* is the *i*th individual or observation.

A sample is a subset of the population under investigation which has been chosen for analysis. The measure to summarise the sample is called a *statistic* – for example, the mean of the sample is denoted by $\bar{X}$ and computed as:

$$\bar{X} = \frac{\Sigma_i^n X_i}{n}$$

where *n* is the sample size.

As illustrated in Figure 17.7, from the population, based on the sampling process, the researcher will select a sampling frame from which a sample is then selected. For example, if we are conducting a study on tourists' expenditure in London, the sampling frame would be tourists visiting some areas in London and a sample chosen using a street survey of 2,000 tourists. Statistics from the sample will be used to infer or make predictions for all tourists (population) visiting London.

17.5.1 Level of confidence

The value that we obtain on a statistic from the sample is called a point estimate. Although we use point estimates as the best guess for the population parameter, it is very unlikely that the population parameter will have the same exact value as the statistic based on only one sample. This point estimate will depend on the sampling

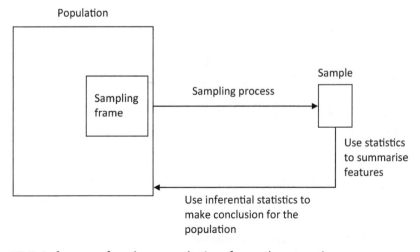

Figure 17.7 Inference for the population from the sample

process and sample size. We are never 100 per cent sure. In such as a case, based on the point estimate we use confidence level to provide information on how close the population parameter is. The conventional levels are 90 per cent, 95 percent and 99 per cent. Using the central limit theorem, for a 90 per cent confidence interval, it implies that in 90 out 100 cases we are confident that the true value of the parameter will lie between the interval values estimated when samples of the same size are estimated. The interval values depend on the standard error of the statistic. For example, if the variance of the population is known, the standard error of the sample mean, $SE_{\bar{x}}$, is given by $\frac{\delta^2}{n}$, where δ^2 is the population variance. The confidence interval for the population mean, μ is given by:

$$\bar{X} - z.SE_{\bar{x}} \le \mu \le \bar{X} + z.SE_{\bar{x}}$$

where z is the level of confidence which can be obtained from the Normal Distribution Table. For example, for 95 per cent level of confidence, the value of z is 1.96. The interval values are then computed as illustrated in Figure 17.8.

When the population variance is unknown we use the Student t-distribution instead of the normal distribution. The confidence interval is then given by:

$$\bar{X} - t_{(\alpha/2, n-1)}.SE_{\bar{x}} \le \mu \le \bar{X} + t_{(\alpha/2, n-1)}.SE_{\bar{x}}$$

where α is the level of significance, $n-1$ is the degrees of freedom and $SE_{\bar{x}}$ is given by:

$$SE_{\bar{x}} = \sqrt{\frac{s^2}{n}} = \frac{s}{\sqrt{n}}$$

For a confidence level of 95 per cent, $\alpha = 0.05$, $\alpha/2 = 0.025$. As the sample gets large, the t-distribution is the same as the normal distribution.

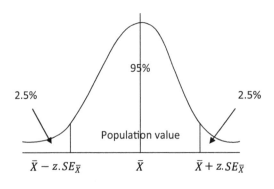

Figure 17.8 Normal curve and confidence intervals

17.6 Hypothesis testing

A hypothesis is a claim that is made about the population parameter, for example (Case 1):

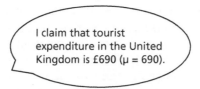

I claim that tourist expenditure in the United Kingdom is £690 ($\mu = 690$).

Also, we can make a claim on the relationship between two or variables – for example, claiming that in the hospitality industry the salary of males differs from the salary of females (Case 2).

How do we test a claim?

17.6.1 Type I and Type II errors

First we need to understand how to state a hypothesis. There are two kinds of hypotheses: null hypothesis and alternative hypothesis. The null hypothesis (denoted H_0) is a statement that no difference exists between the parameter and the statistic being compared to it. The null hypothesis (denoted H_1) is referred to a *status quo* situation. The alternative hypothesis is the opposite of the null hypothesis, it challenges the *status quo*.

For Case 1, we specify the hypotheses as follows:

Null hypothesis $\quad\quad\quad H_0: \mu = 690$

Alternative hypothesis $\quad H_1: \mu \neq 690$

For Case 2, we can test whether there is a gender difference in earnings:

Null hypothesis $\quad\quad\quad H_0: \mu_M = \mu_F$ or $H_0: \mu_M - \mu_F = 0$ (i.e. no wage differentials)

Alternative hypothesis $\quad H_1: \mu_M \neq \mu_F$ or $H_0: \mu_M - \mu_F \neq 0$ (i.e. there are wage differentials)

where μ_M and μ_F are the population mean earnings for male and female employees respectively in the hospitality industry.

Errors can occur while testing the hypotheses due to sampling errors. These are referred to as Type I and Type II errors. A Type I error is committed when a true null hypothesis is rejected (this is the value of the level of significance chosen by the researcher). A Type II error is where one fails to reject a false null hypothesis

The claim can be tested by selecting a sample and collecting data. In the former case, we can select a sample and estimate the average tourist expenditure of the sample. Let's say we found that it is £680 ($\bar{X} = 680$). What we now want to determine is whether the result could have been due to chance. How confident are we to accept the claim that the population tourist expenditure is £690? We can accept or reject the hypothesis on the basis of sampling information alone. A representative sample should have a similar variation to the population. We now must assess whether the difference between the point estimate we obtained from the sample is statistically significant or insignificant from the claim we are making. If we do the calculations ourselves then we will need a set of statistical tables to allow us to judge the significance of the figure we have obtained. Most statistical software uses a probability of 5 per cent (equivalent to saying 95 per cent confidence interval), indicated by '$p = 0.05$', implying that the probability that this could have occurred by chance is 5 per cent. The calculation is run by the software programme and the result generated is called the test statistic. The software will also report the probability at which the value is significant. If the probability of your test statistic having occurred by chance alone is less than 0.05, we may reject the null hypothesis and claim that there is 95 per cent chance that the population mean is not equal to £690. The test statistic is said to be statistically significant.

When you are testing a relationship, if the test statistic's reported probability is less than 0.05, then you can conclude that relationship is statistically significant.

Practical tips: how to conduct hypothesis testing?

1 State the null hypothesis. Normally in the null hypothesis, parameters are used and always contain the 'equal to' sign. For example, if we are testing that male earnings are the same as female earnings, we set the null hypothesis as follows:

$$H_0: \mu_M - \mu_F = 0$$

2 State the alternative hypothesis as:

$$H_1: \mu_M - \mu_F \neq 0$$

3 Choose the level of significance, for example, $\alpha = 5\%$.
4 Compute the test statistic (this will depend on the hypothesis being tested).
5 Either obtain the critical test value from the statistical table or compare the probability value with the chosen level of significance.
6 Interpret the results; for example, if the obtained probability is less than the chosen level of significance, reject the null hypothesis and conclude that the alternative hypothesis is supported.

In the next chapter we show how to use SPSS to conduct hypothesis testing.

17.7 Correlation

In many instances we are interested in measuring the strength of the relationship between two variables. Pearson's correlation coefficient can be used to examine the linear strength between two variables, which can be ordinal variables (e.g. attitude, preference scores) or scale variables (e.g. age, income). The coefficient reveals the magnitude and direction of the linear relationship.

It is very useful to have a visual display of the variables plotted against each other. This can be done by using a scatter diagram. The population correlation coefficient is denoted by ρ (Rho), while the sample correlation coefficient is denoted by r and is used to measure the strength of the linear relationship in the sample observations. The correlation coefficient varies from -1 to $+1$, where -1 is a perfect negative correlation and $+1$ a perfectly positive correlation. When it is equal to 0, it implies no correlation or relationship. It is a unit-free measure. The closer it is to -1, the stronger the negative linear relationship; the closer it is to $+1$, the stronger the positive linear relationship; and the closer it is to 0, the weaker the linear relationship. The computed correlation coefficient can also be tested whether it is statistically significant or not.

We can test the strength of the linear association between two variables as follows:

Null hypothesis $\qquad$ H_0: $\rho = 0$

Alternative hypothesis $\quad$ H_1: $\rho \neq 0$

17.8 Regression analysis

Many students make the mistake of interpreting the correlation coefficient as implying causation. If we have two variables, X and Y, the correlation coefficient of, let's say 0.8, implies that there is a strong positive relationship between X and Y. To be able to discuss whether X causes Y, we need to understand regression analysis.

The sign of the correlation coefficient, r, tells us the direction of the relation. Regression analysis is more powerful that correlation analysis in that it explains the relationship between two or more variables. The aim of regression analysis is to explain the variation in the dependent variable (Y) by the independent variable(s) (Xs). It can be used to test models, tests whether the relationships are statistically significant and can also be used for prediction purposes. We can predict the values of the dependent variable (the variable we are interested in) based on the values of the dependent variable(s). Regression analysis can be simple or multiple. A simple regression model has only two variables and takes the following form:

$$Y_i = \beta_0 + \beta_1 X_i + e_i \tag{1}$$

where Y_i is the dependent variable and X_i is the independent variable, also called explanatory variable. i is the value of X and Y of the ith observation and e_i is an error term which is discussed further below and follows a normal distribution with variance 1 and zero mean. β_0 and β_1 are called parameters and are known as regression coefficients. β_0 is the intercept value of the equation line and β_1 is the change in the dependent variable, Y, for a unit change in the independent variable, X.

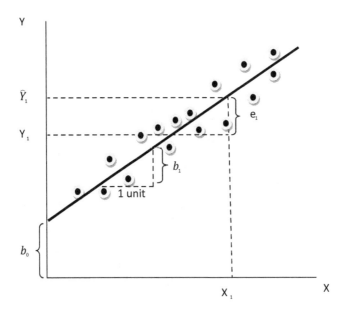

Figure 17.9 Regression analysis

The regression equation is estimated by ordinary least squares to find the line of best fit, see Figure 17.9. Under this method, the line of best fit is obtained by minimising the total squared errors with respect to fit β_0 and β_1 (for further details, see Gujarati, 2003; Gujarati and Porter, 2009).

b_0 and b_1 are the estimates of β_0 and β_1 respectively.

If we estimate the regression model, we will obtain the following:

$$\hat{Y}_i = b_0 + b_1 X_i \tag{2}$$

where $\hat{Y}_i$ is the computed value of Y_1 when the values of b_0 and b_1 are substituted in equation (2) (called *fitted value*). For example, when the value of X is X_1, the fitted value of Y when the estimates of β_0 and β_1 are b_0 and b_1 respectively is $\hat{Y}_1$. The difference between the actual value of Y and the fitted value $(Y_1 - \hat{Y}_1)$ is e_1, the error or residual. Note that $\Sigma e_i = 0$.

In this type of model, we are assuming that X causes Y. The estimated coefficients can be tested whether they are statistically significant or not by setting up the following hypotheses:

$H_0: \beta_0 = 0$

$H_1: \beta_0 \neq 0$

and

$H_0: \beta_1 = 0$

$H_1: \beta_1 \neq 0$

Multiple regression is a linear regression involving more than one independent variable and takes the following form:

$$Y_i = \beta_0 + \beta_1 X_{1i} + \beta_2 X_{2i} + \ldots\ldots\ldots + \beta_m X_{mi} + e_i$$

m is the number of independent variables.

The main assumptions of the regression model are that:

1 e_i is distributed with mean 0 and variable 1.
2 $\text{Var}(e_i) = \delta^2$ (homoscedasticity, that is the variance is constant).
3 Zero covariance between e_i and X variable.
4 No exact collinearity between the X variables, that is, no multicollinearity.
5 $\text{Cov}(e_i, e_j) = 0$ for $i \neq j$, that no serial correlation. (This is unlikely in our case, as we are using cross-section rather than time-series data.)

The first assumption is that the error term is normally distributed. This assumption simply says that variables which are excluded in the model, and therefore included in e_i, do not systematically affect the mean value of Y.

The second assumption states that the variance of the error term is constant. If this assumption is violated then the estimated coefficients will be inefficient. The third assumption is that there is no relationship between the X variables and the error term. The fourth assumption states that the Xs do not have an exact linear relationship; otherwise the estimates will be biased. The fifth assumption states that there is no serial correlation otherwise the estimated coefficients will be inefficient.

17.8.1 The coefficient of determination: R^2

The coefficient of determination in a two-variable regression measures the goodness of fit of the regression equation; that is, it gives the proportion of total variation in the dependent variable explained by the dependent variable. It is denoted by r^2. The value lies between 0 and 1.

In the multiple regression case, the coefficient of determination gives the proportion of total variation in the dependent variable explained by all the dependent variables together. It is denoted by R^2.

17.9 Factor analysis

Factor analysis is commonly used as a data reducing technique. It is conducted by computer software and you will need to take some training to better understand how to use this technique properly. The objective of using factor analysis is to reduce the number of variables into manageable numbers. The aim is to construct new variables based on the relationship between variables. Because in surveys you will obtain a series of variables which most probably might measure similar features, factor analysis can assist you to create new variables from the set of variables based on the relationship between the variables. There are sometimes many questions/statements in a questionnaire where the answers are positively correlated and the respondents tend to provide similar responses; for example, respondents who are satisfied with the quality of food tend to also be satisfied with the food presentation. In such cases, instead of having two variables, one variable can be constructed to represent both responses. The most frequently used approach is the *principal component analysis*. This method transforms a set of interrelated variables into a new set of composite variables. These composite variables are uncorrelated among them. These composite variables can be used for further analysis – for example, to perform regression analyses. A full explanation of factor analysis is beyond the scope of this textbook; interested readers can refer to Hair et al. (1998).

Chapter summary

- Descriptive analysis can be used to summarise the dataset.
- The three measures of central tendency commonly used are the mean, mode and median.
- When the distribution of the data is skewed or has extreme values, the mean is not an appropriate measure; it is better to use the median.
- The most commonly used measure of variation is the standard deviation and it is expressed in the units of the data.
- Inferential statistics are used to make inferences about the population.
- Confidence intervals consist of a range of values that the unknown population parameter lies within, given a specified probability.
- A hypothesis is a claim made about the population parameter.
- Correlation analysis measures the strength of linear association between two variables.
- Regression analysis is used to explain the variation in the dependent variable by the variation in one or more independent variables.
- Factor analysis is to reduce the number of variables into manageable numbers.

Discussion questions

17.1 Why the mean is not always a reliable measure of central tendency?
17.2 What is standard deviation?
17.3 What is the null hypothesis?
17.4 What is meant by *degree of freedom*?
17.5 (a) Using the following data, compute the mean and standard deviation?
        8254, 2365, 5653, 8738, 5527, 8664, 8686, 5767, 8769, 6789, 6609, 6867, 6868, 5232, 6652, 6579, 6070, 8098, 8923, 7823, 5283, 8589, 7522, 8666, 7689, 8005.
      (b) Compute a 90 per cent confidence interval for the mean.
      (c) Compute a 95 per cent confidence interval for the mean.
17.6 Referring to the case study at the beginning of this chapter, what course of actions would you suggest that Rushie could have taken?

Further reading

Gujarati, D. (2003). *Basic Econometrics*, 4th edition. New York: McGraw-Hill.
Hair, J.F., Anderson R.E., Tatham R.L. and Black, W.C. (1998). *Multivariate Data Analysis*, 5th edition. New Jersey: Prentice Hall.

Chapter 18

Analysing quantitative data using SPSS

Ramesh Durbarry

Key questions

- How do I conduct regression analysis?
- How do I check the validity of the results?
- What are the diagnostic tests?
- How do I conduct factor analysis?

18.0 Chapter objectives

This chapter make use the SPSS software to illustrate how to analyse data and perform basic tests to enrich your findings and conclusions. We show how to make use of inferential statistics so that you can provide an informed discussion for the phenomenon under study.

After studying this chapter, you will be able to:

- enter your data into SPSS;
- confidently perform basic statistical tests;
- test simple hypothesis;
- perform analysis of variance (ANOVA);
- conduct regression analysis;
- check the validity of the regression results; and
- conduct factor analysis.

18.1 Analysing quantitative data: descriptive measures, t-tests and ANOVA

After you have collected your completed questionnaires, it is recommended that you enter the data in a spreadsheet after you have properly coded them. You can use either Excel or SPSS or other software such as Microfit, Limdep, Eviews, among the many, to analyse your data. In this chapter, we explain how to use SPSS to summarise

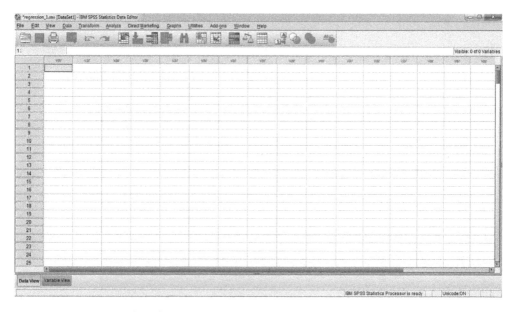

Figure 18.1 Example of an SPSS worksheet

your data, carry out confidence intervals for the mean, perform some simple tests such as the t-test and testing differences within groups (ANOVA), regression and factor analyses.

The SPSS window when you open the software looks as in Figure 18.1.

In the data editor, you can enter the data in a similar way to Excel. On the bottom left hand if you select *Variable View* you can enter the variable name and also provide a description of the variable in the *Label* column.

In our example, we use a case study where 70 employees were surveyed. The variables generated and entered using the data editor window are listed in Table 18.1. Please visit www.routledge.com/9780415673198 to access the file *wage.sav*.

Table 18.1 Variables and definitions for file *wage.sav*

Variables	Definitions
Ethnicgp	Ethnic group: 1 for White; 2 for Asian; 3 for Chinese and 4 for African
Gender	Gender of the respondent: 1 for male and 2 for female
Income	Annual gross salary (£)
Age	Age of the worker
Years	The number of years employed with the firm
Job Satisfaction	The level of job satisfaction

The data editor window will look as in Figure 18.2.

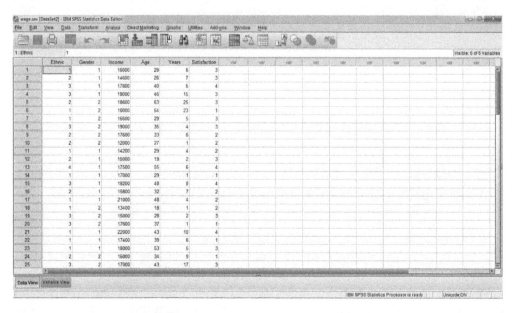

Figure 18.2 SPSS data editor page

The variable window will look as in Figure 18.3.

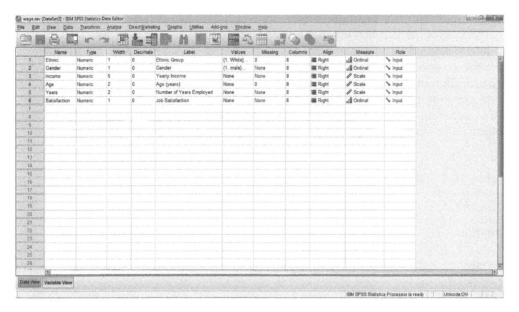

Figure 18.3 Variable window page in SPSS

Practical example: wage differentials

The file wage.sav shows personal data (such as gender, salary, age . . .) for 70 employees for a firm.
    Open the SPSS software and then open the file to view the data.
    How to open the file?

- *File > Open > Data.*
- *Select > wage.sav* (in the folder where you have stored the data).

How to save the file on your pen drive (F)?

- *File > Save As . . .*
- Choose your F-drive from the *Save in* drop-down menu.
- Enter file name and click on *Save*.

Click on the *Variable View* tab at the bottom of the screen to see descriptions for each variable.

To better understand how to use SPSS, let us conduct some tests and extract some information from the dataset to carry out some hypothesis testing.

Let's begin with the following:

1   To obtain descriptive statistics for the variables: Age, Yearly Income and Job Satisfaction, we select some SPSS commands as follows:

On the SPSS menu, perform the following:

Analyze

   Descriptive Statistics

      Frequencies

● Click the series needed (Age, Yearly Income and Job Satisfaction).
● Click on ⊡ to select the highlighted series.

The results should be as shown in Figure 18.4.

● Click on ▣Statistics, and click on *Quartiles, Std. Deviation, Variance, Range, Minimum, Maximum, S.E Mean, Mean, Median, Mode.*
● Click on *Continue.*
● Click on ▣Charts, for charts. You can select only one type of chart at a time. Select *Histogram* and click on *Continue.* You can try different charts in your own time.

Check the output file and you should obtain the answer shown in Table 18.2.

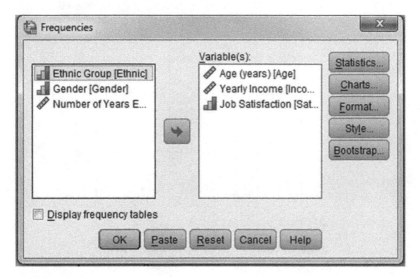

Figure 18.4 Frequency box editor

Table 18.2 Statistics output

		Age (years)	Yearly Income	Job Satisfaction
N	Valid	70	70	70
	Missing	0	0	0
Mean		39.13	16350.00	2.59
Std. Error of Mean		1.463	313.306	.128
Median		38.50	16000.00	3.00
Std. Deviation		12.238	2621.303	1.070
Variance		149.766	6871231.884	1.145
Range		45	14000	3
Minimum		18	12000	1
Maximum		63	26000	4
Sum		2739	1144500	181

The following histograms will be produced for the variables (Graphs 18.1 to 18.3):

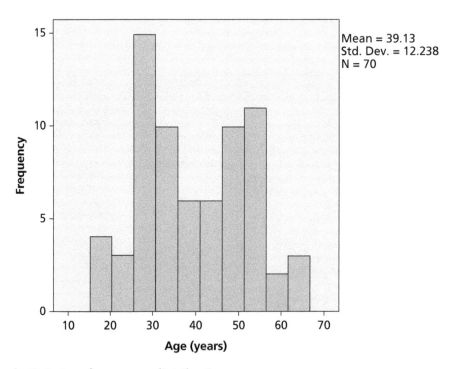

Graph 18.1 Age frequency distribution

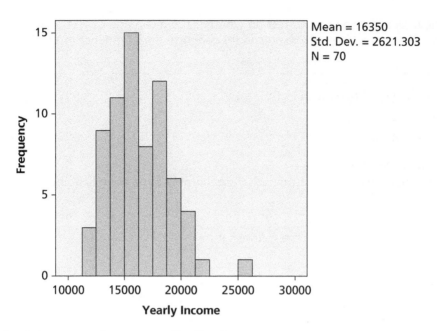

Graph 18.2 Income frequency distribution

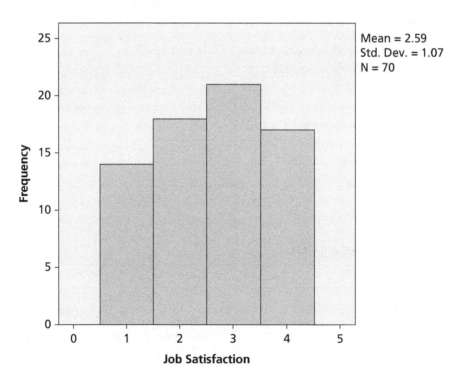

Graph 18.3 Job satisfaction frequency distribution

2   Now let's say we want to test (a) whether the mean age of all the employees is significantly different from 40 and (b) generate the confidence interval for Age.

This is a typical *t-test* with

$H_0 : A = 40$
$H_1 : A \neq 40$

'A' stands for Age
Confidence interval is automatically generated by SPSS while doing the t-test.

For this exercise, perform the following:

Analyze

    Compare Means

        One-Sample T Test . . .

- Click the series needed (*Age*).
- Click on ▣ to select the highlighted series.
- Enter the *Test Value*, which is the value of the parameter in $H_0 = 40$ in our case.
- The *Level of Confidence* (95 per cent by default) can be changed by clicking on *Options*.

You should get the results shown in Tables 18.3a and 18.3b.

Table 18.3a One-Sample Statistics

	N	Mean	Std. Deviation	Std. Error Mean
Age (years)	70	39.13	12.238	1.463

Table 18.3b One-Sample Test

	Test Value = 40					
					95% Confidence Interval of the Difference	
	t	df	Sig. (2-tailed)	Mean Difference	Lower	Upper
Age (years)	−.596	69	.553	−.871	−3.79	2.05

In Table 18.3b 'Sig. (2-tailed)' is equivalent to the p-value. If the p-value is less than 0.05 (p < 0.05) then H_0 is rejected. If the p-value is more than 0.05 (p > 0.05) then H_0 is *not* rejected. In our case, p = 0.553 (> 0.05), therefore we *do not* reject H_0, implying that mean age is *not* statistically different from 40 at 5% level.

From this table, the 95 per cent confidence interval difference is given by $\bar{X} - 40$, with lower limit –3.79 and upper limit 2.05. Hence to compute the confidence interval for the mean ($\bar{X}$) we perform the following:

$$-3.79 \le \bar{X} - 40 \le 2.05$$

$$-3.79 + 40 \le \bar{X}\ 2.05 + 40$$

$$36.21 \le \bar{X}\ 42.05$$

(Alternatively, repeat the above steps and instead of entering 40 in the Test Value, enter 0, you should get the same confidence interval.)

3   Test if the mean salary of male employees is more than the mean salary of female employees.

Here we are comparing two independent means, so we use the *Independent Sample T-Tests*.

$$H_0 : S_M \ge S_F$$
$$H_1 : S_M < S_F$$

'S_M' and 'S_F' are the salary of male and female respectively.

Perform the following:

Analyze

   Compare Means

      Independent-Sample T-Tests . . .

● *Test Variable:* Yearly Income.
● *Grouping Variable:* Gender.
● Click on *define groups* and enter '1' and '2' in the respective boxes → *Continue*.
● This is because the variable 'gender' consists of '1' for male and '2' for female. (You can check this by clicking on the *Variable view* tab and clicking on the column *Values* for *Gender*).
● Click on *Options* if you want to change the *Confidence Level*.
● Click on *OK*.

You should get the results shown in Table 18.4.

Table 18.4 Group Statistics

	Gender	N	Mean	Std. Deviation	Std. Error Mean
Yearly Income	male	37	17013.51	2753.600	452.689
	female	33	15606.06	2281.713	397.195

From Table 18.4 it is evident that that the mean income for male is higher than the mean income for female; whether this is true for the population remains to be seen. From Table 18.5 we need to consider the statistics reported.

The p-value (sig.) for the Levene Test for Equality of Variances is 0.370 (> 0.05), so we do not reject the null hypothesis (H_0) that variances are equal. Therefore we use the *Equal Variances Assumed* row, that is, the first row.

The p-value in this row for the t-test is less than 0.05 (in bold, 0.024), we therefore reject the null hypothesis and we can conclude that there is a statistically significant difference at 5 per cent level that the mean salary of men and women is different. But since the average salary of men is larger than for women, we can conclude that we have enough evidence that the average salary of men is higher than that for women.

Note: if the *Equal variances not assumed* assumption is chosen, the p-value will be 0.022.

4   Now let's say we want to test if the average age of female employees is different from the average age of male employees.

Here again we are comparing two independent means, so we use the *Independent Sample T-Tests*.

$$H_0 : A_M = A_F$$
$$H_1 : A_M \neq A_F$$

'A_M' and 'A_F' are the age of male and female respectively.

Repeat the test as in (3) above and use the following commands:

Analyze

  Compare Means

    Independent-Sample T-Tests . . .

- *Test Variable*: Age
- *Grouping Variable*: Gender
- Click on *define groups* and enter '1' and '2' in the respective boxes → *Continue*.
- This is because the variable 'gender' consists of '1' for male and '2' for female.
- Click on *Options* if you want to change the Confidence Level.
- Click on *OK*.

Table 18.5 Independent Samples Test results (yearly income)

		Levene's Test for Equality of Variances		t-test for Equality of Means					95% Confidence Interval of the Difference	
		F	Sig.	t	df	Sig. (2-tailed)	Mean Difference	Std. Error Difference	Lower	Upper
Yearly Income	Equal variances assumed	.813	.370	2.312	68	.024	1407.453	608.761	192.689	2622.217
	Equal variances not assumed			2.337	67.656	.022	1407.453	602.239	205.594	2609.312

You should get the results shown in Table 18.6.

Table 18.6 Group Statistics results

	Gender	N	Mean	Std. Deviation	Std. Error Mean
Age (years)	male	37	38.81	12.784	2.102
	female	33	39.48	11.782	2.051

18.1.1 What can you observe?

The average age for male (38.81) is less than the average age for female (39.48). Our concern is whether this holds for the population. To test whether this is significant at 5 per cent, we read the results from Table 18.7.

   The Levene's Test for Equality of Variances probability value is 0.370 (which is greater than 0.05), so we do not reject the null hypothesis (H_0) that the variances are equal. Therefore, we use the 'Equal variances assumed' row, the first row.

   The probability value for the t-test in this row is greater than 0.05 (0.820), hence we *do not* reject the null hypothesis and we can conclude that we are 95% confident that the average age of male and female workers is not significantly different.

5   Let's say now we want to test whether the salary differs across the ethnic groups (is there is salary discrimination by ethnic group) and we also wish to locate the source of these differences (if any).

Since ethnic group has more than two categories, we *cannot* use *Independent Sample T-Tests*. We use the *One-way ANOVA* instead.

   $H_0 : \mu_1 = \mu_2 = \mu_3 = \mu_4$
   $H_1 :$ *Not all the μs are the same*

To locate the source of the difference, we use the Tukey Test within the Post-Hoc analysis.

We use the following SPSS command to perform the following:

Analyze

   Compare Means

      One-Way ANOVA . . .

- *Dependent List*: Yearly Income
- *Factor*: Ethnic
- Click on *Options* and select *Homogeneity of Variance Test* → Continue. This is the Levene Test.
- Click on *Post-Hoc . . .* and select *Tukey* → Continue.
- Click on *OK*.

Table 18.7 Independent Samples Test results (age)

		Levene's Test for Equality of Variances		t-test for Equality of Means						
									95% Confidence Interval of the Difference	
		F	Sig.	T	df	Sig. (2-tailed)	Mean Difference	Std. Error Difference	Lower	Upper
Age (years)	Equal variances assumed	.815	.370	-.228	68	.820	-.674	2.951	-6.562	5.214
	Equal variances not assumed			-.230	67.919	.819	-.674	2.937	-6.534	5.186

You should get the results shown in Table 18.8.

Table 18.8 Test of Homogeneity of Variances results

Yearly Income

Levene Statistic	df1	df2	Sig.
.202	3	66	.895

The probability value of the Levene test is greater than 0.05 (0.895), so we can assume that the population variances are relatively equal. Note that the Tukey Test (Table 18.9) is carried out under the assumption that variances are equal, so it is important to carry out this test.

From the ANOVA table, since the probability value (in bold, 0.969) is greater than 0.05, we can conclude that we are 95 per cent confident that there is no salary discrimination by ethnic group. Therefore, there is not enough evidence that the level of income varies across the ethnic groups. Note that we use the F-test rather than the usual t-test.

To locate the difference, if any, we refer to the results under the Post-Hoc Tests (Table 18.10).

If there was a difference in the level of income, we could go further and determine, using the Tukey Test, where the difference lies. That is, between which ethnic groups there is a significant difference in the level of salary. We can see that by looking at the

Table 18.9 Analysis of Variance results (ANOVA)

Yearly Income

	Sum of Squares	df	Mean Square	F	Sig.
Between groups	1803968.254	3	601322.751	.084	**.969**
Within groups	472311031.746	66	7156227.754		
Total	474115000.000	69			

Table 18.10 Post-Hoc Test results: multiple comparisons

Dependent Variable: Yearly Income

Tukey HSD

(I) Ethnic group	(J) Ethnic group	Mean Difference (I-J)	Std. Error	Sig.	95% Confidence Interval	
					Lower Bound	Upper Bound
White	Asian	−188.889	772.239	.995	−2224.29	1846.51
	Chinese	−341.270	842.581	.977	−2562.07	1879.53
	African	394.444	1943.424	.997	−4727.87	5516.76

Asian	White	188.889	772.239	.995	−1846.51	2224.29
	Chinese	−152.381	953.272	.999	−2664.93	2360.17
	African	583.333	1993.911	.991	−4672.05	5838.71
Chinese	White	341.270	842.581	.977	−1879.53	2562.07
	Asian	152.381	953.272	.999	−2360.17	2664.93
	African	735.714	2022.195	.983	−4594.21	6065.64
African	White	−394.444	1943.424	.997	−5516.76	4727.87
	Asian	−583.333	1993.911	.991	−5838.71	4672.05
	Chinese	−735.714	2022.195	.983	−6065.64	4594.21

probability value in the Post-Hoc Test table. If there is any probability value that is less than 0.05, it will mean that there would appear to be income discrimination between the ethnic groups. But in our case they are all above 0.05 (the p-values are actually very high, all above 0.9). So no pairs of ethnic group have significantly different level of salary.

18.2 Regression analysis

Please visit www.routledge.com/9780415673198 to access the file *regression_1.sav.*

From the introduction to regression analysis in Chapter 16, we now show how to perform regression analysis using SPSS and how check the validity of the results by examining the diagnostic tests. The data file *regression_1.sav* includes information on six variables on 303 respondents from a survey conducted in restaurants in the city centre of a hypothetical town. The variables are listed in Table 18.11.
    Let's say we are interested in the following:

1   To determine to what extent the above mentioned characteristics predict the like-lihood (ranging from 1 = 'very unlikely' to 5 = 'very likely') that a person will return to the restaurant s/he has been to before.

Table 18.11 Variables and definitions for file *regression_1.sav*

Variables	Definitions
Visit	The likelihood that the respondent will return to the restaurant: 1 'very unlikely' to 5 'very likely'
Service	Rating of the quality of service
Age	Age of the respondent
Gender	Gender of the respondent: 1 for male and 2 for female
Income	Monthly salary of the respondent
Bill	The bill paid on the last visit to the restaurant

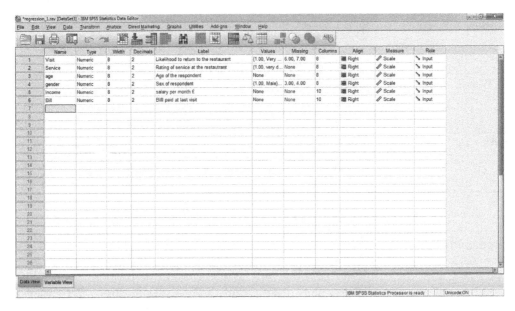

Figure 18.5 Variable View window

2   To find which independent variables help to explain the dependent variable.
3   Comment on the estimated coefficients.
4   Examine whether the main assumptions of regression analysis are met.
5   Comment on the level of multicollinearity in the model.

To view the Variables Description, select the *Variable View* on the data editor window and see the detailed information by clicking in the *Values* column. The Variable View window should display as shown in Figure 18.5.

We first specify the regression model to be estimated as follows:

$$Visit_i = \beta_0 + \beta_1 Service_i + \beta_2 Age_i + \beta_3 Gender_i + \beta_4 Income_i + \beta_5 Bill_i + e_i$$

The main assumptions of the regression model are that:

1   e_i is distributed with mean 0 and variable 1.
2   $Var(e_i) = \delta^2$ (homoscedasticity, that is the variance is constant).
3   Zero covariance between e_i and X variable.
4   No exact collinearity between the X variables, that is, no multicollinearity.
5   $Cov(e_i, e_j) = 0$ for $i \neq j$, that is, no serial correlation. (This is unlikely in our case as we are using cross-section rather than time series data.)

To estimate the following regression use the following SPSS commands:

Analyze

    Regression

        Linear . . .

Move the dependent variable (Visit) in the *Dependent* box.

Move the independent variables (all the other variables) in the *Independent(s)* box.

Make sure that *Enter* is selected as Method.

Enter refers to the Simultaneous Method.

Stepwise refers to the Stepwise Method.

- Click on *Statistics* . . . and select *Collinearity Diagnostics*, *Covariance Matrix* and *Durbin-Watson*. Make sure that *Estimates* and *Model Fit* are also selected.
- *Collinearity Diagnostics* will give the Tolerance and Variance Inflation Factor (VIF) to check for multicollinearity.
- *Covariance Matrix* will provide the correlation matrix to check for multicollinearity.
- *Durbin-Watson* (DW) will check for autocorrelation.
- Click on *Continue*.
- Click on *Plots* . . . and select *Histogram* and *Produce all partial plots*.

Histogram will plot the histogram of the residuals. We can check whether the normality assumption of the distribution of error term is satisfied.

Produce all partial plots produces scatter plots of each X against the Y. It gives you a feel of what sort of relationship to expect. You can also check whether the relationship is linear or not.

- Click on *Continue*.

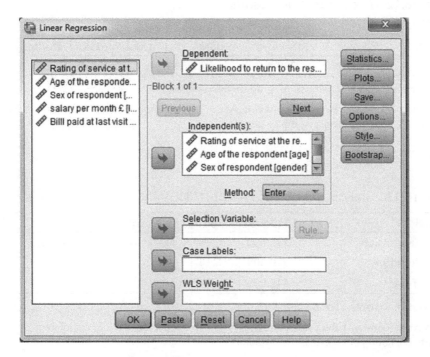

Figure 18.6 Linear regression editor

Ramesh Durbarry

1   To determine to what extent the above mentioned characteristics predict the like-
    lihood (ranging from 1 = 'very unlikely' to 5 = 'very likely') that a person will return
    to the restaurant s/he has been before.

For this question, we need to comment on model fit. First by looking at *Model
Summary* (Table 18.12) we can find that R^2, the coefficient of determination, is 0.299
and the adjusted R square (adjusted for the number of independent variables and
sample size) is 0.283. The R^2 implies that 28.3 per cent of the variation in the dependent variable (likelihood to visit the restaurant) is explained by the five independent
variables. This is not high enough as is it less than 50 per cent.

The ANOVA results obtained are as shown in Table 18.13.

The probability value from the F-test in the ANOVA table is 0.000, which is less than
0.05, implying that we can reject the null hypothesis that the regression coefficients
(β's) are all simultaneously equal to zero (H_0: $\beta_0 = \beta_1 = \ldots = \beta_m = 0$). Therefore, we can
claim that at least one of the regression coefficients (β) is different from zero and that
the findings have not arisen simply from a sampling error. The model implies that all
the independent variables taken together significantly explain the variation in the
likelihood to visit the restaurant.

2   To find which independent variables help to explain the dependent variable,
    we look at the 'Standardized Coefficients (Beta)' in the *Coefficients* table
    (Table 18.4).

Table 18.12 Model Summary results[a]

Model	R	R Square	Adjusted R Square	Std. Error of the Estimate	Durbin-Watson
1	.547[b]	.299	.283	1.20418	2.138

a. Dependent Variable: Likelihood to return to the restaurant

b. Predictors: (Constant), Bill paid at last visit, Age of the respondent, Sex of respondent, Salary per
   month (£), Rating of service at the restaurant

Table 18.13 Analysis of Variance results (ANOVA)[a]

Model		Sum of Squares	df	Mean Square	F	Sig.
1	Regression	132.600	5	26.520	18.289	.000[b]
	Residual	310.309	214	1.450		
	Total	442.909	219			

a. Dependent Variable: Likelihood to return to the restaurant

b. Predictors: (Constant), Bill paid at last visit, Age of the respondent, Sex of respondent, Salary per
   month (£), Rating of service at the restaurant

Table 18.14 Standardised Coefficients and Collinearity Statistics[a]

Model	Unstandardized Coefficients		Standardized Coefficients			Collinearity Statistics	
	B	Std. Error	Beta	t	Sig.	Tolerance	VIF
1 (Constant)	2.318	.568		4.082	.000		
Rating of service at the restaurant	.368	.059	.397	6.226	.000	.807	1.239
Age of the respondent	−.010	.007	−.089	−1.555	.122	.989	1.011
Sex of respondent	−.192	.176	−.068	−1.094	.275	.855	1.170
Salary per month (£)	.000	.000	.157	2.618	.009	.908	1.101
Billl paid at last visit	.029	.012	.144	2.474	.014	.973	1.028

a. Dependent Variable: Likelihood to return to the restaurant

If we look at the probability values, 'Rating of service at the restaurant' and 'Salary per month' are the only variables with probability value less than 5 per cent (excluding the constant term) and are, hence, significant. It means that they have a significant effect on the likelihood to return to the restaurant. All the other variables are not significant because their p-values are more than 0.05.

3   To interpret the results, we focus only on the variables which are significant. For example, on the 'Rating of service at the restaurant' variable, assuming all other variables are held constant, if the rating of the service at the restaurant increases by one unit, the 'Likelihood to visit to the restaurant' will increase by 0.4 units. Similarly, if the salary of the respondent increases by £1, the 'Likelihood to visit the restaurant' increases by 0.16.

On the gender variable, we interpret the result although it is not significant. We find that the coefficient is negative, implying that the likelihood that somebody will visit the restaurant and the gender are negatively related. Literally, it means that if you increase gender by 1 unit, 'Likelihood to visit the restaurant' will fall by 0.068 units, ceteris paribus. Now the variable for gender takes the value of '1' and '2' only. Increasing Gender means that you are moving from '1' to '2', that is from male to female (check the *Variable* view in SPSS under the Value column). Therefore, the coefficient for Gender can be interpreted that female has a lower 'Likelihood to visit the restaurant' than male by 0.068 (but we will ignore this conclusion, as the coefficient is not significant).

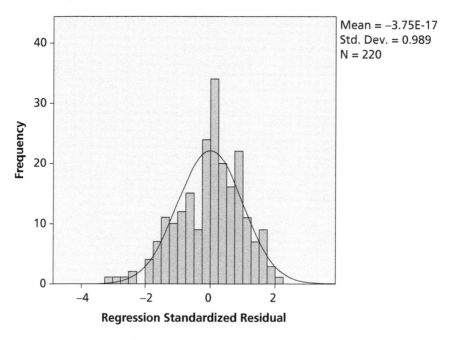

Mean = −3.75E-17
Std. Dev. = 0.989
N = 220

Graph 18.4 Histogram of residuals[a]
a. Dependent Variable: Likelihood to return to the restaurant

4   To examine whether the main assumptions of regression analysis are met, we look at charts; for example, the histogram for the residuals is quite close to the normal distribution (Graph 18.4). Therefore, we can say that the error term is normally distributed.

Looking at the Model Summary table (Table 18.12), the DW statistic lies between 0 and 4. When DW is close to 2, there is no autocorrelation problem. When it is close to 0 or 4, there is an autocorrelation problem. In our case, the DW statistic is 2.138, close to 2 and hence there is no problem of autocorrelation.

5   To comment on the level of multicollinearity in the model, we look at the Coefficients table (Table 18.14), the Collinearity Statistics column. We use the Tolerance or the VIF to infer on the multicollinearity. Tolerance = $(1-\tilde{R}^2)$ and VIF $=\dfrac{1}{Tolerance}$. Low tolerance (lower than 0.1) and high VIF (higher than 10) indicate that multicollinearity is present. In our case, the lowest tolerance is 0.807 and the highest VIF is 1.239, which shows that there is no multicollinearity problem. If we also check the correlation coefficients between the variables (Table 18.15), which provide more information about the exact structure of multi-collinearity, we can observe that none of the correlation coefficients is more than 0.75, confirming that there is no problem of multicollinearity in the model.

Table 18.15 Coefficients Correlations matrix[a]

Model		Bill paid at last visit	Age of the respondent	Sex of respondent	Salary per month (£)	Rating of service at the restaurant
1	Correlations					
	Bill paid at last visit	1.000	-.044	-.017	-.117	-.079
	Age of the respondent	-.044	1.000	-.013	.029	.074
	Sex of respondent	-.017	-.013	1.000	.077	.344
	Salary per month (£)	-.117	.029	.077	1.000	-.213
	Rating of service at the restaurant	-.079	.074	.344	-.213	1.000
	Covariances					
	Bill paid at last visit	.000	-3.405E-6	-3.540E-5	-7.109E-8	-5.436E-5
	Age of the respondent	-3.405E-6	4.421E-5	-1.519E-5	1.001E-8	2.894E-5
	Sex of respondent	-3.540E-5	-1.519E-5	.031	7.007E-7	.004
	Salary per month (£)	-7.109E-8	1.001E-8	7.007E-7	2.712E-9	-6.563E-7
	Rating of service at the restaurant	-5.436E-5	2.894E-5	.004	-6.563E-7	.004

a. Dependent Variable: Likelihood to return to the restaurant

Table 18.16 Variables and definitions for file *restaurant.sav*

Variables	Definitions
Presentation	The food is well presented
Temperature	The food temperature is just right
Menu	A wide choice of menu is offered
Clean	The restaurant is clean & spacious
Location	The restaurant is conveniently located
Parking	The restaurant has adequate parking
Décor	The restaurant's décor is appealing
Facilities	The restaurant's facilities are up-to-date
Atmosphere	The restaurant has a cheerful atmosphere

18.3 Factor analysis

Please visit www.routledge.com/9780415673198 to access the file *restaurant.sav*.

We introduced factor analysis in Chapter 16; we now show how to reduce the number of variables using principal component analysis. The file *restaurant.sav* includes data on nine variables for 55 respondents from a survey conducted in restaurants in the city centre of a hypothetical town to examine the characteristic of a good restaurant. The variables are listed in Table 18.16.

The aim is to reduce the number of variables to a few factors and describe the underlying dimensions. We will:

1   Check whether the assumptions of factor analysis are satisfied.
2   See how many factors we will extract from the 9 variables and why.
3   Label the factors generated.
4   Consider which variable(s) to drop to improve the model.

We will start by following the following SPSS commands:

> *Analyze*
>> *Dimension Reduction*
>>> *Factor*

We will send the variables we want to investigate to the *Variable* box – in our case, all the variables. (Tip: to select all variables, click on one of the variables and press Ctrl A at the same time.)

Ignore the *Selection Variable* box.
Choose the following options:

DESCRIPTIVES

Univariate Descriptive

Initial Solution

Coefficients

Significance Levels

KMO and Bartlett's Test of Sphericity

| Continue |

EXTRACTION

  Method

    Principal Component

  Analyze

    Correlation Matrix

Display

    Scree Plot

    Unrotated Factor Solution

Extract

    Eigenvalues over 1

Maximum iterations for convergence: 25

| Continue |

ROTATION

  Method

Varimax

  Display

    Rotated Solution

  Maximum iterations for convergence: 25

| Continue |

SCORES

  Save as Variables (method: Regression)

  (This will add the newly created factor(s) to you data set; you can see the new factors in the data window after running factor analysis.)

| Continue |

OPTION

  Exclude cases listwise

Coefficient Display Format

  Suppressed absolute values less than: *0.4*

  (Here you can specify the value; change to 0.4 to see factor loadings over 0.4 in the Rotated Components Matrix.)

| Continue |

Click on *OK*.

Table 18.17 Correlation matrix

		The food is well presented	The food temperature is just right	A wide choice of menu is offered	The restaurant is clean & spacious	The restaurant is conveniently located	The restaurant has adequate parking	The restaurant's décor is appealing	The restaurants facilities are up-to-date	The restaurant has a cheerful atmosphere
Correlation	The food is well presented	1.000	.458	.211	.209	-.063	.080	.283	-.021	.207
	The food temperature is just right	.458	1.000	.379	.384	.250	.472	.432	.293	.518
	A wide choice of menu is offered	.211	.379	1.000	.629	.585	.467	.336	.381	.455
	The restaurant is clean & spacious	.209	.384	.629	1.000	.605	.636	.369	.425	.390
	The restaurant is conveniently located	-.063	.250	.585	.605	1.000	.643	.321	.485	.425
	The restaurant has adequate parking	.080	.472	.467	.636	.643	1.000	.546	.540	.692
	The restaurant's décor is appealing	.283	.432	.336	.369	.321	.546	1.000	.663	.527
	The restaurant's facilities are up-to-date	-.021	.293	.381	.425	.485	.540	.663	1.000	.615
	The restaurant has a cheerful atmosphere	.207	.518	.455	.390	.425	.692	.527	.615	1.000

Sig. (1-tailed)

	(1)	(2)	(3)	(4)	(5)	(6)	(7)	(8)	(9)
The food is well presented		.001	.075	.077	.334	.295	.026	.444	.079
The food temperature is just right	.001		.004	.004	.043	.000	.001	.022	.000
A wide choice of menu is offered	.075	.004		.000	.000	.000	.010	.004	.001
The restaurant is clean & spacious	.077	.004	.000		.000	.000	.005	.001	.003
The restaurant is conveniently located	.334	.043	.000	.000		.000	.013	.000	.001
The restaurant has adequate parking	.295	.000	.000	.000	.000		.000	.000	.000
The restaurant's décor is appealing	.026	.001	.010	.005	.013	.000		.000	.000
The restaurant's facilities are up-to-date	.444	.022	.004	.001	.000	.000	.000		.000
The restaurant has a cheerful atmosphere	.079	.000	.001	.003	.001	.000	.000	.000	

Ramesh Durbarry

You should obtain the SPSS output shown in Tables 18.17 to 18.21. We discuss them below.

1   Check if the assumptions are satisfied.

We first look at the extent of correlation among the variables. The correlation matrix (Table 18.17) shows the correlation coefficients for all pair of variables. For example, the correlation between Location and Clean is 0.605 and between Temperature and Facilities is 0.293. From the matrix, we can see that there are a few quite high correlation coefficients (0.629, 0.636). The table is symmetric and the correlation coefficients twice. The second half of the table also shows the p-values of the test that the correlation coefficients are significant or not.

$H_0: \rho = 0$

$H_1: \rho \neq 0$

There are quite a few significant correlation coefficients (p-values less than 0.05). If there are no significant correlations among the variables at all, it means that they are not significant and hence it is not worthwhile conducting a factor analysis.
   Instead of analysing all the figures, we look at a more formal and concise test. Barlett's Test of Sphericity (Table 18.18) checks whether the correlation matrix has significant correlations among at least some of the variables.
   The hypotheses are as follows:

H_0: no correlations at all;

H_1: there are some correlations.

The p-value (Sig.) is 0.000 (less than 0.05), so we reject the null hypothesis and conclude that there are significant correlations between the variables. We can also look at the Kaiser-Meyer-Olkin measure of sampling adequacy. Value above 0.6 indicates that there are enough correlations. In our case, it is 0.75, so there are enough correlations to carry out factor analysis.
2   Let's see now how many factors we can extract from the nine variables.

There are three main criteria to use to determine the number of factors to be extracted.

- Eigenvalues
- Percentage of variance
- Scree plot

Table 18.18 KMO and Barlett's Test

Kaiser-Meyer-Olkin Measure of Sampling Adequacy		.749
Bartlett's Test of Sphericity	Approx. Chi-Square	208.373
	df	36
	Sig.	.000

If they give different results, you the first two may be more reliable.

Eigenvalue shows the number of variables' variance that the factor is capturing. Any factor should account for the variance of at least one variable, thus factors having eigenvalues >1 are considered significant. In our case, we can have either one, two or three factors.

All factors with Eigen values less than 1 are considered insignificant. Therefore, we need a maximum of three factors from the nine suggested factors. The first factor accounts for 29.26 per cent of the total variation and the second factor accounts for 28.84 per cent. Either factors account for 58.10 per cent of the total variation (the cumulative column). A minimum of 60 per cent is regarded as good. Therefore, we need a minimum of three factors. This is after the rotation (Table 18.19).

The Percentage of Variance column looks at the percentage of variance of all the variables the factors are explaining. All the factors should contribute to at least 60 per cent of the variance of the variables to be significant. Always consider the rotated variance criterion. In our case, choosing three factors is the minimum number of factors that contribute to at least 60 per cent of total variances of the nine variables. Having only one factor will explain only 29 per cent of the variance, while having two factors will capture 58 per cent of the variance. Since the Eigenvalue is also more than 1 for the three factors, we can reasonably say that we need to extract three factors.

18.3.1 The Scree plot

The point on the Scree plot at which the curve first begins to straighten out is considered to indicate the maximum number of factors to extract. In our case it is at 3 or 4 factors (Graph 18.5), confirming that three is the optimal number of factors to be extracted.

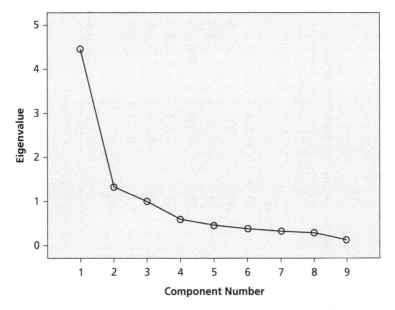

Graph 18.5 Scree plot

Table 18.19 Determining the number of factors: total variance explained

Component	Initial eigenvalues			Extraction Sums of Squared Loadings			Rotation Sums of Squared Loadings		
	Total	% of Variance	Cumulative %	Total	% of Variance	Cumulative %	Total	% of Variance	Cumulative %
1	4.457	49.525	49.525	4.457	49.525	49.525	2.634	29.268	29.268
2	1.341	14.904	64.428	1.341	14.904	64.428	2.596	28.840	58.108
3	1.014	11.268	75.696	1.014	11.268	75.696	1.583	17.589	75.696
4	.589	6.546	82.243						
5	.462	5.128	87.371						
6	.385	4.276	91.647						
7	.331	3.677	95.324						
8	.289	3.208	98.532						
9	.132	1.468	100.000						

Extraction Method: Principal Component Analysis

3   Label the three factors generated.

Labelling is based on intuition, but you need to explain the logic behind it.

Therefore, the nine variables are reduced to only three variables, denoted as fac1_1, fac2_1 and fac3_1 in the SPSS data (check this in the data). The three factors are presented in Table 18.20 based on the Rotated Component Matrix.

Since factor 1 consists of Parking, Décor, Facilities and Atmosphere as variables, we may label this factor 'Restaurant environment'. Since Clean and Location are more significant in factor 2, we label this factor 'Access'. Finally, factor 3 consists of food presentation and the temperature of the food, so we may label this factor 'Food quality'.

The variable Parking is common in both factors 1 and 2 and the factor loadings are significant (greater than 0.4) for both factors. If we want a 'pure' factor solution, it would be advisable to omit Parking from the analysis.

4   We now consider which variable(s) to drop to improve the model.

If there are any variable(s) significant in more than one factor, you should consider dropping the variable and re-run the factor analysis without including them. In our case, Parking is common to both factor 1 and factor 2, and ideally it should be removed from the model and re-estimated.

To learn more about testing hypotheses, conducting regression analysis, factor analysis and much more, you can consult the following websites:

● http://people.cst.cmich.edu/lee1c/spss/index.htm
● http://courses.csusm.edu/resources/spss/

Table 18.20 Rotated Component Matrix[a]

	Component		
	1	2	3
The food is well presented			.919
The food temperature is just right			.684
A wide choice of menu is offered		.801	
The restaurant is clean & spacious		.825	
The restaurant is conveniently located		.818	
The restaurant has adequate parking	.619	.593	
The restaurant's décor is appealing	.814		
The restaurant's facilities are up-to-date	.848		
The restaurant has a cheerful atmosphere	.742		

Extraction Method: Principal Component Analysis

Rotation Method: Varimax with Kaiser Normalization

a. Rotation converged in 5 iterations

- www.ats.ucla.edu/stat/spss/
- www.uccs.edu/~faculty/lbecker/SPSS/content.htm

Chapter summary

- Use a spreadsheet to enter your data.
- To ensure your data is correctly entered, use graphs such as bar charts and histograms to inspect the data.
- Use point estimates and generate confidence intervals to determine the likelihood of where the 'true' value of the parameter lies.
- Conduct t-tests to assess the significance of relationships.
- Regression analysis can be used to assess which variables are responsible to explain causes and variations in the variable of interest.
- Factor analysis can be used to reduce the number of variables in data analysis.

Discussion questions

Please visit www.routledge.com/9780415673198 to access files *wage.sav*, *regression_1.sav* and *restaurant.sav*.

18.1 Using the data from *wage.sav*:
   (a) Test whether the mean salary of all the employees is significantly different from £16,000. What is the confidence interval for 'Income'?
   (b) Determine whether there are significant differences in the income level across gender. Locate the source of these differences using the post-hoc analysis.

18.2 Use the data from *regression_1.sav* and estimate the following regression:
   (a) $Visit_i = \beta_0 + \beta_1 Service_i + \beta_2 Age_i + \beta_3 Gender_i + \beta_4 Income_i + e_i$
   (b) $Visit_i = \beta_0 + \beta_1 Service_i + \beta_2 Age_i + \beta_3 Gender_i + e_i$
   (c) $Visit_i = \beta_0 + \beta_1 Service_i + \beta_2 Age_i + e_i$

   What can you conclude from the above regression?

18.3 Use the data from *restaurant.sav* to conduct the following hypotheses:
   (a) Test whether respondents at least 'Agree' that the restaurant is clean and spacious (Hint: Ho: $\mu \geq 4$).
   (b) Test whether the respondents at least 'Agree' that the restaurant is conveniently located.

Further reading

Gujarati, D. (2003). *Basic Econometrics*, 4th edition. New York: McGraw-Hill.
Hair, J.F., Anderson, R.E., Tatham, R.L. and Black, W.C. (1998). *Multivariate Data Analysis*, 5th edition. New Jersey: Prentice Hall.

Chapter 19

Writing the research report

Richard Sharpley

It would seem, then, that some of the titles of books on thesis and dissertation writing are misleading. It is, perhaps, reasonable to assume that guides with titles such as Writing the Doctoral Dissertation . . . would give detailed advice on the structure and organisation of a thesis and the range of options that might be available to students . . . This did not, to a large extent, prove to be the case.

(Paltridge, 2001, p. 137)

Richard Sharpley

19.0 Chapter objectives

After studying this chapter, you will be able to:

- understand the importance of writing up within the overall research process;
- produce an academically sound, logically structured, persuasive report;
- write in an appropriate academic style;
- use references effectively and correctly; and
- be more confident about writing up your research.

19.1 Introduction

Writing up is, arguably, the most significant element of the entire research process. This is not to say, of course, that the research itself is not important. Indeed, the value of any research in general is measured by its outcomes, whilst one of the fundamental criteria by which PhD research in particular is judged is the extent to which it makes an original contribution to knowledge. However, for most tourism students, whether undergraduate or postgraduate, the purpose of undertaking research (usually in the form of a dissertation or thesis) is more broadly to demonstrate the ability to identify, undertake and successfully complete a research project within the field of travel and tourism. Moreover, not only is evidence of that ability provided primarily by the written work the student submits for assessment – the research report or thesis – but also and, perhaps, more importantly, the quality of that written work may have a significant influence on the grade awarded. Putting it another way, excellent research can be weakened (or, in pragmatic terms, given a lower mark) because it is poorly written up; conversely, markers or examiners may look more favourably on even weak research if it is presented within a well-written, logically structured and convincingly argued thesis.

It is rather surprising, therefore, that writing up is typically relegated to the final phase of the research process, often seen by students as a tedious or unpleasant but nevertheless necessary task that follows the 'fun' of doing the actual research. Equally, it is surprising that, as the quotation above reveals, many books or guides on research provide little in the way of help or advice on writing up; although details on *what* should be written are usually provided, less attention is given to *how* it should be written. Yet, as any supervisor knows, it is writing up that students often find the most difficult or challenging aspect of doing research and, therefore, put off until the last moment.

Thus, the purpose of this chapter is to provide guidance on writing up research. In particular, it focuses on styles of writing, on how to reference correctly and to use referencing as a means of enhancing the academic rigour of a dissertation or thesis, and on the need to inject a critical perspective. It also gives some hints and tips on how to go about writing up and how to overcome common challenges. First, however, it is important to understand why writing up should be approached not as the last functional task of the research process – 'I've done all the research, so now I'll write it up' – but as a fundamental and integral part of doing academic research.

19.2 The importance of writing up

It is all too easy to think of writing up as simply reporting or describing a research project although, in some contexts, it may in fact involve just that. For example, market research is usually written up in a report that describes its results in a factual style (in tourism, the 'Country Reports' produced by the London-based international market research company Mintel Group Ltd fall into this category); similarly, scientific research is often written up in reports that describe the implementation and outcomes of research projects. Moreover, in both cases, it is likely that the reports are written once the research and been completed and all data have been collected and analysed.

However, in the case of social scientific academic research such as that typically undertaken by tourism students, writing up cannot, or should not, be thought of as the production of a report that, in effect, describes research once it has been done. Indeed, to refer to the outcome of such research as a 'report' is misleading. As already observed, most tourism students, whether on an undergraduate degree programme or embarking on a PhD, are doing research not as an end in itself but as a means to an end. That is, they are setting out to produce a piece of work, such as a final year dissertation or a doctoral thesis, that is submitted for assessment, the aim presumably being to achieve as high a grade or as few required amendments as possible. It is, therefore, important from the outset to understand what the purpose of that piece of work (hereafter referred to as the thesis) is, particularly from the perspective of the person who is assessing it. In other words, students should try to put themselves in the shoes of the marker or examiner, asking themselves what that person is looking for in their submitted work. This will then enable them to think about how to write up their research to best meet the expectations of the examiner.

Certainly, fundamental to any thesis is 'good' and original research. Whatever its subject or focus, it is vital that an appropriate methodology is adopted and rigorously implemented in order to meet the objectives of the research (that is, to answer the research question) as effectively as possible. However, in writing up, students need to demonstrate more than just their ability to undertake successful research, whether primary, secondary, qualitative or quantitative. What the examiner will also be looking for is a coherent, complete and critical piece of work that identifies, justifies, explores and answers an appropriate research question in a logical and structured way. Putting it more simply, it is not only the actual research that is of interest to the examiner, but also the 'story' of that research, answering questions such as: why was the research done? How was it done? What particular research methods were employed, and why? What conclusions can be drawn from the research? And, what contribution does the research make to knowledge and understanding of the subject area?

The manner in which that story is written can go a long way to determining the success or otherwise of the thesis; that is, how it is written is as important, if not more so, than what it says. Effective writing up can reveal not only students' subject knowledge and research skills, but also their ability to think critically, to develop coherent arguments and to come to logical conclusions. In short, it is effective writing up that transforms a piece of research into an academic paper or thesis. Therefore, the importance of writing up, in terms of both planning and execution, cannot be over-estimated.

Practical tips

Remember: your thesis not only reports on your research. It tells the whole story – what you are researching, why you are researching it, how you went about the research, what you found out and what the implications are. So, think of writing up your research as writing such a story.

Of course, good writing is not an easy task. Nor does it become easier with experience – even accomplished academics with a good publication record often find it a difficult process. Nevertheless, there are a number of basic 'rules' or guidelines that, if followed, can put you on the right path towards writing up your research successfully. Indeed, building on the idea that what is being written is a story of the research process, two things are of particular importance: the structure of the thesis, and the style in which it is written.

19.3 The structure of the thesis

Students often ask questions such as: what should be in a thesis? How many chapters should I write? Or, how long should the literature review be? These are evidence of an assumption that there is a standard structure or format for writing up research, which is certainly not the case. As Paltridge (2001, p. 126) observes, not only do theses vary, 'in terms of their purpose, readership, the kind of skills and knowledge they are required to demonstrate and "display", and the kinds of requirements they need to meet', but also the ways in which they are written continues to evolve. A thesis today might be written in a very different way from how it would have been written a decade ago. In short, there is no single, prescribed structure or format for a thesis; how it is written will very much reflect its content, focus and objectives.

Nevertheless, in order to tell the complete story of the research a thesis should follow a logical structure from introduction through to conclusion, and most guides to writing up (including those provided to students by their college or university) suggest a standard format (see below). In most cases, this is likely to be a suitable structure to follow when writing up research in tourism studies. That is, any thesis or 'research report' requires an introduction, some review of the relevant literature or theory, an explanation of methodology, and a discussion of the research and its implications. In fact, academic research papers published in tourism journals such as *Annals of Tourism Research*, *Tourism Management*, *Journal of Sustainable Tourism* or *Tourism Planning and Development* (there are well over 60 tourism journals to choose from!) are typically structured in this way. Thus, it is a worthwhile exercise to read a few published papers prior to starting writing up, just to see how they are organised.

The structure of a thesis

Abstract: a summary of the entire thesis

Prelims: acknowledgements, table of contents, list of tables/figures, and so on

> *Introduction*: a description of and justification for the research question
>
> *Literature review*: a critical discussion of relevant literature/theory (see Chapter 5)
>
> *Methodology*: how and why particular research methods were chosen and implemented
>
> *Research findings*: a description of the data generated by the research
>
> *Discussion*: a critical discussion of the findings in relation to existing knowledge/theory
>
> *Conclusion*: the implications, contribution, strengths and weaknesses of the research
>
> *References*: an alphabetical list of all sources cited or referred to in the thesis
>
> *Appendices*: additional material that supports, but is not fundamental to, the thesis.

This structure is not rigid, of course. For example, in some instances, such as when a case study approach is being used (a frequent occurrence in tourism studies, when the research is related to a particular country or destination), an additional section or chapter may be required to introduce the case study. In other instances, it may be more appropriate to blend the research findings and discussion into a single chapter, whilst a more complex structure will reflect the use of multiple case studies or multiple research methods.

Irrespective of the actual structure, however, what is most important is an understanding of the purpose of each section/chapter and the relationship between them. In other words, a common mistake made by students is to think of each section or element of a thesis separately, as something that is required or expected, rather than as part of the story. In particular, the literature review is often written without any evident thought about how it fits into and contributes to the thesis. As a consequence, students' work is frequently marked down because it is unclear how the literature review frames, underpins or informs the subsequent research – in a sense, the thesis becomes a work 'of two halves'. Therefore, each section should be written as part of the overall story, but this can only be done if the purpose or function of each section is first recognised (a useful guide to structuring a thesis is also provided in Finn et al., 2000, pp. 233–238).

19.3.1 Abstract

Abstracts are widely used by academic researchers, who use them as a basis for deciding whether or not to access and read the complete paper or thesis which they summarise. In a sense, therefore, the abstract serves the same purpose as the 'executive summary' in a technical report; its purpose is to provide a succinct summary of the entire thesis. It is *not* simply an introduction to the thesis, and should summarise the aims and objectives of the research, the methods employed, the outcomes and the implications.

19.3.2 Introduction

Technically speaking, the purpose of the introduction is, by definition, to introduce the research. That is, it should outline the aim and objectives of the research, including a clear statement of the research question, as well as describing briefly how the research has been done. In other words, it fulfils the need for what Phillips and Pugh (2005, p. 56) refer to as 'focal theory' as one of the four key elements of a thesis, this being where 'you spell out . . . precisely what you are researching and why. You establish the nature of your problem and set about analysing it.' Key to this, though often overlooked, is the 'why'. In other words, the principle purpose of introducing and justifying the research is to encourage or excite the reader, to make them want to read the thesis. It should tell the reader why they should read the thesis. It also sets the tone for the rest of the thesis; a good introduction provides a positive foundation for what follows.

Practical tips

In establishing the 'focal theory', the introduction also contributes to the cohesion of a thesis. A useful trick is to start your conclusion with the words: 'As stated in the introduction to this thesis, the purpose of the research was to . . .', followed by a re-statement of the aims and objectives. This will ensure that you have actually done what you set out to do, that you have adhered to the focal theory.

19.3.3 Literature review

This is considered in more detail in Chapter 5. However, it is important to remember that the purpose of the review is not just to reveal your knowledge of the relevant literature by describing its content. It is not an end in itself. Rather, the purpose of the review, depending on the nature and focus of the research, is to provide a context for or to inform the subsequent research. It should reveal your knowledge or expertise in the area you are studying, referred to by Philips and Pugh (2005) as the 'background theory' to the thesis or, more precisely, 'the present state of the art: what developments, controversies, breakthroughs are currently exciting or engaging leading practitioners and thus pushing forward thinking on the subject' (p. 55). Therefore, the purpose of the review is, for example, to reveal how the research will address existing gaps in knowledge, to contribute to or challenge contemporary debates, or provide a conceptual framework for the research. One way to make sure that it achieves this is to give the literature review a title that indicates its content and focus; don't simply call it 'Literature Review'.

19.3.4 Methodology

The methodology section/chapter (which, in contrast to the literature review, may be simply titled 'Methodology'!) serves a number of purposes. First and foremost, it provides students with the opportunity to explain why particular approaches and methods have been chosen, for in any academic research it is necessary justify why one or more methods have been selected in preference to others. This, in turn, also provides the opportunity to critically appraise the strengths and weaknesses of particular methods. For example, focus groups are a popular method of qualitative research, yet subject to a number of recognised weaknesses which should be acknowledged and compensated for, usually by employing an additional method such as in-depth interviews. Second, the methodology chapter enables students to explain how they did their research – that is, to reveal the extent of their research skills and expertise – and, third, it provides them with the opportunity to reveal more generally their knowledge and understanding of research approaches and philosophies. Throughout, however, it is important to relate the discussion to the particular focus of the thesis; lengthy general reviews of, for example, ontologies and epistemologies related to different research paradigms may in fact diminish the overall impact of the methodology section.

19.3.5 Research findings

In some respects this is one of the easier sections of a thesis to write. Unless the intention is to combine the report of the findings with a discussion of their significance, the findings chapter is essentially a narrative that describes the data generated by the research. The way in which this is structured will, to a great extent, be dictated by the nature of the research itself. The results from self-completion questionnaires, for example, could logically be written up in the sequence of the questionnaire itself; conversely, the outcomes of interviews are more likely to be structured around identified themes. Either way, the purpose is to report objectively the data gathered. Care must be taken, however, over how the findings are presented in order to maintain the interest of the reader. On the one hand, where detail is needed it should be provided; on the other hand, data should wherever possible be summarised in visual form supported by a commentary (readers should never be expected to interpret graphs, charts and other visual representations themselves). Putting it another way, try to restrict the content of the findings chapter to what is essential to the thesis and try to vary the way in which the data is presented. Additional data can be provided in appendices, whilst the reader will be unimpressed with excessive surplus information.

19.3.6 Discussion

The discussion section is the lynchpin of the thesis. Its purpose is to explore the findings of the research in relation to the overall aims and objectives of the thesis and, in particular, in relation to existing knowledge as revealed in the preceding literature review. Consequently, it is here that that the real value or contribution of the research emerges. In other words, whilst the research findings may be of interest in themselves, for the purposes of an academic thesis they are of limited relevance until it they are discussed or interpreted within the context of the research question. If you do not reveal or discuss the significance of your findings effectively, the reader may simply think: 'so what?'

The structure and content of the discussion section will inevitably depend on the purposes and nature of the research. Thus, it is difficult to prescribe precisely how it should be written. Broadly, however, you should reflect on the implications of your findings for the questions that have driven your research. This implies that you should also relate your findings to existing theories or knowledge, assuming of course that, in the introduction to your thesis, you have justified your research on the basis of an identified gap in existing knowledge on the subject! Therefore, you need to relate your findings to the key themes, debates or concepts that are considered in your literature review, where relevant comparing them to the results of previous work. Not only may your research have been inspired by questions or issues raised in previous studies, but also you may be able to demonstrate how your research supports, enhances or, perhaps, challenges the outcomes of those studies. It is also important to remain as objective as possible when discussing your research findings; that is, you should try to avoid subjective speculation about the implications of your research. In other words, your discussion should be supported by the data your research have generated and evidence from previous studies, and not be based on personal ideas or opinions.

19.3.7 Conclusion

The purpose of the conclusion is to demonstrate the extent to which the objectives of the research have been met; it is where you bring the story of your research to a logical close. It is a useful trick, therefore, to start the concluding chapter or section by writing: 'As stated in the introduction, the purpose of this thesis was to . . .' and, if relevant, to repeat the aims and objectives you may have listed in your introduction. Not only does this provide a structure for the narrative in the conclusion, but it ensures that the thesis has done what it set out to do! It is likely that the conclusion will summarise the key outcome of the research, but care should be taken not to simply regard it as a summary of the thesis as a whole. Rather, it is an opportunity to critically appraise your research: how successful have you been in meeting your objectives? What contribution has your research made to theory or knowledge in the subject area? How does it compare to previous studies? And, what are the limitations to your research, both in implementation and outcome? It is also likely that your results will point to future areas of research – if so, these should be identified and explained. What is not necessarily required in the conclusion is a list of recommendations, although students often feel the need to provide one. If the research is, for example, a more practice-based business project, such an analysis of marketing opportunities for a destination or a visitor satisfaction survey, then the outcomes of the research will inevitably underpin a set of recommendations for the client. However, it is not normally appropriate to provide recommendations as a conclusion to an academic piece of work. It is also essential that no new ideas or data are introduced in the conclusion, which should only reflect critically on what has already been done.

19.3.8 References

Making reference to the wider literature is, of course, fundamental to academic research. How to reference effectively is considered later in this chapter but, for the purposes of the discussion here, it is important to note that the reference list, which is normally located in a thesis after the conclusion but before any appendices, is critical in two respects. First, it provides (or should provide) complete details of all sources used/cited in the thesis. Not only does this help to avoid any charges of plagiarism (the use of other people's work or ideas without acknowledging it), but it also allows the reader to follow up any sources that might be of particular interest – academics frequently use the reference lists provided in books and journal articles as a source for their own research – or, in the case of the marker/examiner, to check the accuracy of material cited. Indeed, for this reason, it is vital that complete and correct information is provided. Second and more pragmatically, the reference list immediately gives the marker of your thesis an indication of the extent to which you have accessed the literature and therefore, in principle, your knowledge of issues, concepts and debates relevant to your research. Students often ask the question 'How many references should I make?' The simple answer is: as many as possible! A comprehensive, contemporary and correctly presented list of references is likely to impress the person reading and marking your thesis – in fact, many markers will look at the reference list before starting to read the thesis.

Reference list or bibliography?

These two terms are often (and erroneously) used interchangeably. Strictly speaking, the reference list should list only those sources of material cited in a thesis; conversely, a bibliography may include all sources that have been used or consulted during the research process, including those not necessarily cited in the thesis. To avoid confusion, and unless a bibliography is specifically required, the academic convention of providing a reference list (a list of all material referred to or cited in the thesis) should be adhered to.

19.3.9 Appendices

Students sometime succumb to the temptation to attach as many appendices as possible to their theses, whether to 'pad out' a short piece of work or, perhaps, to circumvent word limits. This should avoided wherever possible. Any information that is fundamental to the thesis (for example, tables of tourist arrivals and expenditure statistics, conceptual models, maps, and so on) should be integrated into and discussed in the main text. Conversely, the purpose of appendices is to provide the reader with additional materials that are of direct relevance to the research but not vital to the flow or argument of the thesis. Such materials depend upon the nature of the thesis and may include, for example, a copy of the questionnaire used for a survey, detailed statistics which are only summarised in the main text, or the typescript of a recorded interview. More general materials, such as company reports, should not be included.

19.4 Writing in an academic style

Just as important as an appropriate structure, if not more so, is the style in which a thesis is written. This includes both the actual writing – that is, the language used – and how it is presented. In many respects, the latter (effective presentation) is relatively easy to achieve. Students are usually provided with a set of guidelines to follow with respect to the word length and presentation of their thesis, including 'technical' requirements, such as font size, line spacing, margins, text alignment, pagination (page numbering) and the wording of the title page. Such requirements not only ensure that all students follow a consistent 'house style', but are also designed to help them present their work in an academic format. It goes without saying that formal guidelines on presentation should be adhered to. At the same time, however a number of simple 'rules' can be followed, including:

Avoid writing large blocks of text: however well written it may be, a visually attractive thesis will appear less daunting and easier to read. One way to achieve this is to present the text in what may be referred to as 'bite-sized chunks'. It is no coincidence that some academic journals, for example, advise authors to limit the length of each paragraph in their paper to around 120 words or so. Not only does this make the paper look more readable, but it also encourages the writer to be succinct in what they are saying – long paragraphs may simply be evidence of a rambling narrative! Inserting a line space between paragraphs is also good practice, whilst, depending on an institution's formal guidelines, text that is double-spaced and in size-12 font is perhaps the most 'reader-friendly'.

Make use of sections and subsections: an academic thesis is usually presented in chapters, the number of which will be dependent on the nature and content of the thesis. A PhD thesis may comprise up to ten chapters whereas an undergraduate dissertation of typically 10,000 words should be no more than four or five chapters at most. The presentation of chapters is enhanced by the use of sections and subsections which identify specific themes and sub-themes within a chapter. An appropriate numbering system for sections and subsections should be employed (for example, 5.4.3 refers to Chapter 5, Section 4, Subsection 3) whilst the use of titles and sub-titles for sections is also recommended. All chapters and sections/subsections should, of course, be listed with correct page numbers in the table of contents.

Make use of diagrams or figures: it has long been said that 'a picture says a thousand words'. That is, an image can convey information that may otherwise require many pages of text. This is certainly true in the case of academic writing, where complex concepts, for example, are often presented in visual format, or 'models'. At the same time, however, diagrams, figures or other types of image can be used to support or summarise the written word in theses, as well as being an additional means of breaking up the text to enhance its visual attraction. Destination case studies always benefit from the inclusion of a map, whilst key points may be emphasised by the inclusion of a table of statistics. As a simple example, the common argument that tourism has long been a growth sector can be demonstrated emphatically by a table of annual international arrivals. Even standard elements of a thesis may be presented visually; the description of the structure of the thesis, for example, may be shown in a flowchart that summarises the content of each chapter. Moreover, advances in digital technology mean that it is now easy for students to insert their own photographs into their thesis. This can be particularly useful in supporting the description of fieldwork although care must be taken not to include too many images. It is also important to remember that all figures/tables must be referred to in the text to justify this inclusion, whilst more complex ones should be explained. It is not the role of the reader to interpret data presented in tabular or diagrammatic form.

SPAG (Spelling, Punctuation and Grammar): all too often, a fundamentally good thesis is weakened by spelling, grammatical and more general typographical errors. It is accepted (though not necessarily acceptable!) that the occasional mistake is inevitable; irrespective of the number of times you read through your thesis, you are likely to miss the occasional error. However, consistent and simple SPAG mistakes, such as confusing *its* (belonging to it) with *it's* (it is), should be avoided. Word processing programmes can identify and correct spelling mistakes, though these are not infallible – they cannot ensure that the correct word (for example, 'their' as opposed to 'there') is used in the first place. So, although it is important to 'copy edit' your work, to read through it carefully looking for SPAG errors, it is recommended that you ask a friend or family member to also read it to check for mistakes.

Actually writing in an academic style is, perhaps, more difficult to achieve. Whereas presentation is concerned with the clarity, structure and correctness and, hence, the 'readability' of your thesis in a technical sense, writing in an academic style is more about the language used to develop arguments, to convey a sense of expertise and to endow the thesis with a sense of academic rigour. As noted above, even seasoned academics frequently encounter difficulty in writing up their research for publication in academic journals and it is a skill that does not come easily to many people. Nevertheless, the style in which you write your thesis is fundamental the success or otherwise of your thesis; the more academic it 'feels', the better it will be. There are two ways in which the academic style of writing can be improved: first, though the actual language used and, second, through the overall way it is written. With respect to language, a number of hints and tips are summarised in the box below and subsequently described in more detail:

Practical tips on writing style

Try to keep your sentences short: long sentences are cumbersome and limit the impact of what you are trying to say.

Avoid long or complex words: long words impress nobody. Arguments are best expressed in clear and simple language.

Write in the third person: this helps to maintain the objectivity of your arguments.

Blend referencing into the narrative: integrating your referencing into the narrative enhances its academic rigour.

Make use of 'signposts': these help to guide the reader through your thesis and ensure that the narrative flows logically.

A common mistake is to write sentences that are much too long. Indeed, as an examiner, it is not uncommon to encounter entire paragraphs that are just one sentence that has been clumsily lengthened by the use of various forms of punctuation!

Short sentences are much more punchy. If you look at any newspaper article, you will see that journalists often use short sentences to get their point over to the reader. Therefore, when writing your thesis, always ask yourself: 'could I write this in a shorter, more succinct way?' Of course, it is not always possible or desirable to use only short sentences, as the resultant narrative would not flow well. However, lengthy sentences should be avoided. Similarly, the use of long words should also be avoided when shorter, simpler words will suffice. Just because you are writing a PhD thesis, for example, does not mean you have to employ complex or uncommon words. Moreover, the person reading your thesis is more interested in what you have to say rather than the breadth of your vocabulary, and will not welcome dense, complex language.

As will be discussed shortly, it is important that academic writing is objective. That is, it should be based on evidence and sound argument rather than subjective and perhaps personal opinion (even though the researcher is expressing his or her own ideas or conclusions based on the research). Therefore, although the use of the first person is common practice in some disciplines, such as sociology, it is better to follow convention and use the third person. This not only encourages a more objective perspective but also reflects a more academic style. This is not to say that the first person cannot be used, particularly where personal reflection on the research is required or appropriate. Nevertheless, most if not all parts of a thesis can be written in the third person, using sentences such as 'This dissertation seeks to . . .', 'It may be argued that . . .', 'This evidence suggests that . . .', and so on. However, students should avoid referring to themselves in the third person in the thesis, such as 'The author suggests that . . .' or 'The researcher argues that . . .'. Again, these may be better written as 'It is suggested that . . .' or 'It is argued that . . .'.

Referencing is also discussed in more detail below. However, it is important to note here that blending or integrating references into your narrative is an effective way of enhancing the academic 'feel' of your writing. Putting it another way, at its simplest level, referencing involves identifying the source of facts or arguments presented in a thesis, usually by providing an author or organisation's name and the date of publication. However, integrating referenced material into the thesis by, for example, using direct quotations to support your arguments, not only increases the academic rigour of your work but also suggest that you have actually read the sources that you are citing!

And finally, a useful tool in academic writing is the 'signpost'. As suggested earlier in this chapter, a thesis is, in effect, the story of a research project, from the initial development of the research question through to the discussion and conclusions of that research. Therefore, just as a novel builds up a plot and storyline, it is essential that each chapter and section in a thesis flows logically on from the previous one. One way to ensure this is to use signposts. Simply stated, these are sentences or short paragraphs at the end of sections or chapters which, quite simply, point out the direction the thesis is taking. That is, they explain or indicate the purpose and focus of the following section/chapter, effectively leading the reader through the thesis. For example, signposts can be used to develop your argument: 'It is evident that motivation is a fundamental element of tourism demand. However, as the following section discusses, motivation is a complex concept . . .'. Alternatively, they can explain or justify what comes next by using words such as: 'Therefore, the purpose of the next chapter is to . . .' or 'As the following chapter reveals . . .'. At the same, signposting will encourage you to think about what you are writing in your thesis, helping you to structure it logically and to avoid including unnecessary or irrelevant material.

Turning now to the overall style or, if you like, 'flavour' of a thesis, there are three principal ways of enhancing its academic rigour. These are, perhaps, more difficult to achieve and come with practice, experience and confidence, in particular confidence in your own knowledge of the subject area and expertise in research. Nevertheless, even if you have little or no experience in writing up research, it is well worth bearing them in mind. First, and as mentioned above, a thesis should be objective. In other words, the discussion, arguments and conclusions in a thesis should appear to be based on facts and sound reasoning. The role of the researcher is, essentially to explore the evidence relevant to a research question, drawing both on existing knowledge and theory and new knowledge generated by the research, and to come to conclusions based on that evidence. Thus, in principle, the researcher takes an independent, dis-passionate and informed view of a particular question or issue. In practice, of course, this may be difficult to maintain, particularly when interpreting the outcomes of qual-itative research and even more so when specific phenomenological methods, such as auto-ethnography, are used. However, when writing up research, it is essential to convey a sense of objectivity, to avoid it being read as subjective, personal opinion. Thus, wherever possible, the outcomes and implications of the research should be discussed in relation to evidence, such as previous studies or key theories identified in the literature review.

Second, a critical approach to the research should be in evidence. To be 'critical' in academic work means to take a questioning approach; that is, not to accept a par-ticular thing – a theory, a policy, a fact – as given, but to consider whether there are alternative perspectives, theories or answers. For example, tourism students frequently write theses that refer to the concept of sustainable tourism development. All too often, however, they simply describe its principles and objectives; rarely do they ques-tion whether sustainable tourism development is viable in practice. Therefore, when writing up research it is essential to adopt a more questioning or critical approach, not only in the discussion/conclusion sections but, preferably, throughout the entire thesis. Of course, this is easier said than done. To be critical requires both the confi-dence to challenge what may be perceived as 'received wisdom' and the knowledge upon which to base alternative viewpoints. However, by simply demonstrating that you recognise there may be other arguments, alternative explanations and, perhaps, no absolute 'truth', you can begin to inject some critique into your work. For example, in the literature review it is possible to draw on opposing viewpoints to critique a particular point. Returning to the subject of sustainable tourism, for instance, rather than simply writing that it is the dominant contemporary approach to tourism devel-opment, a more critical stance can be conveyed by writing: 'Although many have long considered sustainable tourism to be been an essential approach to the develop-ment of tourism, more recently others have criticised the concept, arguing that . . .'. Similarly, in the methodology section, your choice of research method can be justi-fied on a critical assessment of the relevance of different methods to your research whilst, when discussing the results of the research, alternative implications should be considered. In short, the thesis should be written in a way that reveals thought and reflection on the part of the researcher.

Finally, try to take ownership of the thesis. In other words, when writing up your research, use words and phrases to demonstrate that, in a sense, you are in control of the process, that you are managing it effectively. For example, it is not uncommon in the literature review to define key concepts in your research. Frequently, students will use a definition cited in the literature: 'Goodwin (2011) defines responsible tourism as . . .'. However, it is more effective to cite two or three definitions as a basis for writing: 'For the purpose of this thesis, responsible tourism is defined as . . .'. In other instances, there may be issues relevant but not fundamental to your research. Rather than ignoring them (for which you may be criticised by the marker), you could write: 'Though of relevance, this issue is beyond the scope of this thesis (see x, y, z references)'. In so doing, you are telling the reader that not only are you aware of these issues and the relevant literature, but that you have made a positive decision not to discuss them in your thesis. In other words, you are in control of your thesis

19.5 Referencing

Referencing correctly is an essential skill in academic writing. In any form of written academic work, whether an essay, a report or a thesis, the source of any information used must identified or 'referenced'. That is, when you use any information, including theories, conceptual models, words, statistical data, and so on, that is not your own original work, you must always refer to the source, whether people, organisations or websites, in the main text of your thesis as well as providing complete details in the reference list. Failure to do so may result in a charge of plagiarism, whilst inaccurate or incomplete referencing is considered poor academic practice and may result in your work being marked down. Conversely, accurate and extensive referencing may enhance the academic quality of your writing.

Practical tips

If in doubt, always provide a reference for work or ideas that are not your own. You can never have too many references. However, make sure that you are actually able to access any source that you cite. If you refer to sources that are, for example, obscure out-of-print books not held by your library, the person marking your thesis may assume (possibly correctly!) that you have not read the original and respond accordingly.

In essence, correct referencing, as indicated above, involves two distinct tasks: referencing the source in the text of the thesis, and providing accurate details in the reference list at the end of the thesis. Both are relatively simple tasks that, with practice, come naturally to academics, yet it is surprising how many students, both under- and postgraduate, struggle to reference correctly. Indeed, it is even more surprising given that almost every paper published in an academic tourism journal and many tourism text books are replete with examples of correct referencing. All that has to be done is to follow the style of referencing in those journals and books!

A full guide to referencing is well beyond the scope of this chapter. Moreover, most institutions provide their students with thesis guidelines which include comprehensive details on how to reference correctly, and there are a number of excellent books, such as Neville (2007) or Pears and Shields (2010). The purpose here, therefore, is to provide a few essential tips and hints, whilst the best way to learn to reference correctly is, as suggested above, to see how it is done in published academic articles and books.

19.5.1 Referencing in the text

There are different systems of referencing although the most commonly used (and probably the easiest) is the Harvard system. With this system, the author's surname (or the organisation) and year of publication are inserted at an appropriate place in the text, and the full reference is provided in an alphabetical list at the end of the thesis. In its simplest form, name and date follow in brackets immediately after a phrase or sentence. For example:

> It has been argued that there is no such thing as sustainable tourism development (Sharpley, 2000).

However, this can be written in different ways to blend into the narrative. For example:

> Whilst many commentators support the concept, Sharpley (2000) argues that there is no such thing as sustainable tourism development

Or, alternatively:

> Whilst many commentators support the concept, Sharpley (2000: 14) argues that 'true sustainable tourism development is unachievable'.

In the last example, a direct quote is being used; therefore, the page number (14) must also be cited.

There are different ways in which sources are cited in the text. For example, (Sharpley 2000: 14) may be written as (Sharpley, 2000: 14) or (Sharpley, 2000, p. 14). The only rule is: be consistent in style. Beyond that, some key things to remember are:

- Only cite the author's surname, unless there are two different authors with the same surname that you cite with publications in the same year (yes, it can happen!). In this case, you would write (Smith, A., 2010) and (Smith, B., 2010).
- When multiple authors are cited, it is preferable to use 'et al.' and to list all of the authors' name(s) in the References section.
- Organisations can be cited by name or acronym. For example (United Nations World Tourism Organisation, 2012) or (UNWTO, 2012). Whichever you use must also be used in the reference list.
- When citing multiple sources to support a particular point, these can be cited either alphabetically (Allen, 1998; Brown, 2005; Carruthers, 1990) or by date (Carruthers, 1990; Allen, 1998; Brown, 2005). Again, consistency is the key.
- Whenever you quote directly, or use a figure/table, include the page number. If in doubt, it is always better to include the page number.

One particular area of confusion is how to reference a source that you have not read or accessed yourself but have found in another source that you have read. The usual convention is to write, for example, 'Jenkins (1991) cited in Sharpley (2010)'. The issue is whether or not to subsequently include both sources in the reference list or just Sharpley (2010); most suggest just the source you have read should be listed. In any case, care should be taken to minimise the practice of citing 'second-hand' sources. Not only is there little reason for not accessing the original, particularly given the increasing availability of online resources, but also the continual use of 'cited in' points to limited wider reading.

19.5.2 Compiling the reference list

Again, compiling a reference list should be a relatively simple exercise. Although style may vary, each reference should provide as complete information as possible in a recognised and consistent format. A useful exercise is to look at the reference list in published papers and books and follow a similar format; conversely, you may be required to follow your institution's 'house style'. More generally:

- The reference list should be a single, alphabetical list. Do not create separate lists for journals, book and websites.
- Be consistent in style.
- When referencing electronic/web-based sources, provide the complete URL and be sure to indicate the date you accessed it.
- Make sure that all sources cited in the text are included in the reference list. One way to do this is to add each new reference to the list as you are writing your thesis, although you need to remember to remove any references that you subsequently delete from your text.

19.6 How to approach writing up

Finally, it is worth considering how to go about the process of writing up. As observed at the beginning of this chapter, although writing up is one of the most important parts of the research process, not only do many people find or perceive it to be the hardest part of doing research but also they tend to leave it until the actual research has been completed. Consequently, they find that they are rushing to complete writing up to meet deadlines and, as a result, produce a thesis that is of lower quality than might otherwise have been the case. Therefore, writing up should be started as soon as possible; once you have overcome the hurdle of starting to write, it will become much easier to make progress.

Inevitably, people work and write in different ways. Some work better in the morning, others in the evening; some prefer to work over brief periods, others can sustain their concentration for longer periods; and some will write numerous drafts of their thesis, whilst others will work slowly through a single version which they will submit. Irrespective of these differences, however, there are two principal ways in which the writing up process can be made easier:

Effective time management: the research in general, and writing up in particular, should be regarded as regular work. That is, establishing and keeping to specific times and days for writing will provide a temporal framework for working on writing up. Setting personal deadlines for sections/chapters is also a useful way of keeping on track although if you find this difficult, you can ask your supervisor to set deadlines to see written work. At the same time, however, writing is difficult and it is not uncommon to occasionally suffer a mild form of 'writer's block', when the words just don't seem to flow. In such instances, it is best to go and do something completely different, such as going out for a walk, or working on a different project. Coming back to the thesis with a fresh mind will soon result in the momentum being regained.

Start at the beginning: Many people will start the writing process by working on the literature review chapter, or even the results chapter if they have left writing up to later in the research process. Indeed, there are even various computer programmes that allow blocks of text to be moved around to build a thesis. It may be better, however, to start at the very beginning by writing the introduction. Given that the thesis is the story of the research, it is better to have a clear idea in your own mind from the outset about how that story will unfold. Writing the introduction, justifying what you are researching, will help clarify the structure and arguments you want to follow, reducing the amount of time you might have to spend rewriting drafts of subsequent chapters.

However difficult you find writing up, it is worth persevering. Even it remains a laborious or even stressful process, with practice you will become more confident, you will recognise and respond to the challenges of writing and, if you persevere, you will produce a piece of work of which you will be justifiably proud.

Chapter summary

- Writing up is, arguably, the most significant element of the entire research process.
- The quality of the written work may have a significant influence on the grade awarded.
- You need to meet the expectations of the examiner.
- It is vital that an appropriate methodology is adopted and rigorously implemented in order to meet the objectives of the research as effectively as possible.
- A dissertation or thesis should follow a logical structure and requires an introduction, some review of the relevant literature or theory, an explanation of methodology, and a discussion of the research and its implications.
- Make sure you check spelling, grammatical and more general typographical errors.
- The source of any information used must identified or 'referenced'.

Discussion questions

19.1 Why is it important to proofread your work?
19.2 Will the structure of your dissertation or thesis be the same if you have conducted a quantitative or qualitative research? Why?
19.3 What is the purpose of an abstract? What should be included?
19.4 What is the difference between a 'list of references' and a 'bibliography'?

Richard Sharpley

Further reading

Brotherton, B. (2008). *Researching Hospitality and Tourism: A Student Guide*. London: Sage.

Bryman, A. and Bell, E. (2007). *Business Research Methods*, revised edition. London: Oxford University Press.

Neuman, W.L. (2006). *Social Research Methods: Qualitative and Quantitative Approaches*. Boston: Pearson, Allyn and Bacon.

Saunders, M.N.K., Lewis, P. and Thornhill, A. (2009). *Research Methods for Business Students*, 5th edition. Harlow: Pearson Education Ltd.

Veal A.J. (2011). *Research Methods for Leisure and Tourism*, 4th edition. Harlow: Prentice Hall.

Chapter 20

Research presentation

Ramesh Durbarry

Presenting your research work is an exciting stage, as it gives you a chance to tell others what you have contributed to knowledge and how you have conducted your research study.

Presenting your work requires some preparation. How would you feel if you were to present your work in front of an audience of 200 people?

20.0 Chapter objectives

After studying this chapter, you will be able to:

- design and structure your presentation;
- confidently present your research work;
- prepare a poster presentation; and
- structure your research for a PowerPoint presentation.

20.1 Introduction

Research results are communicated as written reports, but very often researchers and students have to present their research work or projects orally at certain point. Researchers may present their research work in a variety of different settings such as departmental seminar, international conference or towards an assessment. Being able to present the research work to an audience is a key skill for researchers to develop.

Oral presentation requires different sets of skills from those involved in writing. The use of audio-visual aid such as Microsoft PowerPoint in oral presentation is very common. Anyone can give a presentation to a professional standard but like most things, it requires preparation and practice. Poster presentation is another common way of presenting the work among students. It is vital that the presenter considers who the audience is. A presentation to an interdisciplinary audience will be different from a conference presentation with subject specialists in the field.

20.2 Structure of a presentation

The structure of a presentation must be logical and straightforward. A coherent structure for a presentation includes an informative introduction, the main points to be presented in a sequence and the way forward or conclusion.

An informative introduction: this is a key element in a presentation and is where the presenter explains the content and purpose of the presentation. An effective introduction comprises a positive welcome from the presenter, a statement on what will be discussed, a statement on the outcome of the presentation and what the audience is expected to do, such as, to ask questions at the end or at any time during the presentation and to take notes.

The main points: these are the focal point of the presentation. The main points must be clear and expressed in a few words or short sentences. To enhance clarity and substantiate the presentation the presenter may use diagrams, illustrations and data.

The way forward or conclusion: this is the stage where the presenter summarises the content and purpose of the presentation, provides an overview of the research work and also indicates the future research work that needs to be done.

Generally, the concluding part of the presentation provides a review of the topic, conclusions drawn from the research work, the future research that will be needed and thanks to the audience for listening.

Practical tips

Emphasise the contribution that you have made to the research study.

20.3 Preparing and reviewing the presentation

Visual aids are powerful tools to enhance a presentation and provides a stimulating addition to the spoken words. There are many different types of visual aids and the most commonly used is Microsoft PowerPoint. General principles are: use a readable font size, keep the background simple and use animations when needed. Always remember to check the room layout, availability of the equipment and that the audience are able to see the visual projections. There are a number of salient features that must be considered when designing a PowerPoint slide:

- *Colour*: be consistent with the colour and background, avoid colours that can be too glaring for the audience (for example, avoid red on a yellow background).
- *Text*: ensure that the correct font size is used, usually at least 24 point size, otherwise it will be difficult to read. Use a consistent typeface and font size throughout the presentation.
- *Summarise*: summarise the key points and try to avoid too much text.
- *Graphics*: PowerPoint presentation facilitates the inclusion of graphics in the presentation. The relevant graphical images must be presented along with verbal material. Make sure you choose scanned pictures of an appropriate quality.
- *Transitions and animations*: PowerPoint offers slide transitions and animating elements of slides and these features must be used efficiently. It is advisable not to overuse these features as it may distract the audience.
- *Review*: Make sure that the content of the presentation is thoroughly reviewed. Ask the following questions:
  - Does the presentation meet the objectives?
  - Is the structure logical?
  - Is the content of the presentation at the right level for your audience?
  - Is the presentation too long or too short?

20.4 Delivering the presentation

It is important to find out well in advance about your audience and the environment in which you are going to be presenting. Find out about the layout of the room, time allocated for the presentation and check the availability of equipment.

Practical tips: some dos and don'ts

- Don't stand in front of the screen.
- Don't just read the slides.
- The slides should be a help to supplement to content of your speech.
- Use short wordings or bulleted keywords and develop them as you present.
- Do not point to your laptop or computer screen to explain diagrams or pictures; rather point to the projection screen. Use a laser pen if possible.
- Give your audience enough time to read through your slides.

Effective presenters should be familiar with the material to be presented. They must practice and familiarise themselves with the words and phrases in the presentation. Make notes or use a card index – these can be read at a glance and provide support to make an effective presentation. The speed of your delivery must be easy to follow. An effective presenter must be full of enthusiasm, energetic and flexible.

20.4.1 Responding to questions

The question and answer session is a vital element of the presentation and many presenters fear this session. The question and answer session should be considered as a formal part of the presentation as it enables the audience to clarify issues. It is important that the presenter listens to all parts of a question before drawing a premature response and always clarify the area of enquiry before proceeding any further. The members of the audience should be kept engaged, especially in large groups, as they may become bored if the presentation comes down into a series of one-to-one discussions with individuals. If a question is too difficult to answer, it is better to admit that you have not considered it or do not know.

20.5 Poster presentations

Research students often display posters at a conference to gain confidence in talking about their research and to establish networks. Usually, the conference organisers will inform you about the size and format of the poster and the space allocated will determine the content of the poster.

As with an oral presentation, the poster is structured with a title, an abstract stating the key findings, an introduction with clear problem statement, the methodology used, a results section to illustrate the main results and a conclusion to show main findings and any future work.

A good poster should be eye-catching and easy to read from a reasonable distance. Avoid using more than two font sizes as they may be distracting. A picture can say a thousand words but only if illustrated correctly, illustrations must be accompanied by a written statement and the messages should be clear. Use colours sparingly and only to emphasise, differentiate and add interest.

20.6 Stress management

Presenting can be nerve-wracking and many presenters may feel nervous when speaking publicly, either to a room of course peers or conference delegates. This is sometimes referred to as performance anxiety. The following tips may help to reduce the anxiety:

- Always develop positive thinking towards the presentation, for example, 'will aim to do the best' instead of 'will be a disaster'.
- Check the venue beforehand and make sure that the equipment is working.
- Relax physically; do relaxation exercises to release muscular tension.
- Make eye contact to maintain attention.
- Watch your body language and speak at an appropriate pace.
- Do some rehearsals in front of your friends or family members.
- Email yourself a copy of the presentation just in case you fail to open the file from your flash drive.
- Be prepared to deliver the presentation even without any visual aids.

20.7 Preparing for your viva

The viva is considered to be a rite in the academic world and has its own ceremony and tradition. The viva or *viva voce* is often considered as a verbal counterpart to your written thesis. In the viva the student will have to demonstrate the ability to participate in academic discussion with other researchers in the same field. You need not worry about the viva session provided that you have carried out the research work yourself. The answer and defence will become natural. For example, if you have designed your questionnaire, piloted it and carried out the survey, you will remember each and every stage because of your engagement in the process.

- Find out when the viva will take place.
- Find out who have been appointed as examiners – usually there is one internal and one external examiner. There may be more examiners depending on the area of study. Find out how the examiners' research links with your own research.
- Work out a timetable for viva preparation. Create a list of viva questions and practice answering them clearly.
- Remain engaged with the research work. Re-read the dissertation or thesis carefully and summarise the main points, identify the main contribution to knowledge, implications of the findings and any further research work required.
- Always keep a positive attitude and be confident.
- During the viva be relaxed, take time to consider before responding and do not give confrontational responses.

20.8 Example of a presentation structure

Depending on the time that you have been allocated for the presentation, you will have to work towards a structure which is able to deliver a good coverage of your research and the findings. For example, at many conferences you are given between 20 to 30 minutes for a presentation. As for students presenting their research proposal or dissertation, they are usually given a maximum of 30 minutes for presentation and 5 to 10 minutes for the question and answer session.

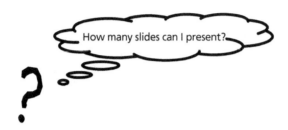

The number of slides is the trickiest part for most students. Students often end up having too many slides because they are excited about their research and want present too much information.

For a 30-minute presentation, a maximum of 12 to 15 slides should be enough. This is an example:

Slide 1: Research title, name, affiliation

Slide 2: Rationale for the research work

Slide 3: Aims and objectives

Slide 4: Literature part I

Slide 5: Literature part II

Slide 6: Research questions

Slide 7: Conceptual framework

Slide 8: Model and hypotheses

Slide 9: Methodology

Slide 10: Data analysis I

Slide 11: Data analysis II

Slide 12: Data analysis III

Slide 13: Discussions

Slide 14: Conclusions and way forward

Slide 15: Thanking the audience

This will be followed by the 5- to 10-minute question and answer session. It will be useful if you bring a copy of your research documents and any supporting documents, such as the approved ethics form, completed questionnaires and interview transcripts.

Chapter summary

- Prepare the content of your presentation: what have you covered in your research? Why you have researched the topic? How you have conducted research? What have you found? What has been your contribution?
- Your presentation should have a logical flow and a structure.
- Your presentation content will vary according to different audiences. For an academic audience, you may include technical elements such as mathematical models and statistical/econometric analyses, but for a non-academic audience the presentation has to be accessible.
- You have to be prepared to adapt your presentation on the day.

Discussion questions

20.1 If you were to make an oral presentation on your research, which aspects of your research you would focus on?

20.2 How would your preparation change if the time allocated is halved?

Further reading

Bryman, A. and Bell, E. (2007). *Business Research Methods*, revised edition. London: Oxford University Press.

Neuman, W.L. (2006). *Social Research Methods: Qualitative and Quantitative Approaches*. Boston: Pearson, Allyn and Bacon.

Saunders, M.N.K., Lewis, P. and Thornhill, A. (2009). *Research Methods for Business Students*, 5th edition. Harlow: Pearson Education Ltd.

Veal, A.J. (2011). *Research Methods for Leisure and Tourism*, 4th edition. Harlow: Prentice Hall.

Bibliography

Altrichter, H., Posch, P. and Somekh, B. (2006). *Teachers Investigate Their Work: An Introduction to the Methods of Action Research*, 2nd edition. London: Routledge.

American Marketing Association (2007). *Definition of Marketing*. Available at: www.marketingpower.com/AboutAMA/Pages/DefinitionofMarketing.aspx (accessed 19 April 2012).

Amsden, B., Stedman, R. and Kruger, L. (2011). 'The creation and maintenance of sense of place in a tourism-dependent community', *Leisure Sciences*, 33 (1), 32–51.

Anderson, L. (2006). 'Analytic Autoethnography', *Journal of Contemporary Ethnography*, 35 (4), 373–395.

Ateljevic, I., Pritchard, A. and Morgan, N. (eds) (2007). *The Critical Turn in Tourism Studies: Innovative Research Methodologies*. Oxford: Elsevier.

Babbie, E. (1990). *Survey Research Methods*, 2nd edition. Belmont, CA: Wadsworth.

Babbie, E. (1998). *The Practice of Social Research*, 8th edition. Belmont, CA: Wadsworth.

Bauman, Z. (2000). *Liquid Modernity*. Cambridge: Polity.

Bazeley, P. (2004). 'Issues in mixing qualitative and quantitative approaches to research'. In Buber, R. and Gadner, J. (eds), *Applying Qualitative Methods to Marketing Management Research*. Basingstoke: Palgrave Macmillan, pp. 141–156.

Bazeley, P. (2007). *Qualitative Data Analysis Using NVivo*. London: Sage.

Beaven, Z. and Laws, C. (2007). '"Never let me down again": Loyal customer attitudes towards ticket distribution channels for live music events: A netnographic exploration of the US leg of the Depeche Mode 2005–2006 World Tour', *Managing Leisure*, 12, 120–142.

Beedie, P. (2010). *Mountain based Adventure Tourism: Lifestyle Choice and Identity Formation*. Saarbrucken: Lambert Academic Publishing.

Bengry-Howell, A., Wiles, R., Nind, R. and Crow, G. (2011). *A Review of the Academic Impact of Three Methodological Innovations: Netnography, Child-Led Research and Creative Research Methods*. ESRC National Centre for Research Methods, NCRM Working Paper Series, 01/2011. Swindon: ESRC. Available at: http://eprints.ncrm.ac.uk/1844/1/Review_of_methodological_innovations.pdf (accessed 30 January 2013).

Bennett, J.A. and Strydom, J.W. (2001). *Introduction to Travel and Tourism Marketing*. Lansdowne: Juta Education.

Bogdan, R.C. and Biklen, S.K. (1992). *Qualitative Research: An Introduction to Theory and Methods*. Needham Heights: Allyn & Bacon.

Booms, B.H. and Bittner, M.J. (1981). 'Marketing strategies and organisation structures for service firms'. In J.H. Donnelly and W.R. George (eds), *Marketing in Services*. Chicago: American Marketing Association, pp. 47–51.

Brewer, J. and Hunter, A. (1989). *Multimethod Research: A Synthesis of Styles*. Newbury Park, CA: Sage.

Briggs, S. (2001). *Successful Tourism Marketing: A Practical Handbook*, 2nd edition. London: Kogan Page.

Brotherton, B. (2008). *Researching Hospitality and Tourism: A Student Guide*. London: Sage.

Brown, S.W., Gummesson, E., Edvardsson, B. and Gustavsson, B. (1991). *Service Quality: Multidisciplinary and Multinational Perspectives*. New York: Macmillan.

Bryman, A. (2008). *Social Research Methods*, 3rd edition. London: Oxford University Press.

Bryman, A. and Bell, E. (2007). *Business Research Methods*, revised edition. London: Oxford University Press.

Burns, P. and Lester, J. (2005). 'Using visual evidence: The case of cannibal tours'. In B. Ritchie (ed.), *Tourism Research Methods: Integrating Theory with Practice*. Wallingford, Oxon: CABI, pp. 49–62.

Burns, P., Palmer, P. and Lester, J. (2010). *Tourism and Visual Culture*. Wallingford, Oxon: CABI.

Caro, F.G. (1997). *Readings in Evaluation Research*, 2nd edition. New York: Russell Sage Foundation.

Carr, N. (2002). 'A comparative analysis of the behaviour of domestic and international young tourists', *Tourism Management*, 23 (3), 321–325.

Chalfen, R.M. (1979). 'Photograph's role in tourism: Some unexplored relationships', *Annals of Tourism Research*, 6 (4), 435–447.

Charmaz, K. (2000). 'Grounded theory objectivist and constructivist methods'. In N.K. Denzin and Y.S. Lincoln (eds), *Handbook of Qualitative Research*. Thousand Oaks, CA: Sage, pp. 509–535.

Charmaz, K. (2005). 'Grounded theory in the 21st century: A qualitative method for advancing social justice research'. In N.K. Denzin and Y.E. Lincoln (eds), *Handbook of Qualitative Research*, 3rd edition. Thousand Oaks, CA: Sage, pp. 507–535.

Charmaz, K. (2006). *Constructing Grounded Theory: A Practical Guide through Qualitative Analysis*. London: Sage.

Choi, S., Lehto, Z. and Morrison, A. (2007). 'Destination image representation on the web: Content analysis of Macau travel related websites', *Tourism Management*, 28 (1), 118–129.

Coffey, A. and Atkinson, P. (1996). *Making Sense of Qualitative Data*. Thousand Oaks, CA: Sage.

Cohen, L., Manion, L. and Morrison, K. (2000). *Research Methods in Education*. London: Routledge/Falmer.

Collis, J. and Hussey, R. (2003). *Business Research: A Practical Guide to Undergraduate and Postgraduate Students*. Basingstoke: Palgrave Macmillan.

Concise Oxford English Dictionary (2011). 11th edition. Oxford: Oxford University Press.

Cooper, C.P. (1998). *Tourism: Principles and Practice*, 2nd edition. Harlow: Longman.

Cooper, D.R. and Schindler, P.S. (2003). *Business Research Methods*, 8th edition. New York: McGraw-Hill.

Crabtree, B.F. and Miller, W.L. (eds) (1999). *Doing Qualitative Research*. London: Sage.

Creswell, J.W. (1994). *Research Design Qualitative & Quantitative Approaches*. Thousand Oaks, CA: Sage.

Creswell, J.W. (2002). *Educational Research: Planning, Conducting, and Evaluating Quantitative and Qualitative Approaches to Research*. Upper Saddle River, NJ: Merrill/Pearson Education.

Creswell, J.W. (2003). *Research Design: Quantitative, Qualitative, and Mixed Methods Approaches*, 2nd edition. Thousand Oaks, CA: Sage.

Creswell, J.W. (2007). *Qualitative Inquiry and Research Design, Choosing among Five Approaches*, 2nd edition. London: Sage.

Creswell, J.W. and Plano Clark, V.L. (2007). *Designing and Conducting Mixed Methods Research*. Thousand Oaks, CA: Sage

Crompton, J.L. and Richardson, S.L. (1986). 'The tourism connection where public and private leisure services merge', *Parks and Recreation* (October), 38–44.

Dahlen, M., Lange, F. and Smith, T. (2010). *Marketing Communications: A Brand Narrative Approach*. West Sussex: Wiley.

Dann, G.M.S. (1996). 'Tourists' images of a destination – an alternative analysis', *Journal of Travel & Tourism Marketing*, 5 (1/2), 41–55.

Davis, D. (2005). *Business Research for Decision Making*, 6th edition. Mason, OH: South-Western College Publishing.

De Vaus, D.A. (1995). *Surveys in Social Research*. New South Wales: Allen and Unwin.

Denscombe, M. (1998). *The Good Research Guide: For Small-Scale Social Research Projects*. Buckingham: Open University Press.

Denscombe, M. (2007). *The Good Research Guide*, 4th edition. Maidenhead: Open University Press.

Denzin, N.K. (1970). *The Research Act in Sociology*. Chicago: Aldine.

Denzin, N.K. and Lincoln, Y.S. (1994). 'Introduction: Entering the field of qualitative research'. In N.K. Denzin and Y.S. Lincoln (eds), *Handbook of Qualitative Research*. Thousand Oaks, CA: Sage, pp. 1–8.

Denzin, N.K. and Lincoln, Y.S. (eds) (2000). *Handbook of Qualitative Research*, 2nd edition. Thousand Oaks, CA: Sage

Devashish, D. (2011). *Tourism Marketing*. India: Pearson Education.

Dholakia, N. and Zhang, D. (2004). 'Online qualitative research in the age of e-commerce: Data sources and approaches', *Forum: Qualitative Social Research*, 5 (2), Art. 29. Available at: http://nbn-resolving.de/urn:nbn:de:0114-fqs0402299 (accessed 30 January 2013).

Dibbs, S. (1995). 'Understanding the level of marketing activity in the leisure sector', *The Service Industries Journal*, 15 (3), 257–275.

Dolnicar, S., Laesser, C. and Matus, K. (2009). 'Online versus paper', *Journal of Travel Research*, 47 (3), 295–316.

Drisko, J. (2000). 'Computer-aided data analysis'. In J. Anastas (ed.), *Research Design for Social Work and the Human Services*, 2nd edition. New York: Columbia University Press, pp. 503–532.

Durbarry, R. (2008). 'Tourism taxes: Implications for tourism demand in the UK', *Review of Development Economics*, 12 (1), 21–36.

Durbarry, R. and Sinclair, M.T. (2003). 'Market shares analysis of French tourism demand', *Annals of Tourism Research*, 30 (4), 927–941.

Easterby-Smith, M., Thorpe, R. and Jackson, P.R. (2008). *Management Research: An Introduction*, 3rd edition. London: Sage.

Edensor, T. (1998). *Tourists at the Taj*. London: Routledge.

Ellis, C., Adams, T. and Bochner, A. (2011). 'Auto-ethnography: An overview', *Qualitative Social Research*, 12 (1). Available at: www.qualitative-research.net/index.php/fqs/article/view/1589/3095 (accessed 9 July 2015).

Enoch, Y. and Grossman, R. (2010). 'Blogs of Israeli and Danish backpackers to India', *Annals of Tourism Research*, 37 (2), 520–536.

Ess, C. and The AoIR Ethics Working Committee (2002). 'Ethical decision-making and internet research: Recommendations form the AoIR ethics working committee'. Available at: www.aoir.org/reports/ethics.pdf (accessed 9 May 2011).

Fetterman, D.M. (1989). *Ethnography: Step by Step*. Applied Social Research Methods Series, No. 17. Newbury Park, CA: Sage.

Fielding, N. (2008). 'Ethnography'. In N. Gilbert (ed.), *Researching Social Life*, 3rd edition. London: Sage, pp. 266–284.

Fielding, N. and Thomas, H. (2008). 'Qualitative interviewing'. In N. Gilbert (ed.), *Researching Social Life*, 3rd edition. London: Sage, pp. 245–265.

Finn, M., Elliot-White, M. and Walton, M. (2000). *Tourism and Leisure Research Methods: Data Collection, Analysis, and Interpretation*. Harlow: Pearson Education.

Fisher, M. (1997). *Qualitative Computing: Using Software for Qualitative Data Analysis*. Aldershot: Ashgate.

Ford, N. (1987). *Research and Practice in Librarianship: A Cognitive View*. In B. Katz and R. Kinder (eds), *Current Trends in Information Research and Theory*. New York: Haworth, pp. 21–47.

Frankfort-Nachmias, C. and Nachmias, D. (1996). *Research Methods in the Social Sciences*, 5th edition. London: St. Martin's Press.

Fyall, A. and Garrod, B. (2005). *Tourism Marketing: A Collaborative Approach*. Clevedon: Channel View Publications.

Fyall, A., Garrod, B., Leask, A. and Wanhill, S. (2008). *Managing Visitor Attractions: New Directions*, 2nd edition. Oxford: Butterworth Heinemann.

Garrod, B. (2008). 'Exploring place perception a photo-based analysis', *Annals Of Tourism Research*, 35 (2), 381–401.

Gatson, S.N. and Zweerink, A. (2004). 'Ethnography online: "Natives" practicing and inscribing community', *Qualitative Research*, 4 (2), 179–200.

Gayle, J. (2001). *Tourism Research*. Milton: John Wiley & Sons Australia Ltd.

Gibbs, G.R. (2007). *Analysing Qualitative Data*. London: Sage.

Glaser, B. (1978). *Theoretical Sensitivity: Advances in the Methodology of Grounded Theory*. Mill Valley, CA: Sociology Press.

Glaser, B. (1992a). *Emergence vs. Forcing: Basics of Grounded Theory Analysis*. Mill Valley, CA: Sociology Press.

Glaser, B. (1992b). *Examples of Grounded Theory: A Reader*. Mill Valley, CA: Sociology Press.

Glaser, B. and Strauss, A. (1967). *The Discovery of Grounded Theory: Strategies for Qualitative Research*. Chicago: Aldine.

Goeldner, R.J. and Ritchie, R.B. (2009). *Tourism: Principles, Practices, Philosophies*, 11th edition. Hoboken, NJ: Wiley.

Goffman, E. (1959). *The Presentation of Self in Everyday Life*. London: Penguin.

Goulding, C. (1999). *Grounded Theory: Some Reflections on Paradigm, Procedures and Misconceptions*. University of Wolverhampton Business School Working Paper Series. Wolverhampton: University of Wolverhampton.

Goulding, C. (2002). *Grounded Theory: A Practical Guide for Management, Business and Market Researchers*. London, Thousand Oaks, CA, and New Delhi: Sage.

Gray, D. (2004). *Doing Research in the Real World*. Los Angeles, CA: Sage.

Guba, E.G. (1990). *The Paradigm Dialog*. London: Sage.

Guba, E.G. and Lincoln, Y.S. (1994). 'Competing paradigms in qualitative research'. In N.K. Denzin and Y.S. Lincoln (eds), *Handbook of Qualitative Research*. London: Sage, pp. 105–117.

Guba, E.G. and Lincoln, Y.S. (1998). 'Competing paradigms in qualitative research'. In N.K. Denzin and Y.S. Lincoln (eds), *The Landscape of Qualitative Research*. Thousand Oaks, CA: Sage.

Gujarati, D. (2003). *Basic Econometrics*, 4th edition. New York: McGraw-Hill.

Gujarati, D. and Porter, D.C. (2009). *Basic Econometrics*, 6th edition. Boston: McGraw-Hill.

Hair, J.F., Anderson, R.E., Tatham, R.L. and Black, W.C. (1998). *Multivariate Data Analysis*, 5th edition. New Jersey: Prentice Hall.

Hammersley, M. and Atkinson, P. (2007). *Ethnography: Principles in Practice*, 3rd edition. London: Routledge.

Hannam, K. and Knox, D. (2005). 'Discourse analysis in tourism research: A critical perspective', *Tourism Recreation Research*, 30 (2), 23–30.

Hardy, H. (2005). 'Using grounded theory to explore stockholder perceptions of tourism', *Journal of Tourism and Cultural Change*, 3 (2), 108–133.

Harrison, C. (1991). *Countryside Recreation in a Changing Society*. London: TMS.

Henderson, K.A. (1991). *Dimension of Choice: A Qualitative Approach to Recreation, Arks and Leisure Research*. State College, PA: Venture.

Hermann, I. (2012). 'Cold war heritage (and) tourism: Exploring heritage processes within Cold War sites in Britain'. Dissertation submitted to the University of Bedfordshire.

Heskett, J.L., Jones, T.O., Loveman, G.W., Sasser, W.E. and Schelsinger, L.L.A. (1994). 'Putting the service profit chain to work', *Harvard Business Review*, 164–174.

Hewitt, J. (2005). 'Toward an understanding of how threads die in asynchronous computer conferences', *Journal of Notes the Learning Sciences*, 14 (4), 567–589.

Hewson, C. (2002). *Internet Research Methods: A Practical Guide for Social and Behavioural Sciences*. London: Sage.

Hewson, C., Yule, P., Laurent, D. and Vogel, C. (2003). *Internet Research Methods: A Practical Guide for the Social and Behavioural Sciences*. London: Sage.

Hine, C. (2000). *Virtual Ethnography*. London: Sage.

Hine, C. (ed.) (2005). *Virtual Methods: Issues in Social Research on the Internet*. Oxford: Berg.

Hobson, J. (2003). 'The case for more exploratory and grounded tourism research', *Pacific Tourism Review*, 6, 73–81.

Holman-Jones, S. (2005). 'Auto-ethnography: Making the personal political'. In N.K. Denzin and Y.S. Lincoln (eds), *Handbook of Qualitative Research*. Thousand Oaks, CA: Sage, pp. 763–791.

Hooley, G.J., Piercy, N.F. and Nicoulaud, B. (2008). *Marketing Strategy and Competitive Positioning*, 4th edition. Harlow: Pearson Education.

Hoque, Z. (2006). *Methodological Issues in Accounting Research: Theories, Methods and Issues*. London: Spiramus Press.

Hudson, J.M. and Bruckman, A. (2004). '"Go Away": Participant objections to being studied and the ethics of chatroom research', *The Information Society*, 20 (2), 127–139.

Hughes, J. and Sharrock, W. (1997). *The Philosophy of Social Research*, 3rd edition. Pearson: Essex.

Hussey, J. and Hussey, R. (1997). *Business Research: A Practical Guide for Undergraduate and Postgraduate Students*. Basingstoke: Palgrave.

Illum, S.F., Ivanov, S.H. and Liang, Y. (2010). 'Using virtual communities in tourism research', *Tourism Management*, 31 (3), 335–340.

Jackson, S.L. (2011). *Research Methods and Statistics: A Critical Thinking Approach*, 4th edition. Belmont: Cengage Learning.

Janta, H. (2011). 'Polish migrant workers in the UK hospitality industry: Profiles, work experience and methods for accessing employment', *International Journal of Contemporary Hospitality Management*, 23 (6), 803–819.

Janta, H. and Ladkin, A. (2009). 'Polish migrant labour in the hospitality workforce: Implications for recruitment and retention', *Tourism, Culture and Communications*, 9 (1–2), 5–15.

Janta, H., Lugosi, P., Brown, L. and Ladkin, A. (2012). 'Migrant networks, language learning and tourism employment', *Tourism Management*, 33 (2), 431–439.

Jennings, G. (1997). 'The travel experience of cruisers'. In M. Oppermann (ed.), *The Travel Experience of Cruisers*. Wallingford, Oxon: CABI, pp. 94–105.

Jennings, G. (2001). *Tourism Research*. Hoboken, NJ: Wiley.

Jennings, G. (2010). *Tourism Research*, 2nd edition. Milton: John Wiley & Sons Australia Ltd.

Johnson, R.B. and Onwuegbuzie, A.J. (2004). 'Mixed methods research: A research paradigm whose time has come', *Educational Researcher*, 33 (7), 14–26.

Johnson, R.B., Onwuegbuzie, A.J. and Turner, L.A. (2007). 'Toward a definition of mixed research', *Journal of Mixed Methods Research*, 1 (2), 112–133.

Kalof, L., Dan, A. and Dietz, T. (2008). *Essentials of Social Research*. Maidenhead: Open University Press.

Kellehear, A. (1993). *The Unobtrusive Researcher: A Guide to Methods*. Sydney: Allen & Unwin

Keller, K.L. (2001). 'Mastering the marketing communications mix: Micro and macro perspectives on integrated marketing communication programs', *Journal of Marketing Management*, 17 (7–8), 819–847.

Kinser, K. and Fall, L.T. (2005). 'Lions and tigers and bears, Oh my! An examination of membership communication programs among our nation's zoos', *Journal of Hospitality & Leisure Marketing*, 12 (1/2), 57–77.

Kotler, P. (2011). *Marketing Insights from A to Z: 80 Concepts Every Manager Needs to Know*. Hoboken, NJ: Wiley.

Kotler, P. and Armstrong, G. (2009). *Principles of Marketing*. New Jersey: Pearson Education.

Kozinets, R.V. (1999). 'E-tribalized marketing? The strategic implications of virtual communities of consumption', *European Management Journal*, 17 (3), 252–264.

Kozinets, R.V. (2002). 'The field behind the screen: Using netnography for marketing research in online communities', *Journal of Marketing Research*, 39, 61–72.

Kozinets, R.V. (2010). *Netnography: Doing Ethnographic Research Online*. London: Sage.

Krane, V., Andersen, M.B. and Stream, W.B. (1997). 'Issues of qualitative research methods and presentation', *Journal of Sport and Exercise Psychology*, 19 (2), 213–218.

Kuhn, T.S. (1977). *The Essential Tension: Selected Studies in Scientific Tradition and Change*. Chicago: University of Chicago Press.

Kumar, P. (2010). *Marketing of Hospitality and Tourism Services*. New Delhi: Tata McGraw Hill.

Langer, R. and Beckman, S.C. (2005). 'Sensitive research topics: Netnography revisited', *Qualitative Market Research: An International Journal*, 8, 189–203.

Leech, N.L. and Onwuegbuzie, A.L. (2010). 'Guidelines for conducting and reporting mixed research in the field of counselling and beyond', *Journal of Counselling and Development*, 88 (1), 61–70.

Lemelin, R. (2006). 'The gawk, the glance and the gaze: Occular consumption and polar bear tourism in Churchill, Manitoba, Canada', *Current Issues in Tourism*, 9 (6), 516–534.

Levine, D.M., Stephan, D.F. and Szabat, K.A. (2017). *Statistics for Managers Using Microsoft Excel*, 8th edition. Harlow: Pearson.

Lewins, A. and Silver, C. (2007). *Using Software in Qualitative Research: A Step by Step Guide*. London: Sage.

Lincoln, Y.S. and Guba, E.G. (1985). *Naturalistic Inquiry*. Beverley Hills, CA: Sage.

Lincoln, Y.S. and Guba, E.G. (2000). 'Paradigmatic controversies, contradictions, and emerging confluences'. In N.K Denzin and Y.S. Lincoln (eds), *Handbook of Qualitative Research*, 2nd edition. Thousand Oaks, CA: Sage.

Litvin, S.W. (2007). 'Marketing visitor attractions: A segmentation study', *International Journal of Tourism Research*, 9, 9–19.

Locke, K. (2001). *Grounded Theory in Management Research*. London: Sage.

Lofland, J. (1971). *Analyzing Social Settings*. Belmont, CA: Wadsworth.

Lofland, J. and Lofland, L. (1995). *Analyzing Social Settings: A Guide to Qualitative Observation and Analysis*, 3rd edition. London: Wadsworth.

Lugosi, P., Janta, H. and Watson, P. (2012). 'Investigative management and consumer research on the internet', *International Journal of Contemporary Hospitality Management*, 24 (6), 838–854.

Lye, J., Perera, H. and Rahman, A. (2006). 'Grounded theory: A grounded discovery method for accounting research'. In Z. Hoque (ed.), *Methodological Issues in Accounting Research: Theories and Methods*. London: Spiramus Press, pp. 129–160.

Madge, C. (2006). Online research ethics module. Leicester University. Available at: www.geog.le.ac.uk/orm/ethics/ethprint3.pdf (accessed 30 January 2013).

Martin, D., Woodside, A.G. and Dehuang, N. (2007). 'Etic interpreting of naïve subjective personal introspections of tourism behavior: Analyzing visitors' stories about experiencing Mumbai, Seoul, Singapore, and Tokyo', *International Journal of Culture, Tourism and Hospitality Research*, 1 (1), 14–44.

Mason, J. (1996). *Qualitative Researching*. London: Sage.

Mayring, P. (2000). Qualitative content analysis. *Forum Qualitative Sozialforschung/ Forum: Qualitative Social Research*, 1 (2), Art. 20. Available at: http://nbn-resolving. de/urn:nbn:de:0114-fqs0002204 (accessed 10 August 2017).

McCarthy, E.J. (1960). *Basic Marketing: A Managerial Approach*. Homewood, IL: R.D. Irwin.

McCarville, R. (2007). 'From a fall in the mall to a run in the sun: One journey to Ironman Triathlon', *Leisure Sciences*, 29, 159–173.

McKercher, B., Law, R. and Lam, T. (2006). 'Rating tourism and hospitality journals', *Tourism Management*, 27 (6), 1235–1252.

Mehmetoglu, M. and Olsen, K. (2003). 'Talking authenticity: What kind of experiences do solitary travellers in the Norwegian Lofoten islands regard as authentic?', *Tourism, Culture & Communication*, 4, 137–152.

Miles, M.B. and Huberman, M.A. (1994). *Qualitative Data Analysis: An Expanded Sourcebook*, 2nd edition. Beverley Hills, CA: Sage.

Mkono, M. (2012). 'A netnographic examination of constructive authenticity in Victoria Falls tourist (restaurant) experiences', *International Journal of Hospitality Management*, 31 (2), 387–394.

Morgan, M. (2009). 'What makes a good festival? Understanding the event experience', *Event Management*, 12 (2), 81–93.

Murdy, S. and Pike, S. (2012). 'Perceptions of visitor relationship marketing opportunities by destination marketers: An importance-performance analysis', *Tourism Management*, 33, 1281–1285.

Murthy, D. (2008). 'Digital ethnography: An examination of the use of new technologies for social research', *Sociology*, 42 (5), 837–855.

Neuman, W.L. (2006). *Social Research Methods: Qualitative and Quantitative Approaches*. Boston: Pearson, Allyn and Bacon.

Neville, C. (2007). *The Complete Guide to Referencing and Avoiding Plagiarism*. Maidenhead: McGraw-Hill Education.

O'Reilly, N.J., Rahinel, R., Foster, K. and Peterson, M. (2007). 'Connecting the megaclasses: The netnographic advantage', *Journal of Marketing Education*, 29 (1), 69–84.

O'Sullivan, P.B. and Flanagin, A.J. (2003). 'Reconceptualizing "flaming" and other problematic message', *New Media & Society*, 5 (1), 69–94.

Onwuegbuzie, A.J. and Leech, N.L. (2005). 'On becoming a pragmatic researcher: The importance of combining quantitative and qualitative research methodologies', *International Journal of Social Research Methodology: Theory and Practice*, 8, 375–387.

Ovadia, S. (2009). 'Exploring the potential of Twitter as a research tool', *Behavioral & Social Sciences Librarian*, 28 (4), 202–205.

Page, S.J. and Connell, J. (2006). *Tourism: A Modern Synthesis*, 2nd edition. London: Thomson Learning.

Page, S.J. and Connell, J. (2009). *Tourism: A Modern Synthesis*, 3rd edition. Hampshire: Cengage Learning.

Paltridge, B. (2001). 'Thesis and dissertation writing: An examination of published advice and actual practice', *English for Specific Purposes*, 21 (2), 125–143.

Paris, C.M. (2012). 'FLASHPACKERS: An emerging sub-culture?', *Annals of Tourism Research*, 39, 1094–1115.

Patton, M.Q. (1988). 'Paradigms and pragmatism'. In D.M. Fetterman (ed.), *Qualitative Approaches to Evaluation in Education: The Silent Scientific Revolution*. New York: Praeger, pp. 116–137.

Patton, M.Q. (1990). *Qualitative Evaluation and Research Method*. Newbury Park, CA: Sage.

Patton, M.Q. (2002). *Qualitative Research and Evaluation Methods*, 3rd edition. Thousand Oaks, CA: Sage.

Pears, R. and Shields, G. (2010). *Cite Them Right: The Essential Referencing Guide*, 8th edition. Basingstoke: Palgrave Macmillan.

Phillimore, J. and Goodson, L. (eds) (2004). *Qualitative Research in Tourism: Ontologies, Epistemologies and Methodologies*. London: Routledge.

Phillips, E.M. and Pugh, D.S. (2005). *How To Get A PhD: A Handbook for Students and their Supervisors*, 4th edition. Maidenhead: Open University Press

Podoshen, J.S. (2013). 'Dark tourism motivations: Simulation, emotional contagion and topographic comparison', *Tourism Management*, 35, 263–271.

Pritchard, A. and Morgan, N. (2001). 'Culture, identity and tourism representation: Marketing Cymru or Wales?', *Tourism Management*, 22 (2), 167–179.

Rakić, T. and Chambers, D. (eds) (2011). *An Introduction to Visual Research Methods in Tourism* , Volume 9. London: Routledge.

Reichel, M. and Ramey, M.A. (eds) (1987). *Conceptual Frameworks for Bibliographic Education: Theory to Practice*. Littleton, CO: Libraries Unlimited.

Riley, R.W. (1996). 'Revealing socially constructed knowledge through quasi-structured interviews and grounded theory analysis', *Journal of Travel & Tourism Marketing*, 5 (1–2), 21–40.

Ritchie, J., Spencer, L. and O'Connor, W. (2003). 'Carrying out qualitative analysis'. In J. Ritchie and J. Lewis (eds), *Qualitative Research Practice: A Guide for Social Science Students and Researchers*. Thousand Oaks, CA: Sage, pp. 219–263.

Robson, C. (2002). *Real World Research*, 2nd edition. Oxford: Blackwell.

Rose, G. (2016). *Visual Methodologies: An Introduction to Researching with Visual Materials*, 4th edition. London: Sage.

Ryan, C. (1998). 'The travel career ladder: An appraisal', *Annals of Tourism Research*, 25, 936–957.

Sarantakos, S. (1998). *Social Research*, 2nd edition. South Melbourne: Macmillan Education.

Sarantakos, S. (2005). *Social Research*, 3rd edition. Melbourne: Palgrave Macmillan.

Sather-Wagstaff, J. (2008). 'Picturing experience: A tourist-centered perspective on commemorative historical sites', *Tourist Studies*, 8 (1), 77–103.

Saunders, M., Lewis, P. and Thornhill, A. (2003). *Research Methods for Business Students*, 3rd edition. Harlow: Prentice Hall.

Saunders, M., Lewis, P. and Thornhill, A. (2009). *Research Methods for Business Students*, 5th edition. Harlow: Pearson Education.

Schonlau, M., Fricker, R.D. and Elliott, M.N. (2002). *Conducting Research Surveys via E-mail and the Web*. Santa Monica, CA: Rand.

Schwandt, T.A. (1994). 'Constructivist, interpretivist approaches to human inquiry'. In N.K. Denzin and Y.S. Lincoln (eds), *Handbook of Qualitative Research*. Thousand Oaks, CA: Sage, pp. 118–138.

Schwartz, D.A. (1969). 'Measuring the effectiveness of your company's advertising', *Journal of Marketing*, 33, 20–25.

Seaton, A.V. and Bennet, M.M. (1996). *The Marketing of Tourism Product: Concepts, Issues and Cases*. London: Thomson Learning.

Sharpe, N.D., De Veaux, R.D. and Velleman, P.F. (2015). *Business Statistics*, 3rd edition. Harlow: Pearson Education.

Sieber, S.D. (1973). 'The integration of fieldwork and survey methods', *American Journal of Sociology*, 73, 1335–1359.

Sinclair, M.T. and Stabler, M. (1987). *The Economics of Tourism*. London: Routledge.

Smith, B. and Weed, M. (2007). 'The potential of narrative research in sports tourism', *Journal of Sport & Tourism*, 12 (3–4), 249–269.

Sorice, M., Shafer, C. and Ditton, R. (2006). 'Managing endangered species within the use–preservation paradox: The Florida manatee as a tourism attraction', *Environmental Management*, 37 (1), 69–83.

Spradley, J.P. (1980). *Participant Observation*. New York: Holt, Rinehart and Winston

Spradley, J.P. (2016). *Participant Observation*, 2nd edition. Belmont, CA: Waveland Press.

Stamou, A.G. and Paraskevopoulos, S. (2004). 'Images of nature by tourism and environmentalist discourses in visitors books: A critical discourse analysis of ecotourism', *Discourse & Society*, 15 (1), 105–129.

Stebbins, R.A. (2010). 'The Internet as a scientific tool for studying leisure activities: Exploratory Internet data collection', *Leisure Studies*, 29, 469–475.

Stieger, S. and Reips, U. (2010). 'What are participants doing while filling in an online questionnaire: A paradata collection tool and an empirical study', *Computers in Human Behavior*, 26 (6), 1488–1495.

Strauss, A. (1987). *Qualitative Analysis for Social Scientists*. Cambridge: Cambridge University Press.

Strauss, A. (1991). *Creating Sociological Awareness: Collective Images and Symbolic Representation*. New Jersey: Transaction Publishers.

Strauss, A. and Corbin, J. (1990). *Basics of Qualitative Research: Grounded Theory Procedures and Techniques*. London: Sage.

Strauss, A. and Corbin, J. (1997). *Grounded Theory in Practice*. London: Sage.

Strauss, A. and Corbin, J. (1998). *Basics of Qualitative Research: Techniques and Procedures for Developing Grounded Theory*. London: Sage.

Sue, V.M. and Ritter, L.A. (2007). *Conducting Online Surveys*. Los Angeles, CA, and London: Sage.

Sue, V.M. and Ritter, L.A. (2012). *Conducting Online Surveys*, 2nd edition. Los Angeles, CA: Sage.

Swarbrooke, J. (2002). *The Development and Management of Visitor Attractions*, 2nd edition. Oxford: Butterworth-Heinemann.

Tashakkori, A. and Teddlie, C. (1998). *Mixed Methodology: Combing Qualitative and Quantitative Approaches*. London: Sage.

Tashakkori, A. and Teddlie, C. (2003). *Handbook of Mixed Methods in Social and Behavioral Research*. Thousand Oaks, CA: Sage.

Thompsen, P.A. and Foulger, D.A. (1996). 'Effects of pictographs and quoting on flaming in electronic mail', *Computers in Human Behavior*, 12 (2), 225–243.

Thompson, N. (2001). 'Building brands in visitor attractions'. Available at: www.insights.org.uk/articleitem.aspx?title=Building+Brands+in+Visitor+Attractions (accessed 20 April 2012).

Thurlow, C. and Jaworski, A. (2003). 'Communicating a global reach: Inflight magazines as a globalizing genre in tourism', *Journal of Sociolinguistics*, 7 (4), 579–606.

Toepoel, V. (2016). *Doing Surveys Online*. London: Sage.

Tuohino, A. and Pitkdnen, K. (2004). 'The transformation of a neutral lake landscape into a meaningful experience – Interpreting Tourist Photos', *Journal Of Tourism & Cultural Change*, 2 (1), 77–93.

Tzanelli, R. (2003). 'Casting "the Neohellenic Other": Tourism, the culture industry, and contemporary orientalism in "Captain Corelli's Mandolin" (2001)', *Journal of Consumer Culture*, 3 (2), 217–244.

Urry, J. (1995). *Consuming Places*. London: Routledge.

Uzzell, D. (1984). 'An alternative structuralist approach to the psychology of tourism marketing', *Annals of Tourism Research*, 11 (1), 79–99.

Varey, R.J. (2002). *Marketing Communication: Principles and Practice*. London: Routledge.

Varley, P. (2007). 'Confecting adventure and playing with meaning: The adventure commodification continuum', *Journal of Sport and Tourism*, 11 (2), 173–194.

Veal, A.J. (2005). *Business Research Methods: A Managerial Approach*, 2nd edition. Australia: Longman.

Veal, A.J. (2011). *Research Methods for Leisure and Tourism: A Practical Guide*, 4th edition. Harlow: Pearson Education.

Walle, A. (1997). 'Quantitative verses qualitative tourism research', *Annals of Tourism Research*, 24 (3), 524–536.

Watson, P., Morgan, M. and Hemmington, N. (2008). 'Online communities and the sharing of extraordinary restaurant experiences', *Journal of Foodservice*, 19, 289–302.

Weber, K. (2001). 'Outdoor adventure tourism: A review of research approaches', *Annals of Tourism Research*, 28 (2), 360–377.

Wells, D.W. (1997). *Measuring Advertising Effectiveness*. New Jersey: Lawrence Erlbaum.

Wheeldon, J. (2010). 'Mapping mixed methods research: Methods, measures and meaning', *Journal of Mixed Methods Research*, 4 (2), 87–102.

Wileman, R.E. (1993). *Visual Communication*. Englewood Cliffs, NJ: Educational Technology Publications.

Winter, T. (2003). 'Tomb raiding Angkor: A clash of cultures', *Indonesia and the Malay World*, 31 (89), 58–68.

Wittel, A. (2000). 'Ethnography on the move: From field to net to internet', *Forum: Qualitative Social Research*, 1 (1), Art. 21. Available at: http://nbn-resolving.de/urn:nbn:de:0114-fqs0001213 (accessed 30 January 2013).

Woburn Safari Park (2012). Available at: www.woburn.co.uk/safari (accessed 26 April 2012).

World Commission on Environment and Development (1987). *Our Common Future* (known as the Brundtland Report). Oxford: Oxford University Press.

Wright, K.B. (2005). 'Researching Internet-based populations: Advantages and disadvantages of online survey research, online questionnaire authoring software packages, and web survey services', *Journal of Computer-Mediated Communication*, 10 (3), Art. 11. Available at: http://jcmc.indiana.edu/vol10/issue3/wright.html (accessed 30 January 2013).

WTO (2012). *Tourism Highlights 2012*. Madrid: UNWTO Publications. Available at: www.e-unwto.org/doi/pdf/10.18111/9789284414666 (accessed 30 April 2013).

Xiao, H. (2006). 'The discourse of power: Deng Xiaoping and tourism development in China', *Tourism Management*, 27 (5), 803–814.

Xun, J. and Reynolds, J. (2010). 'Applying netnography to market research: The case of the online forum', *Journal of Targeting, Measurement and Analysis for Marketing*, 18, 17–31.

Yin, R.K. (1994). *Case Study Research: Design and Methods*, 2nd edition. London: Sage.

Zhang, Y. and Wildemuth, B.M. (2017). 'Qualitative analysis of content'. In B. Wildmuth (ed.), *Applications of Social Research Methods to Questions in Information and Library Science*, 2nd edition. Santa Barbara, CA: Libraries Unlimited, pp. 318–329.

Index

Taylor & Francis eBooks

Helping you to choose the right eBooks for your Library

Add Routledge titles to your library's digital collection today. Taylor and Francis ebooks contains over 50,000 titles in the Humanities, Social Sciences, Behavioural Sciences, Built Environment and Law.

Choose from a range of subject packages or create your own!

Benefits for you
- » Free MARC records
- » COUNTER-compliant usage statistics
- » Flexible purchase and pricing options
- » All titles DRM-free.

Benefits for your user
- » Off-site, anytime access via Athens or referring URL
- » Print or copy pages or chapters
- » Full content search
- » Bookmark, highlight and annotate text
- » Access to thousands of pages of quality research at the click of a button.

REQUEST YOUR FREE INSTITUTIONAL TRIAL TODAY

Free Trials Available
We offer free trials to qualifying academic, corporate and government customers.

eCollections – Choose from over 30 subject eCollections, including:

Archaeology	Language Learning
Architecture	Law
Asian Studies	Literature
Business & Management	Media & Communication
Classical Studies	Middle East Studies
Construction	Music
Creative & Media Arts	Philosophy
Criminology & Criminal Justice	Planning
Economics	Politics
Education	Psychology & Mental Health
Energy	Religion
Engineering	Security
English Language & Linguistics	Social Work
Environment & Sustainability	Sociology
Geography	Sport
Health Studies	Theatre & Performance
History	Tourism, Hospitality & Events

For more information, pricing enquiries or to order a free trial, please contact your local sales team:
www.tandfebooks.com/page/sales

 Routledge
Taylor & Francis Group

The home of
Routledge books

www.tandfebooks.com